Early Independents Bracknell, Crowtl &Wokingham Area

Written and Published

by Paul Lacey

Originally with Lovick Motors of Crowthorne, 1951 Guy 'Arab' MkIII-type GMO 418 had a Thurgood body and passed with that operator to Brimblecombe Bros. of Wokingham, in whose service it is seen heading for Wembley.

Copyright Paul Lacey 2020

The right of Paul Lacey to be identified as the author of this work has been asserted by him in accordance with Sections 77 and 78 of the Copyright, Design and Patents Act 1988. No part of this publication may be reproduced, stored in a retrieval system, or transmitted in any form or by any means, electronic, mechanical, photocopying, recording, or otherwise, with prior permission of the publisher. Any person who commits an unauthorised act may be liable for a criminal prosecution or civil claims for damages.

Written, designed, typeset and published by Paul Lacey

17 Sparrow Close, Woosehill,

Wokingham, Berkshire, RG41 3HT

ISBN 978-0-9567832-5-7

Printed by Biddles Books, King's Lynn, Norfolk, PE32 1SF

The Benham premises in Wokingham's Peach Street, showing the entrance into the extensive yard area on the left.

CONTENTS

LOCATION MAPS/FLEET LISTS

ACKNOWLEDGEMENTS

A work of this nature, researched on-and-off over 50 years alongside other projects, has involved input from many sources, so my apologies are tendered should any go without acknowledgement here. Generally, I have spent much time perusing the local newspapers of the time, so thanks to the Library Staff in Bracknell and Reading, along with the Berkshire Archives. I am also grateful to my fellow researchers for making available information they had gleaned, as well as my contacts at the Omnibus Society and PSV Circle. Much personal information was also taken from the Census, work I undertook often parallel to my own Family History activities.

However, such a history would be largely unrecorded had it not been for the personal contributions of those who were there at the time, and indeed those active in such operations. In that respect, much very interesting material was provided during interviews with members, relatives and employees of the Benham, Brimblecombe, Fuller, Gough, Herring, Keene, Lovick, Lewis, Neal, Spragg and Wooff families.

A sketch of the 1925 Dennis bus MO 6184, which only saw a few week's service with the Progressive Bus Service.

THE EARLY INDEPENDENTS SERIES

This volume is intended as the second of three, which will cover the independent bus and coach operators in various parts of the Thames Valley area, with the first taking in the Henley and Marlow area and the third the Maidenhead area. All are based on many years of detailed research, much of it making use of personal interviews with many primary sources now lost to the passage of time, along with a unique collection of local photographs, preserved here for posterity. These works will compliment the volumes already published on the independents of West Berkshire (as the Newbury & District Motor Services Story) and the pre-1939 Reading Area coach operators (within Smith's Coaches of Reading 1922-1979), along with the volume on the White Bus Services of Winkfield. Generally, they cover the period from the pioneering days through to the Second World War, though each operator is dealt with according to its own date parameters and the available information. The activities of the Thames Valley Traction Co. Ltd., and its forebear the British Automobile Traction Co. Ltd. can also be found in its own series of volumes.

Paul Lacey, Wokingham   **January 2020**

An introduction to the area

The trio of main settlements in this volume each had quite different origins, so we shall take a look at the locations and characteristics as they were in the 1920's, when most of the individual stories commence.

Bracknell had developed as a cross-roads town which sat on the east-west line of the Reading – Staines road where it crossed the north-south link from Maidenhead to Bagshot and onwards to the South Coast. It stood on heathland at the fringes of the originally much larger Windsor Forest, also becoming the focus for a regular cattle market, which in former days attracted drovers from considerable distances via The Ridgeway and the Drift Road. It is 28 miles west from London, 11 miles east from Reading, 9 miles south of Maidenhead, 5 miles north of Bagshot and 4 miles to Wokingham.

In more modern terms, the London & South Western Railway reached the town from Staines to Reading in 1856, which greatly expanded its main local industry of brick-making, along with the rapid transport of the otherwise largely agricultural produce. Although on a stage-coach route back in that era, the motorbus had reached the town in December 1915 as the *British Automobile Traction Co. Ltd.* put out its tentacles to link Reading with Ascot and Sunningdale. In 1921 the population stood around 4000, long before the New Town had been envisaged, though some of our story will pre-date that development.

Wokingham was also under the general area of the old Windsor Forest for centuries, at one point known as a centre for the silk industry and later for brickmaking, the latter being much boosted once it was connected by the railways. It is situated 33 miles west of London, 7 miles east of Reading, 11 miles south of Henley and 11 miles north of Camberley. In 1921 the population stood at 8079.

It was also a cross-roads town, originally centred on the Emmbrook crossing that became the road southwards to Finchampstead, Yateley and the South Coast, where it also crossed the Reading to Staines highway. It too had an ancient market charter, more aligned to a wider selection of produce, though then predominately set in an agricultural area like its neighbour, both in an area notably for large land-holdings associated with titled estates, which did much to shape the road pattern and how links developed over the centuries.

It was also on the stage-coach route from Reading to Staines and onwards to London, or in other directions from the County Town connections. The town is linked by two railway lines, the Reading to Guildford line of the South Eastern Railway opening in 1849, followed by the Staines to Reading line of the South Western in 1856. The motorbus of *British* reached Wokingham from October 1915 on the Reading via Arborfield route, followed by the Reading – Sunningdale service from December of that year which ran via Bracknell.

Crowthorne is the least altered of the three settlements, with most commercial activity centred on its High Street, where indeed many of our stories will be based. As a large village it somewhat belies the huge developments that have since occurred around it, though in more recent times the local road pattern has seen many changes. In the historical context it stood out of Windsor Forest, though its poor heathland soil did mean it had less agriculture than those described so far, so no market developed.

In the physical sense the centre stands on another crossroads, where what were once little more that tracks linked both Bracknell and Wokingham what is now the A30 at Camberley, then onwards south to the coast. It is some 4.5 miles west of Bracknell, 14 miles east of Reading, 4 miles south of Wokingham and 5 miles north of Camberley. Its population in 1921 was 3980, though that included 1024 Broadmoor inmates.

Crowthorne became the site of the Criminal Lunatic Asylum constructed at Broadmoor by 1868, along with the Wellington College established by the Hero of Waterloo, with the blessing of Queen Victoria, for the education of the sons of Officers in 1853. Indeed, when the Station on the Reading to Guildford railway opened in 1849 it was known as Wellington College, being some 1.2 miles from the High Street – factors all having a bearing on road transport developments. As Crowthorne was close to the A30 boundary set by the Territorial Agreement between *British* (as *Thames Valley* from July 1920) and *Aldershot & District*, there was little attention paid by either concern regarding a bus link quite noticeably, though others did in due course come into the frame.

Also, as each of these settlements was some distance from the bases of *Thames Valley* at Maidenhead and Reading, developments in the provision of charabancs was met locally, plus a number of interesting smaller bus operations. From an overall perspective, this volume deals with operations basically south of the A4 (Bath Road) and north of the A30, with the western boundary set where the A329 enters Reading Borough and that to the east marked by where the A30 passes Sunningdale. Within such a study there are of course operators running over those boundaries to places beyond, so those from the Maidenhead area will only be dealt with in relevance to more local activities, whilst much more detail on developments eastwards from Bracknell are already covered by the *White Bus* volume, and the Reading-based coach operators were included within the *Smith's Coaches* book.

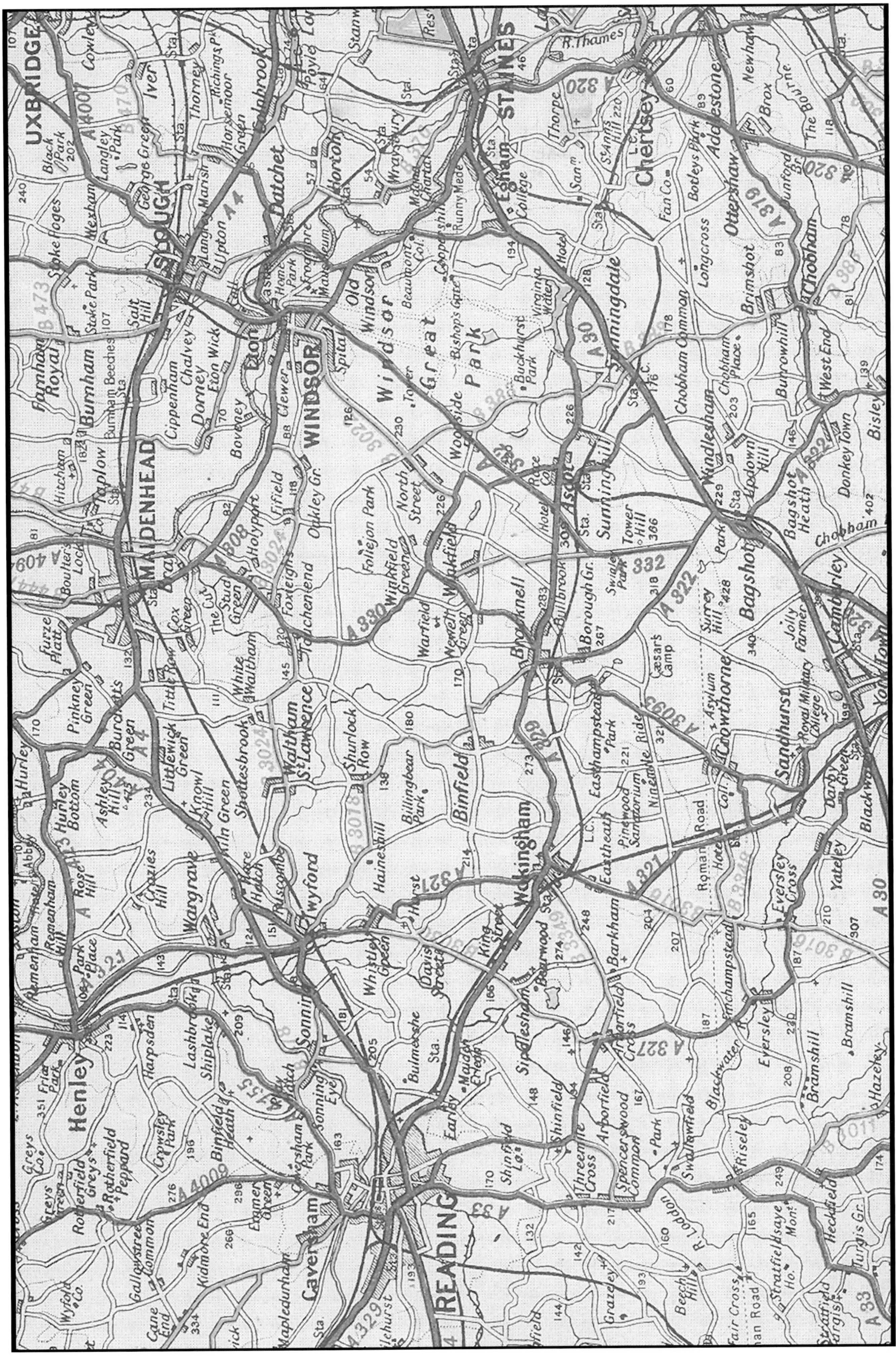
UXBRIDGE
Cowley
Iver
Colnbrook
Datchet
SLOUGH
Langley
Stoke Poges
Wexham
Farnham Royal
Burnham
Taplow
MAIDENHEAD
Cippenham
Dorney
Eton
Eton Wick
Boveney
WINDSOR
Old Windsor
Clewer
Wraysbury
Horton
STAINES
Egham
Thorpe
Chertsey
Addlestone
Ottershaw
Chobham
Virginia Water
Sunningdale
Sunninghill
Ascot
Windsor Great Park
Bracknell
Binfield
Warfield
Winkfield
Holyport
Fifield
White Waltham
Waltham St. Lawrence
Shurlock Row
Twyford
Wargrave
Henley
Remenham
Hurley
Bisham
Knowl Hill
Littlewick Green
Cookham
Wokingham
Crowthorne
Sandhurst
Camberley
Bagshot
Windlesham
Yateley
Eversley
Finchampstead
Barkham
Arborfield
Shinfield
Swallowfield
Sonning
Sonning Eye
Caversham
READING
Earley
Emmer Green
Shiplake
Kidmore End
Grazeley
Stratfield Saye
Heckfield
Bramshill
Hazeley
Blackwater
Riseley
Spencers Wood
Three Mile Cross
Woodley
Hurst
Winnersh
Sindlesham
Hare Hatch
Maidens Green
Fair Cross
R. Thames
A4
A30
A33
A321
A322
A327
A329
A330
A4009

Bruce Douglas Argrave
Vimmy Bus Service
Windsor and Winkfield, Berkshire

The wider story of *Bruce Argrave's* transport ventures has already been covered in the volume on *White Bus Services*, so here we shall only concern ourselves with the service which reached Bracknell. Also, to note is that he did not always follow the rules, so at times was in conflict with the Local Authorities or the Traffic Commissioners.

At first based in Windsor, he apparently became aware that a number of persons desired to travel through to Easthampstead, on the south side of Bracknell, partly due to there being a Union Workhouse set up there by the Parishes of Warfield and Winkfield, along with the Easthampstead Rural District Council. At that time the concept of Bracknell as we know it was less straightforward administratively, with it falling within all three of those areas. Apart from that link, also there were needs to reach the main hospital in Windsor, the shops in both towns and the weekly Bracknell market.

Bruce did obtain a license from New Windsor BC but didn't bother with ERDC, so the latter was displeased to find him operating from Windsor to Easthampstead in late May 1923. The route ran as Windsor (Castle) – Clewer Green (Prince Albert) – Winkfield (Squirrel) – Plaistow Green – Winkfield (White Hart) – Maidens Green (Crown & Anchor) – Winkfield Row (White Horse) – Chavey Down (Post Office) – Bracknell (High Street, Hind's Head) – Easthampstead (Union, Reeds Hill). No times are known for the operation, which ran about 5/6 times daily. It was certainly the first bus service to take that rural line through Winkfield and Chavey Down, an area then noted for a number of plant nurseries, sand pits and scattered communities.

In 1925/6 the family relocated almost opposite the *White Bus* Garage in North Street, Winkfield, and sons Ben and Montague were now involved, with a second route added from May 1929 to Ascot (Royal Hotel) via the newly opened New Road – Fernbank Road link.

Under the 1930 Act both routes were licensed, but the enforced co-operation with *Thames Valley* and *White Bus* over common sections caused financial hardship, leading to the family ending up back at Windsor. In an effort to tap more potential from the service, some journeys were planned to proceed the same way to Maidens Green, then onto Brock Hill Farm – Hollies Corner – Chavey Down (Mushroom Castle), then to the Post Office, after which they diverted via Priory Road to the Royal Foresters on the London Road and Ascot (Royal Hotel), but they were rejected at the Hearing.

Another attempt to vary the route was duly successful in September 1933, with onwards from Maidens Green – Brock Hill Farm – Hollies Corner – Warfield Street – Plough & Harrow – Maidenhead Road, then Bracknell and onto Easthampstead (Union).

Some irregular operation and vehicle issues certainly did not help in those early years after the 1930 Act, so on 16th April 1934 the Traffic Commissioner ran out of patience and revoked the *Vimmy BS* license. Of course, the local *Thames Valley* Inspectors had been vigilant in pointing out the deficiences of the independent, so no surprise that the latter provided a temporary cover from 2nd June 1934, though only as far south as Bracknell. A year later Route 2b as it became was reinstated through to Easthampstead (Union), worked by a 1927 Tilling-Stevens B9A based at Ascot Garage, and now departing Windsor from the Great Western Railway Station. The route in due course warranted a double-decker, whilst once Bracknell New Town developed around Bullbrook the route was further diverted from Chavey Down (Long Hill Road) to run through the new houses, finally being linked up with the Bracknell – Crowthorne section and onwards to Camberley.

Bruce Argrave was now 66 years old and his health was not good, so when the *'Valley* made its offer to him, along with an offer to eliminate *White Bus* over the Windsor – Ascot route, he was happy to accept. As part of the deal a pair of Star 'Flyer' buses passed to TV on 13th May 1936 as Cars 312 (VG 1631) and 313 (RO 9027), though both went by the end of that year, the green-and-white liveried *Vimmy Bus Service* no more.

One of the Vimmy Stars was VG 1631, itself one of a trio like the example shown, built speculatively by the Lowestoft-based coachbuilder United in December 1928 and finding a Norfolk operator before coming to Argrave. It was a 20-seater with 'sunshine' roof.

Bayliss & Poat
Barkham, Berkshire

Frederick Bayliss was born in Shinfield, just south-east of Reading in 1887, and by 1911 he was already established as a carrier, living with his parents who were now at Barkham Hill, by the junction of the Barkham and Bearwood Roads and some 2 miles south of Wokingham.

He had taken over from Gough not long before that date, and he ran daily except Wednesdays and Sundays to Reading by way of the quite scattered communities of Barkham – Bearwood – Ryeish Green – Shinfield – Whitley Wood, using the Black Horse at No.15 London Street as his Reading base and returning from there at 4pm. In its original form the service would have been horse-powered, and it is not known when the transition to a motor took place, the only wartime change being the departure time, amended to 3.30pm from 1917. Two years later he had added another Reading point at The Elephant Hotel, more centrally placed in the Butter Market, which may also indicate when he became motorised.

As with all carriers operating over roads as yet un-served by bus services, he would have taken passengers at times, whilst in the mid-1920's he would no doubt have been aware of the saga of *Fred Field's* attempt to serve a similar area by bus. Indeed, since the Great War he had ceased to serve Ryeish Green, Shinfield and Whitley Wood, as others had started regular bus services, and his route now ran as Barkham – Bearwood – Sindlesham, crossing over the River Loddon at Sindlesham Mill.

And so, in September 1926 he is joined by *Mr. Poat*, in order to lodge a license application with Reading BC for a daily bus service running as Reading – Sindlesham – Bearwood – Barkham – Nine Mile Ride Crossroads – Wellington College. The latter is rather ambiguous, as it could refer to the eastern entrance off Crowthorne High Street, or otherwise the railway station which then bore that name on the western side of Crowthorne, almost certainly the latter.

Indeed, the similarity with *Field's* proposed service seems to support the idea that this venture partly stemmed from the tide of anticipation amongst the local population, whilst the conversion of a carrier's service to bus operation was commonplace in the countryside during that period. The arrival of *Mr. Poat* was also part of the sea-change in operation, and although clearly named in both the Reading BC and *Thames Valley* minutes, he has proved a rather illusive person. Completely absent from all local directories and electoral registers, he would seem to be *Frederick George Poat*, a 31-year old gardener on the 1911 census at Mytchett Heath Cottage at Frimley Green, a dozen or so miles south of Barkham and over in Surrey,

and who had served in the Royal Flying Corps/Royal Air Force during the Great War.

Reading BC did indeed approve the application, and soon afterwards the bus service commenced. Nothing is known of whether a different vehicle was employed to match the change in status of service, but it certainly seems to have proven popular enough. Quite soon after it started the route was extended onwards from Wellington College Station along past The Ridges to reach Finchampstead village.

The Reading based territorial operator, the *Thames Valley Traction Co. Ltd.*, had paid little attention to the area covered by *Bayliss & Poat,* particularly in the earlier years, when the local roads were un-tarred and often rutted and muddy in the wetter months. Indeed, it was largely the post-war reparations money offered to local highway authorities, in recognition of the damage caused by heavy lorry convoys to Arborfield Remount Depot, not to mention the 100's of horses that had been driven on-the-hoof from Wokingham rail station, that finally resulted in these roads being surfaced for the first time!

However, since acquiring *The Progressive Bus Co.* in October 1925, with its Reading – Camberley service via Wokingham and Crowthorne, *Thames Valley* had established a Dormy Shed at Crowthorne in April 1926. This in turn led to that operator considering how it might serve Finchampstead and the back-roads towards Reading. As the *Bayliss & Poat* route was considered, it was decided to make an offer in order to remove any competition, and in March 1928 *Bayliss & Poat* accepted the *Thames Valley* offer of £200, which was for the goodwill only, no vehicle being involved. Perhaps the partnership had not worked out as planned, as *Fred Bayliss* reverted to a good's carrier, and nothing more is heard of *Poat.*

Thames Valley continued over the same route, though its Reading-based bus soon upset Wokingham RDC, as the larger single-decker weighed in at over 4 tons unladen, not really suitable for the narrow sections of road and likely to damage Sindlesham Mill Bridge. The subsequent history of this link, along with other back-roads services in the Wokingham/Crowthorne area is a complex one, with a number of variations tried over the next 5 years. Suffice it to say here that what had been the *Bayliss & Poat* service would from 1st April 1929 become Route 3a, now covered by a Crowthorne-based Leyland 'Pup' 20-seater and modified to run as Reading – Earley – Loddon Bridge – Sindlesham Cross Roads (on the A329) – Bearwood (Walter Arms) – Barkham (Bull) – Nine Mile Ride (California Cross Roads) – Finchampstead (Greyhound) – Crowthorne (Station).

As for *Fred Bayliss,* he continued with the carrier's service duly aided by his son of the same name by

1935. The latter also opened the Barkham Hill Filling Station by 1939, but was called up in 1943 and died on active service during 1945, whilst Frederick senior passed away during his 87th year in 1974.

William George Bentley
Arborfield Cross, Berkshire

William George ('Jack') Bentley was born in the village of Arborfield in 1897, the son of a wheelwright, cart and waggon builder, also born there back in 1865. Whether he spent any time working for his father is not recorded, though his brother Arthur John Bentley (born 1900) did follow that trade. He had obtained his first Driver's License from Berkshire County Council on Christmas Eve 1913, then residing at 'Magnolia House' at Arborfield Cross.

We first encounter *Jack Bentley* working in his own right when he put a new Ford Model T 20hp car on the road from 2nd September 1916. It was registered as BL 5121 and finished in dark blue, licensed for private hire, from which we gather he was offering a taxi service, the village being some 5 miles from Wokingham and a mile or so further to Reading, and still with a number of large houses locally then without a car. Whether he was offering any garage facilities from the outset is not known, but anyone offering such a vehicle for hire would need to be his own mechanic. Indeed, as his father had once had the young *William Vincent* working for him before he went to establish his coach-building and motor garage in Reading, it may well be that Jack had seen training with that firm?

The car was still in use at January 1921, but on 9th September 1922 he diversified by adding a 14-seater charabanc registered MO 494, fitted with a red-liveried Padmore body. Such a date is unusual for what was then a rather seasonal trade, so perhaps he had the chance to by this Ford T 1-tonner cheaply as a cancelled order? However, despite being an open chara he did license it with Reading Borough Council from 19th December 1922, along with himself as a hackney carriage driver, tying in with contemporary reports that he used it for shopping and theatre trips into Reading over the Winter of 1922-3.

For the 1923 season he offered the charabanc for hire, whilst as the only village-based operator, he probably advertised regular excursions. However, no further newspaper advertising took place, and it is not known how long the chara was active with him, only that it was finally licensed as a blue-painted lorry of Bill Hambleton over at Terrace Road in Binfield up to 30th June 1931. From 1924 he was advertising the usual range of garage facilities for the increasing number of local motorists, and was still living at 'Magnolia House' in Arborfield Cross, after which what duly became referred to as Arborfield Garage was operated by him for many years, but without any further involvement with public transport.

John Benham and Frank Benham
Wokingham, Berkshire

John Benham was born at Wokingham, Berkshire in March 1855, and by 1871 had joined his father John as a farm labourer at Norris Barn Farm, just to the east of the town centre. On the census of 1881 he is noted as a domestic coachman and, although still residing with his parents, he was employed at Montague House, a prominent town centre residence in Broad Street.

Later that same year he set himself up in business in the town as a jobmaster and fly proprietor, adding to his directory entry that he 'was recommended by the neighbouring gentry'. Initially he had one cab and a pony-and-trap available, with a base at No.61 Peach Street, on the eastern approach to the centre of town, which fronted directly onto the southern side of the roadway, with a large yard area that was developed into stables and carriage sheds (see photo on page 2).

Indeed, with horse-power being the general means of transport, John soon opened facilities for livery for other horse-owners, whilst also offering the animals on hire by the day or longer terms, hiring hunters in an area where there were many visitors to the surrounding country estates, and in a 1905 advert the term 'Central Hunting Stables' is used. The local point-to-point racing, which was held at Ashridge Farm, a short way north of Wokingham, developed into a 3.5-mile circuit taking in Bill Hill, and John trained about 4 winners of that popular local event which drew large crowds. That continued until the loss of horses to the military for the Great War saw its suspension for some years.

In the mean-time John had married Jane Hazel in the Summer of 1881, and she had been born west of Reading at Hampstead Norris in 1851. She had also been in service, initially as a housemaid in Queens Road, Peckham, (still then in Surrey) by 1871 before moving to The Elms, Old Windsor, Berkshire by 1881, where John met her through his coach duties. John is seen below about 1890 in the Peach Street yard.

The business was steadily expanded through the addition of further horse-drawn vehicles, and the sign-written board on the wall of No.61 Peach Street duly stated 'John Benham, Livery Stables, Good Loose Boxes, Closed and Open Carriages, Horses Let by Day, Week or Month'. Other adverts in Gotelee's Wokingham Compendium in 1892 noted 'open and closed carriages, single or pair pony-traps and phaetons available at short notice, passengers conveyed to station', whilst these categories are expanded to show by 1912 more specifically as 'superior rubber-tyred broughams, landaus, victorias, wagonettes, dog-carts (single or pair), open or closed brakes for private parties, hacks, hunters and harness horses on hire, station brougham meets any train, passenger's luggage collected'. It should of course be appreciated that one of the advantages of the horse era, was that the motive power was separately maintained, meaning that most working horses could be attached to any of these rolling vehicles at short notice. See location map on page 18.

Benham's advert in Gotelee's Guide Book of 1912.

Of course, *Benham* did not have the town entirely to himself, as *Richard Herring* had developed similar facilities from his base on the northern side of Peach Street, at Nos.48/50, just a short way further into town, though such work had only been added in 1905 and largely followed the growth of the Herring sons, of which we shall hear more of in their own section.

The Benhams had 5 children, though only Frank (born July 1888) would play an active role in the business, all other expansion being met by hired drivers. By 1911 Frank was listed on the census as a fly driver, though when he joined the Army in December 1915, he gave his trade as a livery stable-keeper. Despite his having grown up with horses, he was posted to the Army Service Corps (Mechanical Transport).

Frank Benham took his intial instruction at Grove Park in South London, before being posted to 274th MT Company as a lorry driver. It is worth noting that his Wokingham contemporary *Tom Herring* (one of Richard's sons) joined at the same time and was posted to the 273rd, where he served alongside *Alf Smith,* all three men later being involved with the local coach scene. Frank served away from the awful stalemate of the Western Front, being in Macedonia, though he contracted malaria in 1917, also serving in Kilwa and Daresalem before the homeward sea trip to his de-mobbing in March 1919.

In the mean-time Frank had married Annie Brooks in September 1916, a widow, who brought with her daughter Minnie born in Faringdon, Berkshire in 1909. The couple had sons John (1922) and Bernard (1926), and as the family expanded the home address moved across the road to No.86 Peach Street, with the business address remaining at No.61.

As already noted, although the Great War is often thought of as a mechanical war, it also decimated the horse population, a factor much favouring the shift towards motorised transport in its aftermath. *John Benham* was not enthusiastic about motors and did not take up motoring personally, even being known to decline a lift from his own cab from the station, adding he 'would take his final trip in a motor when he was dead'. Indeed, a motor vehicle did appear before the War started, with a 1912 Singer 15hp 5-seater car with laundulette-style bodywork. It was painted dark green and featured a 4-cylinder Aster engine, Bosch magneto and Dunlop tyres, but after that it had been laid up for the years Frank was absent, it was overhauled and offered for sale at £250 in the Reading Mercury of 28th June 1919. So it was Frank who spearheaded the changeover to motors, with his wartime driving experience, taking over the reins (or more appropriately the steering-wheel) from his father in 1922. John was still on hand of course, as old habits die hard, until he passed away in 1935 at the age of 80, a very well-known local man who had risen from humble beginnings.

With the horse-drawn era now at a close, the old stables and sheds were now housing the motor cabs, the yard now reverberating to the sounds of mechanics and engines, whilst the old smells of hay and manure also gave way to the whiff of petrol and oil. However, the old hook for the horse reins on the front of the house persisted after some 40 years, whilst the former harness room became the rest room for the taxi drivers, and the slate on the wall continued in use for chalking up pre-booked jobs! The original board on the front of No.61 Peach Street was duly repainted as '*Frank Benham, Motor Hire Service, Well Appointed Cars & Coaches For Hire For All Occasions*'.

The licensing of hackney cars for hire came under the old Town Police regulations, which Wokingham BC exercised through its Borough Police Force, and an amusing story recalled by Benham's one-time driver Frank Simmonds relates to how his employer at one time had only one hackney carriage plate, but several cars. Therefore, the plate was often moved from one vehicle to another, not actually illegal, but the enamel around the screw holes became rather chipped due to that practice!

The coaching side of the business was a natural succession to the hiring of the larger horse-drawn brakes for private parties to Ascot Races and other events. In those days longer trips were not practical, but with the advent of motor vehicles even the South Coast was now reachable. In the case of *Frank Benham*, it was a lucky win on the horses that gave him the necessary capital to order a Fiat 15/20hp from Vincent's of Reading, who also built the 14-seater grey-liveried gangway charabanc body, licensed as MO 3798 on the last day of August 1924, seen nearest the camera below in July 1931 at Southsea, re-painted reddish-brown and driven by Frank Simmonds.

The coach was initially kept busy with regular trips to Wembley to see the British Empire Exhibition, the largest event held in the country since the 1851 Great Exhibition, after which it was stored for the Winter. It is later recorded as in a brown livery, and it enjoyed a 10-year career with Benham, and was usually driven by Walter Englefield, though he left in 1935 to drive for *Herring Bros.* instead. His place was taken by Robert F. ('Frank') Simmonds, who then lived nearby at No.76 Peach Street, and had been driving taxis and sometimes the coaches from 1931. Young Bernard also recalls that

if someone shouted 'Frank' in the yard they were sure of a good response, as other drivers of his youth were Frank Godfrey and Frank Miller, plus his own Father! Other drivers recalled by Bernard were Charlie Bennett and Joe Chamberlain, and at its peak in the late 1930's the taxi fleet numbered 7 or 8, of which the following are remembered – a 4-seater Austin (MO ????), bought new between 1922 and 1927, a similar 1925 Austin (PE 2223), a late 1932 Humber 'Snipe' 80 7-seater (APA ?743?), a 1934 Buick 7-seater (AYE 91), and 4-seater Austin 16's, one with a square body (CPF 67) of 1935, and streamlined-body example of 1937 (AMO ???). The big Humber was still in use during the Second World War, fitted with headlamp masks and white-edged bumpers and running-boards.

The Fiat was joined by the 1931 season by a Lancia coach, though full details are not known, other than by 1939 it was covering a daily school contract, whilst Bernard recalls it as bearing a reddish livery.

With the advent of the 1930 Road Traffic Act, effective from the 1st day of 1931, *Frank Benham* applied for Road Service Licenses in respect of Excursions & Tours. At the same time *Herring Bros.* and the *Thames Valley Traction Co. Ltd.* of Reading also applied for E&T's from Wokingham. There was room enough for the two local operators, who were given support by a letter from Wokingham BC to the new Traffic Commissioner, though the latter also asked the same not to grant such rights to *Thames Valley*, as the applications were being considered during the Summer of 1931.

Benham successfully gained the licenses requested, which gave him the following excursions from The Garage at No.61 Peach Street, Wokingham:

Destination	Notes
Aldershot Military Tattoo	Specific evenings
Ascot Races	Specific days
Bognor Regis	May to September
Bournemouth	May to September
Brighton	May to September
Epsom Races	Derby Day only
Southsea	May to September

Also on other special occasions, maximum number of vehicles permitted on any departure being two, and notably they remained the only licenses ever sought.

Apart from the above seasonal excursions, the town also supported a fair amount of private hire, with church, social, worker's and pub outings, there being enough to keep both *Benham's* and *Herrings* busy. The smaller coaches were of course a handy size for the conveyance of sport's teams to football or cricket matches, along with evening work to dart's matches, whist drives and dances in those days of few private cars. There was also a the revived Point-to-Point Steeplechase held north of Wokingham at Ashridge

Wood, and organised by the Royal Engineers from Aldershot and under National Hunt Rules.

Although neither of Frank's sons entered the business as such, they did occasionally help out before pursuing their own careers. In the days before the use of antifreeze, Bernard got up with his father at the crack of dawn to prepare the vehicles, re-filling the radiators that had been drained overnight, warming water and spark-plugs in his grandma's kitchen before coaxing the engines into life! Each of the vehicles was known by its registration letters, so 'AMO' would be chalked up with a time for a pre-booked job, also being cleaned in advance. In Wokingham the competition had increased over the years, as apart from *Herring Bros.,* there was also *Ernie Brimblecombe* from 1926, then his son *Bill* continuing that line of work from 1932, whilst *Tom Mason* had branched out from the family's original haulage business into taxi work during the mid-1930's., more of which will be found on page 12.

The coaching side never expanded beyond the two vehicles, with only the Lancia in use from the 1935 season. It possibly continued through the Second World War on contract work, but is believed to have been laid up, or at least considered beyond use, by the end of hostilities. As a result of that *Frank Benham* decided not to continue with that aspect of the business, finding a ready purchaser of his Road Service Licenses in the *Brimblecombe Bros.*, who were based in the Finchampstead Road and looking to expand their coaching work, acquiring him and also the licenses and coaches of *Herring Bros.* in February 1946.

A wartime view of this splendid Humber (APA 743?) has Frank Benham at the wheel, with Mrs. Benham in the floral dress and her sister-in-law Edith Waller who was then also living with them at No.61 Peach Street.

The taxi business continued until about 1953, with even more newcomers to the local scene post-war, and Frank and his family continued to live at No.86 Peach Street. After the taxis ended the garages etc. in the yard were rented out to a coachbuilder and other small firms, and Frank finally passed away in 1967, having lived in nearby Howard Road since 1965, the old sign board still remaining on the wall until after his passing and over 80 years since the original start of the family venture.

Albert Bird
Waltham St. Lawrence, Berkshire
Arthur Spackman
Shurlock Row, Berkshire

When researching the earlier providers of motorised passenger transport links, a number of individuals are encountered who did indeed offer such facilities, if only for a short time or in a limited fashion. The above two men fall into these categories and are also located very close to each other geographically.

Albert Bird was born at Waltham St. Lawrence in 1869 and is found on the 1911 census still close by at 'Smewins Cottages' on the Shottesbrooke Park estate, where he was working as a woodman.

However, on 30th April 1924 he put a grey-painted Ford Model T 1-tonner truck on the road as MO 3134, and it was also noted as having 14 seats for passenger work. His main line of business was a hardware and oil stores at Waltham St. Lawrence, whilst his private address was 'The Bungalow' in that small village. Apart from transport connected with his business, the availability of such a vehicle locally inevitably led him to regular instances of taking sports teams and other social parties to events.

Although he did not further develop the passenger-carrying facilities, this nonetheless shows how merely owning such a vehicle in a rural location would often create involvement, at least until other more dedicated services were available. However, his little Ford was last licensed by another in June 1928, and we hear no more of any passenger work.

On the other hand, *Arthur Spackman* did provide a regular carrier's service, and it also seems that the start of that may have even effectively ousted *Albert Bird* from the passenger journeys he had undertaken?

Arthur was born in 1878, also at Waltham St. Lawrence, and in 1901 we find him at some 2 miles away at Shurlock Row, where he is employed in a large household as a carriage groom. Probably in order to obtain a better position, he had moved away by 1911, when he was coachman at Boldre Hill, near Lymington in Hampshire, still single and living above the stables.

It was most likely after the Great War that he returned to Shurlock Row, though no military records for him have survived, and he came to live at 'Meadow View'. By 1920 he had established himself as a carrier from Shurlock Row, Waltham St. Lawrence and Twyford into Reading on Tuesdays, Thursdays and Saturdays and using the Boars Head in Friar Street as his base. As was still commonplace with such ancient inns, there was a large rear yard, along with stables for the carriers and their horses, or parking for the growing number of motorised services, and *Arthur Spackman* left from there at 3.30pm, his service being one of the latter type of operation for the 9.5-mile journey.

Prior to the expansion of the long-established carrier's service starting from the Jack of Newbury at Binfield into a proper bus service when *Brookhouse Keene* took over in July 1924, it is known that *Spackman* was taking passengers on a regular basis from Shurlock Row and other un-served points along the way.

However, once the *Cody Bus Service* was operating between Binfield and Reading via Shurlock Row, it was inevitable that the improved frequency and better ride offered would tempt many away from the carrier's van.

Little is known of the vehicles used by *Spackman*, though a Ford van was used at one point. In November 1920 he offered a 'good covered van' for sale in the Reading Mercury, though whether horse-drawn or motorised is not stated. However, one local historian noted that he had originally used a horse, so that seems to indicate the changeover point of motive power.

In May 1925 he advertised for sale a Darracq touring car for £20 and a 1-ton Napier lorry with sturdy covered top for £40. The latter was almost certainly the vehicle he had started the carrier's service with, and likely it was ex-WD. Neither sold in response to the advert in the local newspaper, and both could later be noted up for auction in Reading at lesser amounts. This did not, however, mark the end of his carrier's service, which continued until at least 1939 on a goods-only basis using an unrecorded truck or van.

> *Transport activities of one kind or another have been carried out on the site around No.51 Barkham Road for over a century, all of them directly or less directly connected to our story, so we will now look at their complex history, which leads us to its occupation by Brimblecombe Bros.*

The Mason Family

The *Mason* family line connected to local transport ventures started with the birth of David at Eversley in Hampshire during March 1859. He was the son of William and Elizabeth, who were both farm labourers residing in Sparks Lane and originally from Finchampsead, a short way north of the River Blackwater which formed the boundary with Berkshire.

David's exact whereabouts on the 1881 census remain a mystery, though he had married Fanny Maria Eyles from Binfield in Berkshire at St. Saviour's Church in South Hampstead, Middlesex in August 1879, at which time he was working as a railway porter. As their eldest

son is duly noted as born in 1877 and the birth registered at Easthampstead it is possible that he was born to Fanny and adopted by virtue of the subsequent marriage. Whatever the full story, the next son Edward Daniel was indeed born at No.8 Rigeley Road off Harrow Road in Hammersmith, Middlesex in February 1882, at which time his father was still working on the railway as a brakeman.

In the meantime, the 1871 census sees grandparents William and Elizabeth living at Toutley Roundabout in Emmbrook, just west of Wokingham, and his employment is given as a hawker. However, by 1881 he is running the Thatched Cottage, a beer-house just a short distance away on Emmbrook Road, aided by his wife. This building had indeed been a thatch-roofed cottage when built early in the 19th century, but it was acquired by Reading Brewer Simonds in 1866, who had it rebuilt with a slate roof shortly before 1891. In another twist to the story, William dies in 1882, apparently in London or Middlesex, which results in David and his family taking over the pub, and remaining there until at least 1887. It is also worth noting that the total population for the Wokingham Borough at the census of 1881 was only 5043, a far cry from that of more recent times.

By 1891 there had been another change of address and trade, with the family now found at Havelock Place (to be incorporated into Havelock Road soon after), and David is now offering a fly (light horse-drawn carriage) for hire, no doubt in connection with the railway station just across the road. It should also be noted that at that time the brickworks off what is now Oxford Road was still operating, whilst the lane to it would not be finally linked as a through route to the right-angle section onto the Reading Road until the mid-1930's.

And during these moves they added Alice (1883), Charles (1885), Lydia (1888) and Edith (1890), all prior to the 1891 census, at which time they were listed under Havelock Road and David was also a coal merchant. The trade was invariably linked with the railways, which took the bulk deliveries all over the country. However, there are no further mentions of the fly-hire after 1895, as other local competitors were also to be found in the shape of the *Herring* and *Benham* families, both of whom we shall hear more of them under their respective headings.

By 1893 the family had moved the short distance further south along the Barkham Road to No.51, the last of a small terrace of cottages, by which time the family had increased with the addition of Annie (1892) and Mary (1893), followed by Thomas (1894), Caroline (1896) and finally Ernest (1900), actually the 13th child born to the couple, of which 11 survived. The coal business moved along with them, and by then David was a cartage carman on his own account and renting the yard adjacent to the home address.

This was part of a large area owned by the Wokingham-based firm of nurserymen Sale & Son, established in 1818, and whose head office was further up the Barkham Road at Folly Court, as well as a retail outlet in the Market Place in Wokingham. It is said that their tree and rose nurseries extended to some 46 acres, from the Barkham Road westwards to cover both sides of the Emm Brook valley and up to Woosehill Lane. Indeed, at this time there were still orchards right to the frontage of Barkham Road from the Mason's house down to the bridge over the brook and then onto the junction with Woosehill Lane, the entrance to the site being just south of Mason's yard.

There is nothing to indicate any involvement by any of the sons at this point, as Charlie is noted as being a carter on a farm in 1901. On the other hand, Edward had left to join up, and was at the time serving as a driver with the Field Depot Royal Engineers Mounted & Imperial Infantry based at Aldershot Barracks. Despite that, he would return to marry Adelina Howes in October 1907 at St. Paul's Wokingham, with them initially living south of Wokingham off the Finchampstead Road in Evendons Lane. By 1911, also be involved in transportation when working as a coachman and residing in Southlake Street a few miles northwards at Waltham St. Lawrence.

The cartage business operated from the yard off the Barkham Road, though the coal merchanting had ceased by 1899. However, in January 1910 David Mason died at the age of 51, though not an unusual event for a working man of that era. Fanny continued with the business, and she was then joined by son Charlie, whereas 17-year old Thomas was then working as a grocer's assistant. It seems very likely that he soon came over to the business, which became known as D. Mason & Sons. Edward and his family had moved in nearby at No.47 Barkham Road by 1913 to be fully involved, with furniture removals now added.

Up until the Great War the business was of course a horse-powered venture, whilst the addition of gravel and sand merchanting started at an unknown date, the likely source of both being very close by as they could be easily excavated from the once wider course of the brook and its surroundings.

With the coming of the Great War in August 1914 at least three of the sons joined up. Edward, being an ex-serviceman must certainly have returned to the colours, though incomplete records mean he cannot be conclusively identified. Charlie served with the Royal Flying Corps as an air mechanic class 2, which would give him a good grounding for future ventures. He also married Adelaide Wood locally in the last quarter of 1914, one of many ceremonies of that time of those about to depart for an uncertain future. Although Tom Mason's likely World War One own record has not survived, the medal roll cards list some 30 Thomas H.

Mason's, several of which served as motor drivers with the Army Service Corps, so it is likely he gained firsthand experience of lorry work before his return to Wokingham, and the office for the enterprise remained at No.51 Barkham Road.

The only known vehicle of the early post-war period was a 30-35hp Leyland with a grey-painted lorry body registered as BL 0235 on 8th November 1919. Given the date, this was quite likely to be one of the former military Leylands rebuilt by that Company at their Kingston works, but despite that it was sold after only 2 years use.

After the war ended Edward apparently returned to assist in the business, and by 1923 was living with wife Adeline at No.37 Langborough Road, Wokingham. The directories of 1920 and 1924 also gave 'Sunnyside' in Park Road as an address for the haulage business, indicating that one of the family was residing in that unmade road off Wellington Road. However, for the electoral registers for 1923-6 we find Charles and Adelaide at No.20 Wellington Road, which also bore that house name. Behind there, and accessed via the adjacent un-surfaced Park Road was the 'Station Garage', which Charlie used as his base before later re-locating to Rose Street. The shed still survives as a car-valeting business under the original title.

In respect of the family base at No.51 Barkham Road, the electoral registers show that Tom was there living with his mother, with younger brother Ernest still there in 1923, though absent in 1926, when his sister Elizabeth Lydia is once again listed. Whilst an advert in the Reading Mercury in 1926 stated that D. Mason & Sons of Wokingham had Austin tourer cars for immediate delivery, which shows a switch towards that class of trade. Indeed, by 1928 they are using the Station Garage, nearby the railway station and rented from Wokingham Borough Council, also as a base for the haulage work, whilst the 1931 entry notes them as motor haulage contractors, garage and electrical engineers. However, that garage was vacated during 1933, when it became part of another local family garage concern rented to Perkins Bros., who by then were no longer passenger operators.

At this point Charlie went to Reading and intended to retire. However, according to his obituary, he opened his garage in Rose Street, Wokingham in 1941 and the latter started a motor garage business as Mason's Garage, which he ran through to his death in 1955 in, leaving his widow Adelaide (nee Wood) who he had married in 1914 at Wokingham and one daughter.

The next reference is that for Tom Mason, now a car hire proprietor based at the railway station yard in Wokingham. He continued to use the station yard, an ideal base for such taxi work, as the town was served by two railway lines between Reading and London

Waterloo and to Tonbridge in Kent, and there were also still numerous well-off local residents in the hinterland surrounding the town who could afford such transport when also using the trains.

However, in January 1939 Fanny died at the age of 80. Following that Tom relocated his base to No.51 Barkham Road, though in fact the adjacent yard area had also evidently continued to be in family hands, and during October he was granted permission by Wokingham BC to store 500 gallons of petroleum spirit there.

Edward's later career is less well documented, but by 1932 he was already out of the family business as a journeyman carpenter, and he passed away in July 1947 aged 65 and was buried at nearby Crowthorne.

Tom Mason was still evident on the register of electors at No.51 Barkham Road through to 1947/8, but by October 1949 had gone from there, and he finally passed away in 1961 at the age of 67.

Norman W. Angel

The taxi business was sold to Norman W. Angel, who resided with his mother towards the rear of the Barkham Road yard site in a bungalow named 'Costessey', which had been the first new such bungalow in Wokingham after the Second World War and got its name after a marriage in the Norfolk village of the same name. Therefore, the service became known as Costessey Taxis (phone 494), though the name of Angel's Taxis did appear in the Times directories of 1949/50 and 1950/1, which also uses No.51a Barkham Road as the location for the business, though strictly-speaking at that time it referred to the entrance to Sale & Son's nursery. Also established there by Angel was a piggery of some 200 animals on land to the rear of Mason's old yard, but after a while he started to suffer from financial difficulties, which duly led to yet another phase in ownership of both businesses, as we shall see next. The latter is somewhat ironic as Norman had won a, what was then, a small fortune on the Littlewood's football pools in November 1948, almost £12,000 in fact. At the time he stated he would carry on with the taxi business, give a third to his mother, have a good holiday and buy a shooting brake!

Lewis & Neal

The next phase of ownership did not come about through any local connections, but apart from its early manifestations, would go onto provide significant aspects of the final phases of this saga.

Indeed, Wilfred Lewis hailed from Northamptonshire, having married Lily May Alderman in 1921 in the Wellingborough area. Their daughter Gladys married

John Henry Neal in the same area during 1941, after which Michael John Neal was born there in 1943, someone we shall hear more of in due course. Wilfred, who had been born in 1900, had by 1939 become a motor driver on milk deliveries, residing at No.23 Westfield Avenue in Rushden.

The two couples then ran a large piggery with some 800 pigs, along with 200 head of poultry at Rushden, a few miles due east of Wellingborough, but in 1946 the local authority put a compulsory purchase order on the land in order to build urgently needed post-war homes. As a result of this the families relocated to a remote farm in Norfolk, which lacked any mains services, so tilly lights, Calor gas cooking and chemical toilets made life there hard. At one point John was working on buying an old WW2 airfield in Suffolk towards the south in Ipswich, but due to that and the general depravations being experienced, Wilfred took the decision to buy the piggery and taxi businesses then on offer from Norman Angel down in Wokingham, and this took effect from 21st March 1951. As part of the deal the Lewis and Neal families moved into 'Costessey', also retaining the name for the taxis along with the phone number 494. The first advert in the local newspaper appeared on 4th May 1951 under the company name of Lewis & Neal, at that time a partnership between Wilfred Lewis and his daughter Gladys Neal. However, the latter went away in 1953, and about 5 years later the paperwork was amended to John Neal as the partner to his father-in-law.

It should be noted that although Norman Angel had operated from the yard, the land remained in the ownership of the Mason family until sold to *Lewis & Neal* in 1951.

'Costessey' Taxi Service
DAY and NIGHT

Parties—Weddings—Dances catered for

BOOKINGS TAKEN FOR SEASIDE PARTIES TO SOUTH, SOUTH-EAST OR EAST COASTS

MODERATE CHARGES

All Enquiries Receive Personal Attention.

PROPS :—LEWIS & NEAL, " COSTESSEY," 51a, BARKHAM ROAD, WOKINGHAM.
TELEPHONE : WOKINGHAM 494.

Having taken over an established business, there were both inherited drivers and vehicles. Those recalled at first were Reg Rand (later to Station Car Hire), Eddie Bird, Lil Ford and Mrs. Mead from Barkham Ride. The initial cars were a 1933 Buick Straight 8 (ALE 614), Austin 18hp (CMG 390) of 1935 and a Hillman, probably a 14hp, new in 1935 (BLO 258). There was also a lorry used for the piggery, an ex-War Department Bedford 15hp (ERX 371), re-registered in 1948 and operated on military-pattern sand tyres.

The new owners added further cars over the years in succession, these being 1936 Austin 18hp (VV 4977), a similar car (FMD 159) of 1936/7, another 1937 example (HFC 478), along with 1939 (EXN 812). In due course more cars of the next generation followed, with a 1952 Humber Super Snipe (HSR 900), which had been the property of a Lord who had died in London, then a lefthand-drive Austin A40 Hereford of 1951, formerly owned by a French Baroness De Vine, a 1949 ex-Ministry of Supply Humber Pullman razor-edge type (KXK 266). These were joined by a pair of 4-door Austin FX2 taxicabs of 1947 (FOT ???) and 1949 (GCR 794), both of which had been sold out of service in Southampton due to the decline in liner traffic at the docks, all as recalled by John Neal.

Next came two 1958 Austin A55-types (738 EPP) and (ORX 790), a similar vintage Ford Consul MkII's (MUD 999) and (VXE 74), a 1954 Vauxhall Wyvern (OAD 591), and a 1955 Armstrong-Siddeley Saphire (PYE 856). There were also a trio of Rovers, with 1955 60-type (HJD 756), a 1956 75-type (RGB 758) and a 1956 90-type (XUR 901?). A further Austin A55 of 1958 (VXE 790) was joined by a new Standard Ensign ordered new from A. C. Barnes just around the corner in Oxford Road (PBL 594). Two Vauxhall Victor F-types then arrived, one of 1958 (VTR 69), the other in a powder blue upper colour, with cream lower panels (??? HAR), which had been the prize awarded to Miss Great Britain Valerie Martin in 1959. A trio of Vauxhalls then followed, with a 1958 Cresta (390 DFC), a 1959 Velox (PHV 14), then lastly a 1961 Victor ordered new again from Barnes with the specially requested registration number (494 ABL) to echo the firm's phone number! Lastly there was a 1961 Standard Atlas of 1959-60 (2652 AR), which would pass to *Brimblecombe's* later.

PSV operations commence from December 1958 with the purchase of a Martin Walker 11-seat minibus conversion on a Bedford CAV chassis (RMO 667). It was in a livery of sand-and-sable, which it retained during its fairly short stay, a situation hastened by the layout of its bodywork, which featured longitudinal seating, which did not work well with carrying children before the days of seat belts, as they could easily be tipped off the seats when cornering, or would otherwise use the central floor area as a play area and distract the driver. This had been supplied through the long-established Bracknell garage of Drake & Mount, situated at the lower end of the High Street, adjacent to the Regal Cinema, and at that time such conversions were not really that good, many being regarded as just utility vehicles for transporting workers.

However, in late 1959 one of the partners was at Drake & Mount when a new type of minibus on the longer-wheelbase CALV-type called in on a demo run on its way to the Commercial Motor Show, after which *Lewis & Neal* reserved the vehicle once it was released from those duties. The body on that example featured 11 forward-facing seats, and on its return, it was repainted powder blue and cream (to match coach GYA obtained in the meantime) and sign-written (with *Costesey* in error, which it retained), entering service in February 1962 (UJB 498). The firm had hoped to secure '494' as the number once again, but it had already been issued. The previous minibus was sold in March, though it was often seen around afterwards, having gone to a Maidenhead-based builder for staff transport.

The OWB-type GYA 911 seen with its original owner.

As noted above, the first full-size coach had been purchased in August 1959, this being a 1944 Duple-bodied Bedford OWB (GYA 911), which had its original wooden-slated utility seating replaced by 29 coach seats by then. It had been new to *Dibble* down in Somerset, but had latterly been with *Enterprise* of Otterhampton in that same county, running between Bridgwater and the Hinckley Power Station site on the coast, wearing a powder blue and cream livery.

The Bedford OWB was replaced by Duple Vista-bodied 29-seater (DDP 912) from July 1960, which had been new to *Smith's Luxury Coaches* of Reading in 1948, and then in October that was joined by an Austin VBK2/SL-type with Lee 21-seater bodywork (HAA 168) new in 1949 to *Creamline* of Bordon, both of this vehicles having then passed to *Odiham & District*, though the latter had since passed to *Lloyd* of Swanley. The Bedford had actually returned to *Smith's* after disposal, and the Odiham cream and green was duly altered to red and cream, which matched the livery of HAA as acquired.

Once the coaches started their drivers were Melton Woodason, Alan Cutts, Ray Moorshead and Billy Crowe, the latter only being 4ft 11ins in height, and who in later days contrasted with *Brimblecombe* driver 'Tiny' Ducker, who was 6ft 4ins and weighing in at some 20 stones!

The Austin HAA 168 was a neat little coach, handy for school contracts and smaller private hires.

The main work involved transporting children to the Special Needs School off Ascot Road in Holyport, something which also kept a number of the taxis busy at school times. There was also contract work for Sid Gilbert's workers to his Easthampstead Road handbag factory in Bracknell, along with Aerosol's production works at Downmill Road, nearby on the Western Road Industrial Estate. Reading University also used *Costessey* on a regular basis, whilst a steady amount of private hire was forthcoming from the numerous social clubs and worker's social outings, usually with two or three jobs each week.

In December 1960 two applications were also placed before the Traffic Commissioners for fare-paying services for pupils attending St. Joseph's Roman Catholic School in Larges Lane, Bracknell. One ran as Priestwood Avenue – Meadow Way – Honey Hill Road, with a weekly fare of 3 shillings, whilst the other came in from Easthampstead as junction of Beckford Avenue/Waterford Road – Haversham Drive – South Lynn Crescent/Redvers Road, for the same fare, with each operating on school days only. Both continued to be renewed as licenses through to 1966.

Both the 1949 Austin (HAA 168) and 1960 Bedford CALV (UJB 498) were disposed of in May 1961, and in their place came a Duple-bodied 37-seater Bedford (DCB 259) of 1952, formerly with *Cronshaw* of Hendon. This arrived in cream livery with a maroon stripe, which was retained. It was joined in April 1962 by another Duple-bodied Bedford, this time an SBO with 38-seater body (VPD 488), which when new to *Cooke* of Guildford in 1954 had been specified with a strengthened storage area for musical instruments in the roof, as it was used for the Women's Army Band. In the meantime, it had also operated for *Harris* of Cambridge *(Progressive Coaches)*, arriving at Wokingham in cream and blue livery. However, after an accident in the severely icy conditions of January 1963 it was repainted as red and grey during repairs, and this had been intended as the new fleet standard.

In May 1962 a minibus was again acquired, this time a late 1960 Austin J2VA with Kenex 12-seater body (2652 VF), which had originated with *Cunningham* of Hempnall in Norfolk. As this was grey and leaf green it retained that livery for the meantime, and was the replacement for the 1948 Bedford OB (DDP 912).

As a result of the January 1963 accident to VPD, John Neal had to secure an urgent replacement, so 1954 Duple C36F-bodied Bedford SBG (NDF 751) was acquired that month from *Meatyard* of Porchester. It was a 7ft 6ins-wide vehicle which started out with *Neale* of Berkeley in Gloucestershire, also passing through *Little Wonder* of Petersfield in Hampshire before coming to *Costessey* from Portchester, and rather handily it wore a grey and red livery.

Bedford SB-type coach DCB 259 is seen going to The Derby at Epsom with its previous owner.

The 1952 Bedford SB (DCB 259) was disposed of in the Summer of 1963, and its replacement was a smaller Bedford OB (FDL 318), new in 1948 to *Seaview Services* on the Isle of Wight. It had a livery of two-tone green and red, which was certainly not liked, so the green areas were over-painted in grey ready for the Autumn term. Of course, the main work was still the contracts, as *Costessey* never applied for excursion licenses, so changes in seating capacity (both up and down) reflected the seating allocations on contracts, whilst 7ft 6ins vehicles also suited the narrow road sections associated with the rural road network.

Wilfred Lewis was now in his 60's, and had also received some enquiries regarding the possible sale of the land by other business users. Such tempting offers set in train applications for planning permission in order to make the sale more valuable, but these were blocked by the Borough Council, upon which sat Reg Brimblecome, *Costessey Coaches* rival in the town. In those days the will of such characters carried far more weight at Council meetings, even despite obvious business interest – indeed most councillors tended to be drawn from that fraternity, other than those with the time and money to pursue such activities), and *Lewis & Neal* were of the opinion that they could not succeed so sold the business to *Brimblecombe Bros.* instead!

This duly became effective from July 1964, with the transfer of the surviving fleet of 4 vehicles, namely the trio of Bedfords (FDL 318, NDF 751 and VPD 488), as well as the Austin minibus (2652 VF) and the taxis then in use. Whilst *Brimblecome's* were no doubt happy to extend their grip locally, with both the taxi and coach work, the real incentive lay in the opportunity to plan a new garage on the land that came with the deal.

Bedford OB FDL 318 is shown on the seafront at Ryde when working on the Isle of Wight.

It must be assumed that Wilfred retired at this point, whilst John Henry Neal (known as Harry) continued to drive for *Brimblecombe's*. However, the latter's son who was now also known as John, was just coming up to PSV driving age at this juncture, so the new owners put him through the test on their 1962 Duple-bodied Ford 570E coach (188 ARX), after which he drove for them as well. By the end of 1965 he could be found living a short way at No.41 Havelock Road.

The other drivers were transferred over to the new owner, who used the inherited coaches on their usual duties initially. However, the OB (FDL) and narrow SBG (NDF) did not get repainted into *Brimblecombe Bros.* fleet livery and were withdrawn in November 1965 and March 1968 respectively, the OB languishing in the corner of the garage as a source of spare parts for several years, whilst the SBG is said to have ended up in the Channel Islands in due course. Whereas the other Bedford (VPD) was also weeded out in March 1968, the Austin minibus (2652 VF) was retained until October 1972. *NDF was seen by Phil Moth at the Barkham Road garage after the take-over, as below.*

The *Costessey* name disappeared with the change of owner, and indeed the bungalow would even be renamed in due course as 'Territon' to perpetuate the *Brimblecombe* family practice. As we shall see under their heading, the site was developed, whilst the former *Costessey* phone number 494 was added to the 196 and 299 already in use.

We now come to the development of Brimblecombe Bros., the largest single operator dealt with in this volume, although its origins were quite modest until expansion following the end of the Second World War.

Brimblecombe Bros.
Wokingham, Berkshire

Ernest Hooper Brimblecombe was born in 1872 in the South Devon port of Exeter, the son of Richard Skinner Brimblecombe and his wife Margaret (nee Hooper). The latter had indeed originated a few miles from that city at Broadclyst in 1847, whereas Richard came from Plymouth, another Devonian port, and was born in 1841. Shortly before Ernest's birth the couple were recorded at a cottage in Baring Road in the Heavitree district of Exeter, from which he worked as a master tailor, whilst his wife was a milliner from their home, as was quite common practice then.

By 1877 the family had relocated to London and the Marylebone area, a short way from the Paddington terminus of the Great Western Railway. Still working as a tailor, Richard and the family are confirmed as at No.41 Brown Street by the 1881 census. Another move took place by 1887, when they were a short way north-westwards at Willesden Green, the family of 11 children growing steadily throughout. In 1891 they had relocated east to No.64 Maygrove Road in Hampstead. That census was the first to show Ernest employed, and at the time he was still living at home and as a 19-year old footman in domestic service, the area featuring many well-off people with their own carriages.

Ernest married Annie Rose Crew (born Great Marlow, Buckinghamshire 1873) at High Wycombe in 1891, and the couple had 8 children, as Ernest Arthur (1894-1976), Edgar (1896-1975), Alice Dorothy Rose (1898-1991), Lilian May (1900-1988), Violet Annie (1904-1984), Edith Constance (1905-1963), Reginald Hooper (1908-1987) and William Richard (1911-1989). It is interesting to note that the last two brothers, who would form the basis of the main story, almost shared a birthday, as Reg was born on 30th April, whereas Bill hung on until 1st May! The couple's first child was born in the Reading district, whereas the next three were born in the Henley area, and by the Spring of 1901 the family was indeed living at No.17 Clarence Road in the Oxfordshire town of Henley-on-Thames, and Ernie Violet was born at Maidenhead in 1904, and the family was at No.6 Portlock Road in that town by the 1911 census, with Ernie listed as a house-painter.

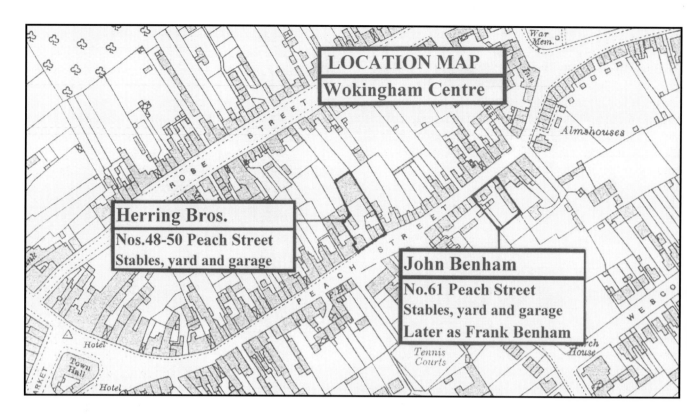

LOCATION MAP
Wokingham Centre

Herring Bros.
Nos.48-50 Peach Street
Stables, yard and garage

John Benham
No.61 Peach Street
Stables, yard and garage
Later as Frank Benham

Location maps for Wokingham Town Centre, the Finchampstead Road and Barkham Road.

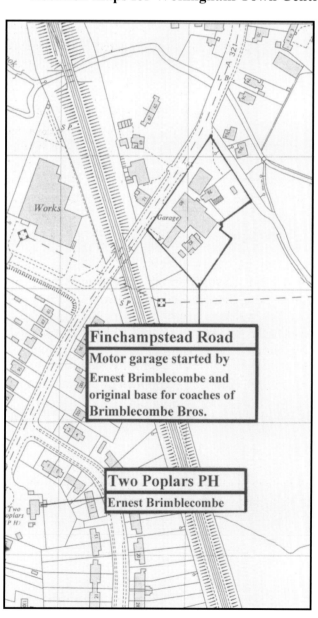

Finchampstead Road
Motor garage started by
Ernest Brimblecombe and
original base for coaches of
Brimblecombe Bros.

Two Poplars PH
Ernest Brimblecombe

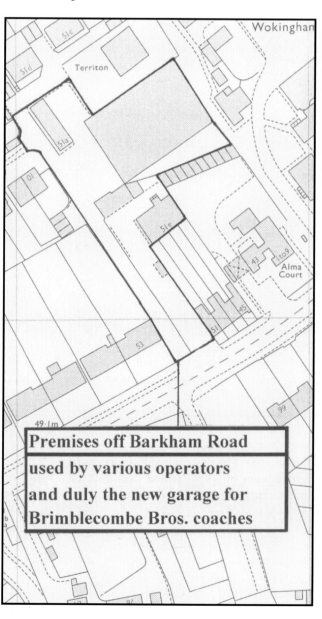

Premises off Barkham Road
used by various operators
and duly the new garage for
Brimblecombe Bros. coaches

Brimblecombe Bros.
Wokingham, Berkshire- *continued*

During the Great War he signed up on 30th August 1914, although 42 years old at the time, noting that he had previously served with the 4th Battalion Oxford Light Infantry (a reserve force), and stating his last employer as J.R. Cooper & Sons, Builders at Maidenhead. He was initially posted to the Royal Defence Corps and all his service was on the Home Front, and from August 1918 he was transferred to the 29th (City of London) Battalion London Regiment, with his war service ending in February 1919. Family sources state that he was with the Royal Berkshire Regiment and the Royal Fusiliers, though his surviving army papers do not confirm that as such.

Whatever his precise duties during the war years, it may be that he had some contact with motor vehicles, as he applied to the *British Automobile Traction Co. Ltd.* at its Bridge Street Garage in Maidenhead in order to become a bus driver, and was still resident at Portlock Road when noted on the hackney carriage licenses granted by the neighbouring Chepping Wycombe Borough Council for Maidenhead-based crews. The local BAT Branch was undergoing considerable expansion at that time, becoming the separate *Thames Valley Traction Co. Ltd.* from July 1920, and the job of a bus driver offered regular employment at a reasonable wage in an uncertain time for those returning from the war.

For how long he drove for *Thames Valley* is not known, though there were recollections of having driven open-fronted double-deckers which were in general use from 1922. However, by 1926 the family had moved again, with Ernie taking over as licensee of the Queen's Head at No.23 The Terrace in Wokingham, Berkshire. That same year is also claimed by family sources as the start of a taxi operation, also sometimes attributed to his son Bill, who was only 18 at the time. Either way, the taxi did feature from around that date, and Bill and Reg duly come into the expanding family ventures as they were old enough. Although Reg had initially worked in the local silk mill, a remnant of a once prosperous local industry, in reality he is recalled as 'only happy with his head under a car bonnet!'.

A further local move saw Ernie take on the larger pub at the Two Poplars on the Finchampstead Road in Wokingham by 1931, whilst the 1932 local directory shows Bill Brimblecombe listed as a motor car proprietor at 'Territon', a couple of houses west of the Rifle Volunteer pub at Emmbrook, on the Reading Road westwards about a mile from Wokingham town centre. This address was shared with William Thomas Adams, a poultry farmer who married Bill's sister Edith in 1931. Also of note was the marriage of daughter Lilian to James McInnes in 1927, and 'Jim'

would in due course serve as a driver on the coach side. Also, Lilian would spend some years as a teacher at Wescott School in Wokingham, where she taught a young Michael John Neal, a name we have already heard of in connection with another operator, whilst Jim came to be highly regarded by his father-in-law. They moved initially to No.74 Barkham Road, but duly relocated across the road when the new bungalows were built southwards of No.51 downhill towards the Emmbrook Bridge.

The first instance of the family taking an interest in coach work came in May 1932, when Road Service Licenses were being applied for under the 1930 Road Traffic Act. Bill Brimblecombe applied for excursions to Aldershot Tattoo, Ascot Races, Henley Regatta, Marlow Regatta, Newbury Races, Southampton, Southsea and Windsor Races, with a pick-up point at No.14a Broad Street in Wokingham, which was the shop of the local booking agent, bookseller and stationer F.J.A. Wright. However, for some reason the application was withdrawn on 1st July 1932, and this line of work is not encountered again until the Summer of 1938.

In the meantime, from his pub base at No.118 Finchampstead Road, Ernie acquired land nearer to the town and along the same road, situated on the eastern side of the road between the two railway bridges and opposite the Pin & Bowl pub, where he opened a motor garage and car hire business aided by his sons Reg and Bill. Only Nos.66/68 are mentioned from 1933, and plans for the garage to the rear of No.68 were submitted to Wokingham Borough Council and approved on 7th September 1933, with a petroleum storage license for 500 gallons on 12th October. The first instance of the use of *'Brimblecombe Bros. Garage'* came in the local directory of 1934, and in that year Ernie and Annie and both sons were all living at No.68, but around 1938/9 Nos.70/70a were also listed, with Ernie and Annie living there as well as the two sons, whilst Bill and Edith Adams were living at No.66 by 1934, though his business was separate as he developed from a cycle and wireless appliance dealer through to the television age with a shop at No.14 Peach Street in Wokingham. Bill is also recorded by Wokingham BC as submitting plans to convert 2 houses at 'Northbrook' by the Emmbrook in Finchampstead Road, which was approved on 7th December 1933.

Ernie died in April 1937, but Annie continued to live on the site until her death in 1953, and a stone plaque to their father was as founder of the business was erected by Reg and Bill (and later relocated to Barkham Road). This also noted the use of the title Eddystone Garage for the business, with a reference to the famous lighthouse off the Devon coast had been visible to their father in his youth, being a dozen or so miles in the sea south-west of Plymouth. That name continued in use for both the garage and later would appear on the rear of coach bodies, showing the 161ft high Douglass tower completed in 1882 with light rays emanating from it.

The memorial plaque now at 51a Barkham Road.

The hire of caravans is first noted in the Berkshire Chronicle in May 1937, being a 1936 4-berth fully-equipped van capable of towing with a 7hp car, which could be hired from Wokingham. Also on offer were fully-equipped static 'Eccles' caravans sited on the coast at Bognor Regis.

BOOKING NOW !

for

ASCOT RACES

(2/- Return)

and

Aldershot Tattoo

(4/- Return)

or QUOTATIONS GIVEN for
PRIVATE PARTIES.

Brimblecombe Bros.

EDDYSTONE GARAGE,
WOKINGHAM.—'Phone · 299.

or with

F. J. A. WRIGHT, (Booking Agents),
Broad Street, Wokingham—'Phone 387

The first known mention of coaching activities comes on 27th May 1938, when this newspaper advert stated that the brothers were offering coach excursions to Royal Ascot Races and the Aldershot Tattoo, both events coving similar dates in the day and evening respectively. Bookings could be made at the Eddystone Garage (phone Wokingham 299) or with F.J.A. Wright, the booking agent in Broad Street. A similar ad appears the following week, which also

states that available for hire were 3/4-berth caravans by the sea at Bognor Regis, along with similar sized caravans suitable for towing by a 7-8hp car. During May 1939 *Brimblecombe Bros.* were offering 'high class coaches and cars for hire', whilst the caravans were now stated to be at Hayling Island, similar adverts continuing through to the end of July, though no coach excursion destinations were given. However, an extensive search of the Notices & Proceedings of the Traffic Commissioners for the per-war period has turned up no reference to the granting of licenses!

At the time that the *Brimblecombes* entered the coaching scene, there were already two long-established family businesses in the town offering the same coach and taxi facilities. One was *Herring Bros.*, with 4 coaches and some taxis, whilst the other was *Frank Benham*, with just an ageing Lancia coach and half-a-dozen taxis, and both businesses were second-generation outfits located in Peach Street. Wokingham was also served by the extensive coastal express services of *Smith's Luxury Coaches* of Reading, who also used the agency in Broad Street, these developing into daily Summer operations also offering period return, day return and single journey tickets.

Although the situation with coach operations pre-war remains unclear, it seems likely that the former *Smith's of Reading* Lancia (YW 939) had been acquired sometime before its earliest recorded date with *Brimblecombes* of June 1941, and it carried a 26-seater body by London Lorries, having been withdrawn by its former owner in January 1939. The Lancia is seen below, but it is believed that the roof was fully panelled over by *Smith's* in due course.

With the outbreak of war, *Brimblecombe's* coaching work actually expanded, as they became involved in daily contracts, often on behalf of the Government or Military Forces, with numerous local camps and airfields, along with factories on aircraft production and other war work. This led to an increase in the fleet with various secondhand purchases, such expansion also forming an incentive to maximise such operations when peace returned. In the meantime, Reg Brimblecombe married Eileen Lailey in February 1941, the couple having two children as Rosemary

Anne (1941) and John (1946), though the later suffered from leukemia and died in 1986 aged just 40.

Willetts of Colchester specialised in supplying coach bodies on the fairly uncommon Fordson chassis.

The first recorded addition to the wartime fleet was a Willett-bodied forward-control Fordson (CNO 716) with seats for 26 and new in July 1935. It was acquired by June 1941, and despite having an Essex registration it was new to *Oliver Taylor* of Caterham in Kent. As a result of that, in December 1941 the Lancia coach (YW 939) was disposed of.

That was followed in November 1942 by a much-travelled Leyland 'Tiger' TS1 (WJ 1916), which had been new in July 1931 as a service saloon with *Sheffield Corporation*. After that it passed to *New Empress Saloons* of London, and in due course absorbed into the *City Coach Co.*, which sent it in 1937 for a new 31-seater front-entrance body by Duple. The 'Tiger' was an advanced chassis for its date, this made a useful coach which would stay for nearly 10 years– a very reliable vehicle, shown below.

1943 saw a real couple of oddities being acquired for contract duties, the situation with new vehicles requiring operators to seek out whatever could be found. One was a forward-control Commer PLNF5-type chassis with a rather bizarre 26-seater coach body by Heaver of Durrington, Wiltshire, and new in May 1939 as COD 71 to *Burfitt* of Ilfracombe, coming to Wokingham in August 1943. Also incoming that year at an unrecorded date was an ancient-looking Albion

'Victor' PM28 (RS 8306) new in December 1926 as a bus of *Major Sibley*, who operated from Aberdeen. He sold out to *Scottish Motor Traction*, who re-bodied it with a rather square 32-seater front-entrance bus body by Cowieson in 1934, coming to Wokingham after a spell with *W. Alexander*, also in Scotland. After that the quartet of very assorted vehicles formed the fleet until after the war had ended in 1945.

The Heaver-bodied Commer with its previous owner.

Indeed, contract work remained the bread-and-butter work of the early post-war era as well, and in particular the two large building projects related to the emerging atomic technology. Both were situated in west Berkshire and based on former RAF sites, the one at Aldermaston for the manufacture of missiles, and that at Harwell for the peaceful applications of the new science. Numerous operators ran to both sites from all over Berkshire and beyond, and *Brimblecombe's* acquired further old coaches and buses of the 31 to 35-seater range in order to meet demand and, as was common practice at that time those running to Harwell saw their drivers employed on site during the day, the vehicles remaining there until the homeward run. However, at Aldermaston, all but one of the coaches remained static, with the other one taking all the drivers back to base until the afternoon journey. Indeed, such was the capacity that the brothers considered buying some double-deckers, though the close proximity of the low railway bridges on the Finchampstead Road, either side of their garage, was apparently a factor in dissuading that course of action!

However, the other factor in the rapid expansion of *Brimblecombe* coaching operations after the war was the decision by the other two established Wokingham operators to call it a day. *Frank Benham* originally had a 1924 Fiat all-weather coach which was in use until the end of September 1934, when it was replaced by a Lancia. He was in no financial way to buy a further replacement, having financed the original purchase from a lucky win on the horses! He did, however, continue his taxi business from his premises at No.61 Peach Street until about 10 years prior to his death in 1967 at the age of 78, the road service license he held passing to *Brimblecombe Bros.* in February 1946, which removed competition on local and coastal excursions, but did not add any significant destinations to those covered by *Herrings* also.

The Albion RS 8306 is seen parked at AERE Harwell.

Also acquired that some month was the coach and car hire business of *Rich Herring (t/a Herring Bros.)* of Nos.54-56 Peach Street, another second-generation transport business, which the family felt should be sold in favour of concentrating on the shop selling glass, china etc. An approach had already been made by *Valliant Coaches* of Ealing, who were keen to get a foothold in the area in view of the lucrative contracts referred to above, but ultimately the decision was made to sell locally in order to maintain better continuity for their established patrons. The deal included a good raft of excursions and part-day tours, both locally and further afield, and on the vehicle side the fleet of 3 remaining coaches passed to the new owners. These were the 1930 Star 'Flyer' (RX 6923), the 1936 Morris-Commercial 'Leader' (DWL 918) and the just pre-war Bedford OB (CBL 502), along with several Armstrong-Siddeley cars, a van and the use of the garage at No.50 Peach Street, where the cars and van remained based. Full details of the various excursions and tours licenses held by *Frank Benham* and *Herring Bros.* will be found under their respective headings.

Also taken over from *Herring Bros.* was a Goods Operator's License, along with a unrecorded 30cwt van, which *Brimblecombes* replaced with a Morris of similar weight (JBL 813) but also fitted with 8 seats for hackney use as well in October 1953. These takeovers were also made shortly before the Ministry of Transport removed the mileage restrictions it had imposed on coach operators in order to conserve fuel, that taking effect from Sunday 11th April 1946.

The other incoming vehicle for 1946 was yet another oddity in the scheme of things, this being one of a small number of Maudslay SF40, a chassis type designed with a front overhang, which also gave a higher seating capacity than the general case when it was new in August 1935. The 36-seater centre-entrance body by Duple was effectively streamlined, and would not have gone amiss amongst the under-

floor types of some 15 years later. Registered CUL 8, it had been new to *Lewis* of London SW10 and had come to *Brimblecombes* by April 1946.

In the meantime, during October 1945, Bill had been married to Diana S.H. Molloy (born 1919) in Sussex at Chichester, and we shall hear more of her later on.

May 1947 saw the first coach purchased new by the firm, with another Maudslay type, a 'Marathon' MkIII (DRX 489) which received a 33-seater front-entrance coach body built by Whitson. The latter was one of a number of smaller firms attracted to producing coach bodies of what were basically still to pre-war designs in post-war famine of such new builds. Similarly, the chassis designed owed much to pre-war design, making this vehicle actually look older than the 1935 SF40-type. However, in common with many other coach bodies constructed during 1947, that on the Maudslay duly saw considerable deterioration due to the use of unseasoned timber, so it had to be replaced by a new fully-fronted body by Strachans in 1953.

Adding even more variety to the small fleet was the Maudslay SF40, seen here with its original operator.

During 1948 a further two secondhand purchases were added, the first being acquired in January and being a 1934 Albion 'Valkyrie' PW67-type re-bodied for *Brimblecombes* by Whitson with a 33-seater front-entrance coach body. ANW 443 had started life with *Whitehead* of Leeds, but was certainly in much better nick than the older PM28 already in use. With the arrival of this coach the strange-looking Commer (COD 71) was disposed of in February 1948.

The second arrival for 1948 came in November and was a further Leyland, though this time a 1938 'Lion' LT8-type chassis which carried a Duple 37-seater coach body, (DOV 973) which had been new to *Stockland* of Birmingham. Shortly after that we first note the addition of local garage owner Jackie Strachan of Wokingham Road, Bracknell as another booking agent.

Whether there had been any attempt to adopt a standard livery pre-war is not known, though the necessity to obtain secondhand vehicles at short notice for contracts makes that unlikely. However, it is evident that the former *Herrings* Star was altered from a two-tone grey scheme to grey with maroon trim, whilst photographs show that the Albion 'Valkyrie' (ANW 443) and later Dennis 'Lancet' (FGC 869) both in that scheme, whilst the 1947 Maudslay 'Marathon' MkIII (DRX 489) appears to be the same from new.

The re-bodied Albion seen when still new at Oxford.

Maintenance was generally to a high standard, and one family source quotes Reg Brimblecombe as having served an apprenticeship at *Thames Valley's* bus workshops in Reading, though records for that period have not survived. That may, however, explain the various contacts between the two concerns over the years, as during the war years *Brimblecombe's* Leyland 'Tiger' TS1 (WJ 1916) was noted running with a TV-badged TS4-style radiator, which it later lost, whilst in July 1953 the brothers bought a pair of Leyland 8.6 oil engines from the *'Valley'*. There were also frequent instances where *Brimblecombe's* coaches were hired by TV to help out during Ascot Race Week, despite having their own express route.

The 'Lion' LT8 DOV 973 on an outing from The Metropolitan pub in Rose Street, Wokingham.

On the other hand, keeping some of the older vehicles was sometimes challenging, and Peter Pribik recalls that the rather ancient-looking 1926 Albion PM28-type (RS 8306) suffered a number of breakdowns, causing the driver to call in at his parent's Frank's Café at Loddon Bridge to phone the garage! On another later occasion one of their Bedford OB's pulled in with a fire under the bonnet, but that was soon extinguished safely.

Reg is recalled as being quite calm about minor mishaps on the road, but always stressed to drivers to 'bring all the bits back', as it made for a quicker repair job. Indeed, one day a coach had several side panels badly damaged on a morning run, so the workshop quickly replaced them and re-sprayed the side ready for that afternoon's return contract run!

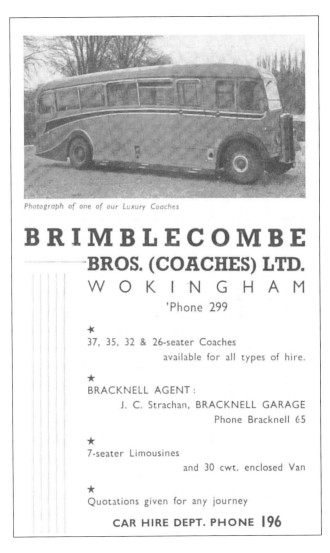

Photograph of one of our Luxury Coaches

BRIMBLECOMBE
BROS. (COACHES) LTD.
W O K I N G H A M
'Phone 299

★
37, 35, 32 & 26-seater Coaches
available for all types of hire.

★
BRACKNELL AGENT:
J. C. Strachan, BRACKNELL GARAGE
Phone Bracknell 65

★
7-seater Limousines
and 30 cwt. enclosed Van

★
Quotations given for any journey

CAR HIRE DEPT. PHONE 196

This advert appeared in a Local Directory for 1947 and featured Maudslay DRX 489 with Whitson body.

The car hire side having been strengthened through the acquisition of *Herring's* 7-seater Armstrong-Siddeley limousines, was now advertised as' the best around and driven by uniformed chauffeurs', remaining based at No.50 Peach Street, the old Herrings phone number 196 now added to their original 299 of the Finchampstead Road premises.

1949 saw a number of changes within the fleet, with supplies of bodies now easing a bit. However, largely with contract duties in mind, the first two arrivals were both secondhand. In May came another Leyland, this time a 'Tiger' TS7 of 1935, which carried a very stylish Burlingham 32-seater centre-entrance coach body and had been new to *Smith's* of Birmingham as AOV 272. It was joined in August by the second Bedford in the fleet, a 1939 WTB-type, which carried a 26-seater body of unconfirmed make. FWJ 902 had been new in the Sheffield area, but again the operator is not known. The arrival of the Leyland saw the end for the squat-fronted Albion 'Viking' RS 8306.

A further trio of new coaches were also on order, but as often happened during that period of shortages of material caused by the continuing austerity in Britain at that time, these arrived later than had been planned. All were normal-control Austin K4/CXB chassis with Whitson 29-seater front-entrance coach bodies. Two arrived in October as FJB 733/4, followed by the third as FJB 735 in November 1949. With their arrival it was possible to dispose of the former *Herring Bros.* Star 'Flyer' VB3-type (RX 6923), which had been new in 1930 and was a rare make by that date.

Above – 'Tiger' AOV 272 as delivered, and *below* - a 1949 advert in the local press for the Easter period.

Two views of the Whitson-bodied Austins, with FJB 734 at Southsea seen above, *and FJB 733 at Lincoln's Inns Fields in London as shown* below.

Certain trips still ran from the *Herring's* garage in perpetuation of their original license, these being the Tuesday-evening Whist Drive excursion to Sunninghill, whilst others departed from the Market Place, a useful triangular site suitable for all road directions. The booking agency of F.J.A. Wright in Broad Street, Wokingham continued in use, but through the *Herring's* licenses also came additional pick-up points at Popeswood (Shoulder of Mutton), Binfield (The Standard), Bracknell (Post Office, High Street), Crowthorne (Iron Duke) and Finchampstead (Greyhound). Most were included according to the direction of travel, with some trips starting out from Bracknell, as had been the case under *Herrings*. An additional booking agent was Mr. E.W. Dorrell (Newsagent, Dukes Ride, Crowthorne), whilst

Herrings continued it that role giving good connections with their former clientele.

Excursion adverts for the Spring of 1950 also list pick-up points at Crowthorne (Prince Alfred), Warfield (Plough & Harrow) and Chavey Down (Royal Foresters) on some trips, with that to Cheddar having one coach starting from Chavey Down and running via Binfield, and a second one from Finchampstead via Crowthorne, then both through Wokingham. Some examples of adult day return fares at the time were Bognor Regis 7 shillings 6 pence, Bournemouth 10s, Brighton 7s 6d, Cheddar 15s, Whipsnade Zoo 5s 9d and Worthing 7s 6d.

Further additional agents were also recruited, particularly as the Bracknell New Town developed, so that by 1962 the full list now read as follows – F.J.A. Wright (Broad Street, Wokingham), Thomas Bowyer (Corn Stores, Peach Street, Wokingham – in place of Herrings next door), Mr. Trigwell (Post Office, Binfield), Mr. LB. Corne (Newsagent, Priestwood Square, Bracknell), J.W. Smith (Newsagent & Bookseller, High Street, Bracknell), Mr. Dorrell (Newsagent, Dukes Ride, Crowthorne), Mrs. Scott (Post Office, Chavey Down), Mr. Farr (Newsagent, Bullbrook), Mrs. Corne (Newsagent, Rectory Row, Easthampstead) and Mr. Mulvey (Orchard Stores, Bagshot Road, Bracknell).

As well as the worker's contracts continuing from the wartime era, there were also a trio of local services designed to serve outlying locations in the Wokingham district. The first of these was the long-established TB Isolation Hospital at Pinewood, just north-west of the crossroads of the Old Wokingham Road and Nine Mile Ride between Crowthorne and Easthampstead Park. Regular journeys were operated for the benefit of visitors to patients at the hospital, the application of February 1949 showing an outward journey on Sundays only at 1.45pm, which returned from the hospital at 4.10pm. The route started from Wokingham Railway Station and ran as Wellington Road – Langborough Road – Easthampstead Road, with the Town Hall added from 1952. The service continued in a similar way until the Spring of 1961, the hospital finally closing down in 1965.

The second service ran to a site opposite the main entrance of the hospital on the Old Wokingham Road, the former Easthampstead Camp, initially still used by the army, but later housing displaced persons, and in due course some local families awaiting housing allocations by the Rural District Councils of Easthampstead or Wokingham as part of a general shortage of post-war housing. Daily journeys provided a link between the camp and Wokingham Station, the route travelling via the Town Hall – Easthampstead Road – Waterloo Road – Old Wokingham Road. In its form of February 1949 it was an evenings-only route, operating between 6.30pm and 8pm into Wokingham

and outward between 9pm and 10pm, though exact times and frequency could be determined by the army authorities, whilst the single fare was set at 7 pence, but the intermediate stops at Star Lane Crossing and Waterloo Crossroads requested were not approved.

Another application followed on 5th March 1949 in order to provide additional links for the civilians now being billeted at the camp. On Tuesdays only there were two journeys from Wokingham (Town Hall) at 2pm and 4.10pm. The first went directly to the camp via Peach Street – Easthampstead Road – Star Lane Crossing, turning at the camp to form the 2.10pm trip back. However, the second journey on that day at 4.10pm ran out from Wokingham in similar fashion until it reached Waterloo Road, where it turned left and took in a stop at the Easthampstead Mansion, turning at the camp to form the 4.35pm return run. In each case the vehicle ran back the opposite way to which it had come out on, thereby forming a circular route. On Saturdays there were four journeys outwards at 9am, 11.25am, 6.50pm and 10.15pm, and these operated in a similar circular fashion, there being a return fare of 1 shilling 1 pence, and even some intermediate single fares. Given the close proximity of the camp site to Pinewood Hospital, it seems likely some of those who could not make the Sunday visiting may have also utilised those journeys, which otherwise formed a useful shopping facility. It should also be appreciated that the *Gough's Garage Bus Service* from Bracknell and Warfield operated to that location from Monday 25th April 1949, and full details will be found under their own heading.

The third of the local applications in February 1949 concerned the Arborfield Garrison, a former Calvary Remount Depot now occupied by the Royal Electrical & Mechanical Engineers and its School of Army Apprentices, situated some 5 miles due south of Wokingham town centre. In addition, there was a substantial amount of apartment accommodation for the students and enough married quarters housing to form its own village. However, the daily travelling arrangements of most of the residents was met through *Thames Valley* service 4a, which operated between Reading and Wokingham via the garrison, also using Langley Common Road and the Barkham Road, with a stop by the railway station. As well as that, there were other peaks of travel, either for evening journeys by the apprentices to the numerous pubs and the cinema in Wokingham, along with other timings designed primarily to cater for weekend leave passes to places further away.

On Friday afternoons a coach left every 10 minutes from 4.30pm until 5pm, calling at various points within the garrison and also the Bramshill Hunt pub in Baird Road on the perimeter of the camp, for Wokingham Station. On Saturday daytimes a basically 10-minute headway operated from midday through to 2.15pm, with set journeys in both directions, whilst on Saturday and Sunday evenings a service commenced from Wokingham Station at 9.30pm, thereafter running at 10 to 16-minute intervals (to march train arrivals) through to the last departure from that point at 11.26pm, suiting those returning from leave and also from the local pubs and cinema. Overall the service called at the Bailleul, Hazebrouck and Poperinge Barracks, whilst a clause in the license permitted operation on other days if requested by the army authorities. In the first post-war application of February 1949 there was also a one-way Monday-Fridays journey from Wokingham Station at 10.10am, though this was obviously dropped in due course. The service was indeed a popular link with the lads of that time, and on one occasion the driver Jim McInnes found quite a queue awaiting the last evening run back to the camp, plus other latecomers arriving. The fare was 6 pence, which he continued to take as they filed on, not really keeping any track of numbers. As his very full coach crawled up the road, 'smoking like a train', it was stopped by the Police who, after turning all the lads off found there were 81 on board! From Christmas 1951 the Arborfield terminus was altered to the Bramshill Hunt pub on Baird Road.

It is thought that both the Easthampstead Camp and Arborfield Garrison services had their origins with *Herring Bros.*, but were operated under Wartime Permits, so no details are available.

From July 1949 the title of the Company was amended as *R.H. & W.R. Brimblecombe* (t/a *Brimblecombe Bros. Ltd.*)

Another lucrative local operation was the express carriage license for Royal Ascot Race Week held annually in June, another of the licenses inherited from *Herrings,* when as many coaches as could be mustered ran journeys to and from the Royal Ascot Hotel and Wokingham Town Hall, the timings being suited to the flow for race-goers. The fares were only single and the charge from Wokingham was 10d and from Bracknell 6d, and despite the frequent *Thames Valley* Route 2 over the same road, the *Brimblecombe* service was indeed popular, particularly with parties emanating from Wokingham's then numerous pubs.

At the renewal of the license to Easthampstead Camp in March 1950 the service was amended to start from Wokingham Town Hall, but now ran on Tuesdays, Thursdays, Fridays, Saturdays and Sundays at times as requested by The Burser at Easthampstead Training College, the Teacher Training Establishment set up for women in the old Downshire mansion, which would duly merge with Bulmershe College at Woodley in 1968. Also added from August 1950 was an excursion to Aldershot Speedway for 2 coaches, a then very popular evening out, fitting in well with the time many finished their working day.

1950 saw only one coach entering the fleet, another 33-seater front-entrance coach, but this time a 1938 Dennis 'Lancet' MkII, which carried a Metcalfe body with a stepped waist-rail fashionable at that time. FGC 869 had been new to *Glenton Tours* of London, but had been with *Morecambe Motors* up in Lancashire in between. Its arrival saw the sale of another ex-*Herring Bros.* coach, this time the Duple-bodied 1936 Morris-Commercial 'Leader' DWL 918. 1951 was a relatively quite year for fleet changes, with only the disposal of the Williett-bodied Fordson (CNO 716) in October.

Dennis 'Lancet' FGC 869 was a useful high-capacity vehicle for the Arborfield Garrison run, seen here with Jim McInnes acting as conductor.

In 1950/1 the local directory shows Eddystone Garage at No.70 Finchampstead Road, with Annie Brimblecombe at No.72 and son Reg and wife Eileen at 72a. Bill & Edith Adams were also noted as at No.70, whilst Bill Brimblecombe was elsewhere in the town at No.14 Crescent Road with his wife Diana and daughter Rose (later known as Rosanna), the couple having married in 1945. Following Annie's death in 1953 No.72 was occupied by John Walter Darbourn and his wife Margaret.

Changes to the fleet for 1952 saw a former *Ribble MS* Burlingham-bodied Leyland 'Tiger' TS8 (RN 8396) of 1938, with front-entrance bus body, now fitted with 31 coach seats taken from Leyland 'Tiger' TS1-type WJ 1916 which it replaced on the Harwell run from May. An example of that large batch of buses is shown above. That was followed by the withdrawal of the Maudslay SF40-type (CUL 8) during October.

Several excursions or tours had been modified, and the full listing for the 1953 season was as follows –

No.	Destination	Notes
1	Bournemouth	Day trip
2	Worthing	Day trip
3	Brighton	Day trip
4	Bognor	Day trip
5	Portsmouth/Southsea	Day trip
6	Epsom	Race days
7	Hayling Island	Day trip
8	Goodwood (incl. motor days)	Race days
9	Burnham Beeches	Day trip
10	Aldershot (also Speedway)	Tattoo
11	Sonning	Race days
12	Reading (Elm Park)	Reading FC
13	Sunninghill (Whist drive)	Tues.Evening
14	Henley (evening trip)	Fireworks
15	Arborfield	Race days
16	Stratfield Saye/Arborfield	Circular tour
17	Henley/Sonning/Woodley	Circular tour
18	Marlow/Henley/Sonning	Circular tour
19	Sandhurst etc.	Circular tour
20	Swinley/Winkfield/Warfield	Circular tour
21	Whipsnade Zoo	Day trip
22	Thame	Show day
23	Bracknell (Mondays)	Evening
24	California - afternoon trip or evening events	
25	Cheddar	Day trip
26	Wembley Stadium	For events
27	Hastings via Eastbourne	Day trip
28	London Zoo	Day trip
29	Chessington Zoo	Day trip
30	Hampton Court and Kew	Day trip
31	Littlehampton	Day trip
32	Frensham Ponds/Hindhead	Circular tour
33	Berkshire Downs	Circular tour
34	Oxford Theatre (evenings)	For shows
35	Beaconsfield (Model Village)	Day trip
36	London (White City Stadium)	Tattoo
37	Blenheim Palace	Circular tour
38	Farnborough	Air display

Notes: The Circular Tours could be operated for either the afternoon or evening. Day trips had adult fares of between 7 shillings and 6 pence and 10 shillings, more local day excursion were 3s 6d to 5s 6d, with half-day tours and other local short duration trips at 1s 9d to 2s 3d. The longest trips were those to Cheddar and Eastbourne/Hastings, both at 15s.

Between December 1952 and March 1953 tour No.39 was added and in March one further tour took the number 40 on the list, with a day excursion to Stratford-upon-Avon for up to 2 coaches and with an adult fare of 10s. No.39 never seems recorded in N&P's, but it probably related to the coaching highlight of 1953, the Coronation of Queen Elizabeth II. In view of the likely demand, the traffic Commissioners largely waived the usual detail and issued special licenses were granted for excursions during the period of the Decorations, Illuminations and the actual Coronation in June 1953, setting an adult return fare of 7s 6d and a maximum of 4 vehicles on any one day in respect of *Brimblecombe's*, plus any requirements of the Police in respect of route taken and parking.

What had originally been a contract working to the Atomic Weapons Research Establishment at Aldermaston was put onto a different footing from March 1953, when the route was registered as an express carriage operation for those employed there. A timetable was set with a morning journey from Wokingham (Town Hall) at 6.40am, which then ran by way of Emmbrook (Rifle Volunteer) – Winnersh (Crossroads) – Winnersh (Drome Garage) – Loddon Bridge (The George) – Loddon Hill (Post Office) – Earley (Three Tuns) – Shinfield (Merry Maidens) Shinfield Green (School) – Spencers Wood (Adey's Stores, Hyde End Road) – Spencers Wood (Red Lion) – Mortimer (Station) – Mortimer (School) – Mortimer Common (Post Office) – Bramley (Crossroads), arriving at the AWRE (Main Gate) at 7.35am. The return journey ran the same route in reverse, leaving at 5.40pm to arrive at Wokingham at 6.35pm. As this was still an Assisted Travel Scheme, payment was not taken from the passengers, but was paid by the Ministry at £3 19s per day in respect of a 35-seater coach, the operation running on Mondays to Fridays, other than Bank Holidays etc. More stops were added from October 1955 at Wilderness Road, Mays Hill and Beech Hill, such was the demand, whilst in due course they timings were adjusted to take account of a shorter working week once introduced.

Private hire was still a good steady trade, and here one party from a Wokingham pub enjoy a roadside beer with the re-bodied Maudslay 'Marathon'.

As already noted, the Whitson body on the 1947 Maudslay (DRX 489) was showing signs of deterioration, mainly through the inevitable use of unseasoned timber at that time, so the vehicle was sent to Strachans for a new front-entrance and fully-fronted 35-seater coach body in time for the spring of 1953. July of that year saw the end for Albion ANW 443, which of course carried a similar vintage Whitson body probably with the same issues, along with the last of the trio of coaches inherited from *Herring Bros.*, as 1939 Thurgood-bodied Bedford OB (CBL 502). Further fleet changes came in October, with the acquisition of former *Roger's* of Farnborough Bedford OB (MMT 866), which had a Duple front-entrance coach body seating 27 and had been new in 1947 to *Garner* of London W13. During November this was joined by a forward-control coach of the same make, but an SB-type, which carried a Duple 33-seater, front-entrance body. New in 1951, ECK 316 had been delivered to the *Ribble M.S.* associated *Scout Motors* of Preston. The arrival of the latter saw the exit of FWJ 902, the 1939 Bedford WTB after 10 year's service.

The significance of such events as annual shows etc. may these days be lost on a population so accustom to television and international travel, but back in the '50's treats were less frequent. So, when Humpty Dumpty on Ice at Wembley Arena was on offer as the Winter spectacular during January and February 1954 the Company found it could soon sell its allocation of tickets. Adults paid 11s 6d, which included the 8s 6d seat for the show, whilst children went for 8s 9d.

Reg Brimblecome had already been a Councillor on Wokingham Borough Council for 6 years when, in May 1954, he was made Mayor for the year, as shown above in his civic portrait. He is recalled as a pleasant man with a good sense of humour, and also the driving force for the revival of the once popular annual carnival and the charities it supported, in what was then a relatively small town. The name is perpetuated by a Brimblecombe Close on a development at Emmbrook.

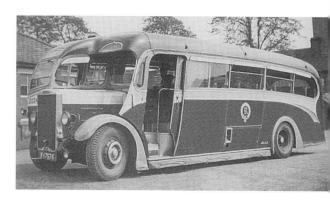

During January 1954 another Leyland 'Tiger' joined the fleet, this time a 1936 TS7 carrying a Duple front-entrance 33-seater coach body. WH 7578 had been new to *Arthur Christy* of Bolton, passing to *Ribble M.S.*, and then onto its associated *Standerwick* fleet, before coming to Wokingham via a dealer. It's twin coach is shown above, and although its stay would be a short one, it allowed for the disposal of similar type coach AOV 272 during July. The other acquisitions for 1954 consisted a pair of 1948 AEC 'Regal' MkIII 0962-type coaches which carried Strachan 33-seater, front-entrance bodies and had been new to *Yeoman's* of Canon Pyon, Hereford. Registered FCJ 843/4 these arrived in September and July respectively, and once in service they allowed the sale of 1938 Dennis 'Lancet' coach FGC 869 during November 1954.

Whereas the coach bodies of the pre-war and early post-war era tended to suit a livery with a base colour relieved by a side flash and mudguards in another colour, the beading styles from the early 1950's became better suited to a more diverse scheme. The *Brimblecombes* fleet therefore adopted a scheme of a dark red and maroon, in roughly equal amounts, with light cream window surrounds, though the actual application did depend on the varied body styles. A winged 'BB' monogram appeared on most of the 1950-60's coaches, whilst the full *'Brimblecombe Bros.'* was fitted into one of the destination apertures and sometimes also at the rear, with boot panels bearing the Eddystone Garage lighthouse logo, Wokingham and the phone numbers.

FCJ 844 was one of the pair of Strachans-bodied AEC 'Regals' purchased in 1954, and whilst their bodies were duly replaced, the 9.6-litre engines made them a popular choice with drivers, seen here when still new.

The AEC 'Reliance' with Burlingham 'Seagull' body was undoubtably one of the most pleasing vehicles of its era, and certainly KMO 939 would serve the firm for many years as a front-line coach before going onto contract duties. It is caught here by the camera of Ray Simpson as part of a 7-coach trip to Wembley in company with Bedford YMP 553, with events such as basketball and ice-hockey drawing large numbers of bookings for all ages before television.

In another view of KMO 939 we can see the sliding centre doorway of that body, and it is nearing Elm Park Stadium of Reading FC on a regular home-match excursion from the Wokingham area. It would remain in service until 1966, although a later view shows that at some point the front end was rebuilt, losing the AEC triangular badge set low on the front grille for new lettering at the centre top of the wing-like beading, presumably after accidental damage.

Whilst the lightweight Bedfords, such as LJB 264, also seen here at Wembley, were not notable for long working lives, this example would even outlast the AEC of the same year, not being disposed of until 1972. A programme of re-engining some of them by John Newman, saw this one loose its petrol engine in favour of a 'Comet' oil engine transferred from a lorry chassis purchased solely for that exercise in the mid-1960's. The driver here is Ron Bucksey.

1954 saw two new coaches purchased, though quite different types of vehicle. In February came an underfloor-engined AEC 'Reliance' MU3RV-type chassis carrying a Burlingham 'Seagull' centre-doorway 41-seater body (KMO 939), which was a modern-looking addition to the fleet and popular with drivers. During July came another forward-control Bedford model, an SBG-type with petrol engine, the fleet still being a mix of diesel and petrol engines. This was LJB 262, which had a Duple 'Vega' 38-seater, front-entrance body, and both of these would be a familiar sight both locally and at the coastal coach parks for many years. The arrival of KMO led to the sale of Bedford SB-type ECK 316 in March, after only a short time in the fleet, and the same was true of Leyland 'Tiger' TS7 WH 7578, which departed in October.

At the close of that season the owners realised they had been charging higher fares on day excursions to the coastal resorts which were served more cheaply by *Smith's Luxury Coaches* on their express services, for example 10 shillings for Brighton compared with the Reading operator's 7s 6d. However, although they did apply to reduce the fares to be in line, both firms soon were putting in for increases due to rises in wages and the cost of fuel, so a fares war was thereby averted.

As can be seen the expansion of the *Brimblecombe* coaching business was very rapid in the post-war era, but there were still further acquisition to be made. Over at Crowthorne was another long-established family business that traced its transport origins back to horse-drawn days. Whereas *Brimblecombe's* garage business would fade in favour of the coaching side, that of *Lovick's Motors* of High Street, Crowthorne was developing in the opposite direction as the generations succeeded those involved earlier. There were apparently several local concerns interested in adding the *Lovick* licenses, but *Brimblecombes* came through as successful in January 1956, also acquiring the active fleet comprising an Austin K4/CXD (GMO 14) and Guy 'Arab' (GMO 418), both new in 1951 and bearing Thurgood bodies. Still evident was also a rare forward-control former *Windsorian* Dennis 'Ace' (JB 7737), which had last been licensed in September 1954 and was sold without entering service with the new owner. The enhanced patronage from the Crowthorne area was useful, though the other small operator also in the High Street, *Sid Townsend*, duly sold his coach business to *Smith's of Reading* instead.

Another worker's express service commenced from February 1956 to the AWRE site at Aldermaston, but this time it was routed out from Wokingham southwards, starting from opposite the Three Brewers pub in Barkham Road, then as Old Leathern Bottel – Bakham Hill Garage – Barkham (Bull Inn) – Arborfield (Wokingham Road) – Arborfield (Memorial) – Swallowfield – Handpost Farm – Riseley (Bull Inn) – Riseley (Fairs Close) – Mortimer (Station) – School –

Mortimer Common (Post Office) – Bramley (Cross Roads) – Merricks Corner – AWRE Main Gate. Two journeys left on weekdays at 6.37am and 7.27am, and the return journey was at 5.40pm Mondays-Thursdays and 5.05pm on Fridays. Up to two coaches could be used on each journey, whilst the fares were set under the Assisted Travel Scheme on this restricted service for AWRE workers only.

The established Wokingham (Town Hall) – AWRE service via Emmbrook – Winnersh – Shinfield etc. was also revised from December 1956 to depart from Wokingham at 6.40am and 7.30am, and with the same times for return journeys as noted above. There was also provision included to operate the 6.40am journey on Saturdays or Sundays if requested by the site authority.

No vehicles left the fleet during 1956, but another of those stranger purchases occurred in June, when a rare Foden PVFE6-type with a one-and-a-half-decker body by Lincs Trailer arrived! KOC 662 was one of several new to *Allenway's* of Birmingham in 1950, when there was a short-lived fad for this type of body, which some obviously regarded as futuristic. The 43 seats were arranged in two tiers over two levels, with a rather unusual window arrangement, whilst the front styling was also unconventional. As it was, many of these bodies were built by firms not particularly found producing coaches, with variable results. This coach came to Wokingham from *Creamline* of Bordon in June 1956, but despite its high seating capacity, which could have eliminated duplicated running, it was not destined to see much use. Indeed, it was disposed of in December 1957, being replaced the month before by an AEC 'Regal' MkIV underfloor-engined coach with a Plaxton 41-seater, centre-entrance body, JGD 116, which was new in 1951 to *Northern Roadways* of Glasgow, then via *Triumph* of Portsmouth and *Valliant* of London W5. As new it had a Burlingham coach body and had been re-bodied in 1956.

Foden KOC 662 and its twin 663 are seen at Pier Head in Liverpool, caught by Ken Swallow in 1953, showing the Crellin-Duplex patented half-deck design.

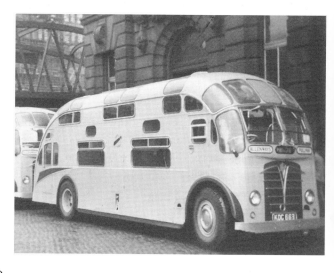

30

KOC 662 is seen again when with Creamline, with the nearside sliding door visible.

The *Brimblecombes* recognised that housing developments at Bracknell New Town would provide additional bums-on-seats for excursions, particularly as many former Londoners had grown up with easy access to South Coast resorts, and so naturally expected the same from their new location. In December 1956 they applied to modify their existing coastal excursions to take in an additional pick up at Priestwood Square. This point was the neighbourhood shopping parade for both the completed Priestwood I estate, situated between the Binfield and Wokingham Roads, which also served the growing housing east of the Binfield Road in the Priestwood II area. This gave regular opportunities to take *Brimblecombe's* coaches to Bognor, Brighton, Bournemouth, Eastbourne, Hastings, Haying Island, Littlehampton, Portsmouth and Worthing.

From January 1957 the routing out of Wokingham of the AWRE service via Barkham was altered to start at the Metalair Factory in Wellington Road, proceeding via Finchampstead Road (Two Poplars) – Evendons Lane turn – Barkham Ride – Gorse Ride turn, before re-joining the old route at Barkham (Bull Inn). Also at times the AWRE-owned vehicles could be seen in the area if covering other shift patterns not on contract.

Following the acquisition of the *Cody Coaches* licenses in October 1956 by *Smith's of Reading*, the latter applied in order to link up the new pick-ups it generated with its established network of Summer coastal express services. As that included Bracknell and Binfield, an objection was forthcoming from *Brimblecombe Bros.* In response the Commissioner said he didn't consider that the latter had exclusive rights to those pick areas, as *Smith's* had acquired the existing licenses from *Cody*. He also added that in considering the overall picture he had refused other applications from *Carter's of Maidenhead* and *Thames Valley* for pick-ups within the already established *Brimblecombe's* area, a good example of the thought that often went into such decisions in

those days. As it was, *Windsorian* had objected to the pick-up at Chavey Down, so that was not allowed.

Perhaps rather surprising for a Wokingham-based operator, it was given the job of providing the shuttle service between Ascot Station and the East Berkshire Golf Course for the tournament sponsored by Bowmakers on Sunday/Monday 23rd/24th June 1957. It ran from 8.30am to 11am, then again from 6.30pm at single fares of 1 shilling, that task in previous years having gone to *White Bus Services* of Winkfield.

During the Summer of 1958 an application was made to Wokingham Borough Council for permission to erect a new coach garage on the site inherited from *Herring Bros.* off Peach Street in the town. The desire was to have a booking office and garage situated more conveniently in the town centre, but the proposal was turned down in July on the grounds that the entrance was too narrow and the roadway in Peach Street, which was then a two-way stretch of the A329, not suitable for the coming and going of such vehicles.

A further small takeover followed in October 1958, when another second-generation operator decided to forsake coaching in order to concentrate on his garage business. That was *James Hinman*, whose father of the same name had established his Popeswood Garage on the southern side of the junction where Binfield's St. Marks Road emerged onto the London Road and just east of the Shoulder of Mutton pub.

Apart from the garage, a carriers business had operated from that area into Reading for many years, continuing in a small way as a coach operation with some private hire and excursions. As *Brimblecombes* already served that area it was a useful and cheap consolidation, with *Hinman's* former *Smith's* of Reading Bedford OB (DRD 382) joining the fleet for a short period.

It is of course worth noting that *Hinman's* near neighbours had been *Cody Coaches*, who had sold out to *Smith's Luxury Coaches* of Reading in September 1956. *Cody* also had a long pedigree back to the 1920's, when it had been started by *Brookhouse Keene,* the decision to sell resulting from the ill health of his successor and son-in-law *Bill Jones. More on Cody Coaches and Hinman will be found elsewhere in this volume.*

Some contract runs were already in place with the Berkshire County Council Education Authority by the early 1950's, but from early 1952 an express service was provided where parents could pay 3s 6d per week for their child to travel on the journey between Earley (Three Tuns), Loddon Bridge or Sutcliffe Avenue to the Woodley County School, that being under the 3-mile distance criteria for free transport. The route took in new areas of housing and ran on schooldays only.

Additional excursions added in December 1958 were a full-day run to Woburn Abbey from Easter to October, plus all-year-round half-day tours to London Airport at 4s 6d and Gatwick Airport 9s, it being an era when the public was welcome to tour such facilities in order to encourage air travel.

New coaches followed in 1958 as Duple-bodied Bedford SB3 (RJB 292) in November, preceded by the first proper minibus, a BMC-bodied Austin J2BA (RBL 655) during September. The pair of half-cab 1948 Strachans-bodied AEC 'Regal' MkIII 0962's had been acquired from *Yeomans* of Canon Pyon in 1954, but these reliable coaches were suffering from bad body deterioration by the late 1950's. One was sent to Burlingham for a fully-fronted body in 1957 (FCJ 843), whilst the other got the same treatment in 1959 (FCJ 844), but due to evolving body styles they were hardly a 'pair' anymore. Indeed, whilst one received the basic 'Baby Seagull' style body as being fitted to vertical front-engined chassis in 1957, by 1959 it had been restyled in rather ugly fashion using wrap-around windscreens, which the drivers also found caused distracting reflections. According to John Neal and John Newman, FCJ 844 had its career cut prematurely short after a bad smash, but even then was rebuilt for further service with *Katmandu Transport* up in the Himalayas!

The rebodied AEC 'Regals' were no longer a pair after such work, as FCJ 844 received the rather ugly updated body seen above at Wembley with driver Ernie Nash, whereas FCJ 843 fared better with its neater 'Baby Seagull', shown below helping Thames Valley during Ascot Race Week.

The only departure from the fleet during 1958 was the AEC 'Regal' MkIV coach JGD 116 which left during September, less than a year after being acquired. There were no incoming vehicles during 1959, and it was not until December that any departures took place, with the demise of Austin K4/CXB-type FJB 733 and Bedford OB MMT 866.

In respect of the transport from the REME Camp at Arborfield, *Smith's Coaches* of Reading had tried back in August 1951 to gain a license for a direct express service to London (Victoria), but it was refused. They tried again in February 1958, but of interest during the coverage by Commercial Motor of that Hearing, it transpired that the Army Authorities were apparently not helpful to the operators, because they would not advise on numbers of passes being issued. *Smith's* were offering to do a 5-shilling return fare, much cheaper than by rail, but the Commissioner queried why they had asked for 7s 6d when applying 7 years before, but Frank Masser, Transport Manager, responded that double-deckers were to be used. That application was again refused, so the shuttle by *Brimblecombes* continued to Wokingham Station.

By the Summer of 1959 the old pattern of Friday and Saturday journeys from the Arborfield Camp had become outdated, so a general relaxation was requested to meet the requirements of the Authority there to run any time of the week, which was granted.

During September 1959 an application was put forward for 5 new express services from Wokingham (Town Hall) to operate Easter, Whitsun, then Saturdays/Sundays and August BH Monday, through to the last weekend in September, one coach requested for each route. All would proceed via Popeswood (Shoulder of Mutton) - Binfield, (Royal Standard) - Bracknell (Priestwood Square and High Street PO) – Chavey Down – Easthampstead (Rectory Row) – Crowthorne (Prince Alfred and Iron Duke). From there they went onwards to Haying Island, Southsea, Weymouth (via Bournemouth), Littlehampton and to Brighton and Worthing. There were objections from *Smith's* and *Windsorian,* as well as British Rail and *Royal Blue* in respect of west of Bournemouth, so when the hearing finally took place on 3rd November 1959 all those licenses were refused.

By the late 1950's it was necessary to extend the yard area available for coach parking, and some were now routinely parked in front of the house properties. Several were also probably outstationed with drivers in connection with contracts, which was certainly the case in the 1960-70's. Otherwise the late '50's and '60's were typified by a consolidation on the coaching front and a decline in the role of the garage business to the point where it is no longer advertised.

In January 1960 the other members of the trio of Austins bought new in 1949 were ousted, these being

FJB 734/5, and also that month the former *Hinman* Bedford OB DRD 382 also departed. Replacements entered service in March 1960 as a Bedford OB with standard Duple 'Vista' 29-seater front-entrance coach body (GCA 388), which had been new in 1950 to *Keeler* of Wrexham, but came to Wokingham via Caversham-based *Peggie's Coaches*. The other Bedford incoming was a 1953 SBO-type chassis with a Burlingham 35-seater front-entrance coach body (YMP 553), new to *Valliant* of London W5, but again it had come via the same Caversham operator.

Fulfilling the need for a 29-seater was Bedford OB-type GCA 388, though its stay was rather short.

The other incoming vehicle for 1960 was a former demonstrator, though virtually new, being a Plaxton 41-seater front-entrance coach on a Ford 570E chassis which was starting to attract sales at the time. It was registered as 2040 FH and arrived during December.

The Ford 2040 FH seen at Wembley with driver Dennis Coyd at the wheel.

In a further attempt to consolidate their position in the area, *Brimblecombe Bros.* applied in November 1961 for additional pick-up points at Arborfield (Water

Tower), Barkham (Doles Hill), Popeswood (Shoulder of Mutton), Binfield (Royal Standard), Bracknell (Priestwood Square, High Street PO) and Bullbrook (Royal Oak), Chavey Down PO, Easthampsted (Rectory Row), Finchampstead (Avery's Corner and Greyhound), Warfield (Plough & Harrow), Winkfield (Hollies Corner), to which was added the following month Harmanswater PO and Crowthorne (Prince Alfred and Iron Duke). The application was this time successful, which helped overcome earlier setbacks.

Another interesting contract was added to take workers from local areas up to the Handley-Page aircraft factory at Cricklewood, which started out from Reading (Cemetery Junction) – Loddon Bridge – Woodley (Roundabout) – Sonning Halt – Maidenhead (Regal Cinema), then direct to the works. It ran out at 6.45am to arrive for 8.40, returning on Mondays to Thursdays at 5.20pm or on Fridays at 4.45pm, that operation continuing through to February 1966.

Further local school's contracts from the Education Authority were forthcoming as it struggled to accommodate the 'baby boomers', and even primary age children were being bussed about to achieve that. In the meantime, the need for services to Easthampstead Camp had ended and the Pinewood Hospital license surrendered in March 1961. Both of the AWRE contracts were still going strong, being renewed in December 1961, accounting for 4 vehicles each day.

The interior view of 2040 FH looking towards the rear shows the arrangements for coaches of that era.

In those days of far fewer private cars some of the factories on the Western Road in Bracknell found it difficult to attract staff, in particular Aerosol Products in Downmill Road, whose largely female production workforce tended to be working mums, so suitably timed journeys were contracted to *Brimblecombes* to bring staff in from Sandhurst and Crowthorne. Also, in the late 1960's another contract coach was kept parked overnight in the Binfield Road yard of Strachan's Garage, their one-time booking agent in Bracknell. The author found it a very useful refuge late one night, when coming home from the Old Manor, taking shelter in it from a sudden thunder storm, but having fallen asleep inside, had to make a hasty departure out of the emergency door when it started up – the exhaust smoke hiding his identity!

A new Trojan mini-coach (XBL 477) arrived in February 1961, and a Bedford SB1-type (WOT 144) followed in May 1961 with a Duple 41-seater front entrance body, new in 1959 to *Gale* of Haslemere. Displaced in 1961 were Bedford OB-type GCA 388 during January, only acquired 11 months before, followed by the former *Lovick's* Guy 'Arab' coach GMO 418 in August and then the re-bodied Maudslay 'Marathon' DRX 489 in December.

Some additional variety entered the fleet, with a 13-seater Trojan (XBL 477), seen above near the end of its days, along with Duple-bodied Bedford (WOT 144) shown below and bought when 2 years old.

Evidently the Ford 570E suitably impressed, as another was delivered new in April 1962 as 188 ARX, carrying a Duple 41-seater front-entrance coach body. The arrival of this saw the subsequent departure of the other former *Lovick's* coach in July, that being Austin K4/CXB-type GMO 14, which had been supplied with spares from the withdrawn FJB 733 until then.

Another school-related contract started in March 1963, on behalf of the Marist Convent School at Sunninghill, which ran from Finchampstead (Gorse Ride) – Wokingham (Town Hall) – Rances Lane – Legg's Roundabout (junction Binfield and Wokingham Roads, Bracknell) – Met Office – RAF Staff College (Broad Lane) – London Road (Running

Horse) – Royal Ascot Hotel, departing at 8.10am for an 8.50 arrival, plus a 4.45pm return journey, parents paying for a season ticket charged at £7 (Finchampstead or Wokingham), £5 (Bracknell) or £4 from Ascot. It would continue to run through to the end of the firm's operations – quite a money-spinner.

The only 3-axle vehicle ever operated was the iconic Bedford VAL, and 933 FJB is seen at Littlehampton.

However, the scene-stealer of November 1963 was the 3-axle Plaxton-bodied Bedford VAL (933 FJB). This model, as immortalised by the cliff-hanging ending to the film The Italian Job, featured a twin-steering arrangement with small diameter wheels to produce a low-floor coach. However, the connection between the front axles could come adrift, resulting in them pointing in different directions, whilst the brake-shoes of the small wheels needed regular adjustment to keep their effectiveness up to scratch! No departures from the fleet took place during 1963 or 1964.

The school journey originally based on Sutcliffe Avenue had been modified from the Spring Term of 1955 to start at the Shinfield Rise Estate (St. Barnabas Church), running in as Elm Lane – Red Hatch Estate – Wilderness Road. However, with improvements to the local bus services it became obsolete after the close of the Autumn Term 1963 and the license surrendered.

Throughout the 1960's the coach fleet was at its height of activity, with the excursions trade not yet affected badly through erosion by private motoring, and plenty of contract runs. There are of course many tales relating to those heady days, and a particular one regarding *Brimblecombes* concerns an excursion to Chessington Zoo driven by Bob Hare, who had taken his wife and 2 kids for free on the trip. However, Bob had not included them in the outgoing headcount, but he did on the return journey, thereby leaving a trio of latecomers behind! When he got back to the yard he found Reg waiting for him, with a smile on his face and asking 'are you missing anyone Bob?'. He then told him that there were 3 passengers waiting at *Windsorian Coaches* office over in Windsor, brought back by their driver when he found them stranded!

The former Lovick's Austin with Thurgood full-fronted body (GMO 14) is shown after a full repaint into the Brimblecombe livery. The rather bored looking driver awaits a party boarding in Reading, perhaps after a visit to a pantomime, then a very popular form of trip for family groups. The Co-Operative movement in Reading was represented by a number of buildings, including this branch and a large headquarters sited in Cheapside.

Also seen in central Reading is Duple-bodied Bedford SB3-type RJB 292, this time outside The Bugle in Friar Street, one of the few of the numerous town centre pubs of that time to have survived. Note the Simonds hop-leaf on the inn-sign, which today shows a Victorian era soldier with bugle from the Colonial wars. RJB was one of the coaches to also receive lettering on the front dash proclaiming its ownership. It would stay with the firm until the end of 1975.

The third picture in this gallery shows Ford 570E-type 188 ARX with Duple 41-seater 'Yeoman'-style body adapted to suit the Ford chassis from the standard 'Super Vega' as seen above on RJB. About that time the winged BB monogram on the body sides was no longer added. It is shown on one of almost daily excursions from local schools to either Wembley or the museums in central London or South Kensington, solid bread-and-butter work which fitted in with school hours.

After that Bob was sent in one of the taxis to collect and apologise to them, as well as replacing the petrol used! On another occasion it was *Carter's of Maidenhead's* driver who came to the rescue when a coach being driven by John Neal failed at Singleton – such were the daily adventures for drivers and passengers alike in those days, and of course a mark of the camaraderie between PSV drivers of the time.

Other drivers recalled from the 1950's and 1960's were Alan Cutts, Billy Oliver, 'Tiny' Ducker, Ernie Nash, Dennis Coyd, Ron Bucksey, Mrs. Phelps, Mr. Buller, and in due course Rosemary Brimblecombe and another lady. Tiny was in fact Walter and lived at No.1 Victoria Cottages, Terrace Road in Binfield.

Mention has already been made of Jim and Lillian McInnes, who by 1950 were living at No.74 Barkham Road in Wokingham, which happened to be opposite the entrance to the long-established haulage and taxi ventures which had started with the *Mason* family. Indeed, this very site would in due course of time also become part of the *Brimblecombe* story through a succession of ownership.

Another family marriage of Bill and Diana's daughter Rosanna in 1964 brought her husband John Newman into the business for a decade, and he proved to be an excellent engineer, trusted by the brothers with the re-engine programme brought in to update coaches and improve running costs, whilst also undertaking some body repairs and driving duties. On the engine front petrol-engined Bedford LJB received the engine from diesel WOT, whilst WOT and RJB were fitted with Leyland 400's taken from 'Comet' lorries purchased for that purpose, thereby extending their working life.

A somewhat curious affair in which *Brimblecombes* had some input occurred during the '60's, was when the Goodey family of Spencers Wood decided to take their ex-Great War US Army Locomobile chassis (NN 373) and have a replica double-deck bus body based on the *London Road Car Company* style built to enable it to be used for film work. Photos show it being worked on at the garage in Wokingham, though it duly went over to *Smith's* of Reading for painting into the blue and yellow livery. A Western Mail photo showed it leaving Cardiff Bus Station being driven by John Newman on a publicity tour to Haverfordwest.

The final takeover came in July 1964, when the owners of *Costessey Coaches* offered to sell to *Brimblecombes*. The proprietors Messrs. *Lewis & Neal* were in fact the latest in a long succession of transport interests centred on No.51 Barkham Road and the yard accessed to its southern side. The full background to these ventures will be found on pages 12 to 17.

Costessey's 4 coaches joined the *Brimblecombe* fleet, these being 1948 Duple-bodied Bedford OB (FDL 318), 1954 Duple-bodied Bedford SBG (NDF 751), similar vintage Duple-bodied Bedford SBG (VPD 488) and a 1960 Kenex-bodied Austin J2VA minibus (2652 VF). *Costessey's* coach drivers, including John Neal then went onto working for the new owners.

Work on the body taking place at Barkham Road on the Locomobile chassis NN 373 as caught by the camera of John Newman above, whilst the author saw it out one day in the shot below before signwriting.

Changes in the workings of the Arborfield Camp with the end of National Service had seen a decline in takings on the service to Wokingham Station, so when the license expired in June 1964 it was let go. However, the race-day service to Ascot still fared very well, and a contemporary photo shows 10 coaches lined up to await the homeward crowds.

As previously noted, the Finchampstead Road parking was becoming an issue, so after the acquisition of *Costessey* plans had been formulated for a new garage on the Barkham Road site, planning permission being applied for in 1966. Apart from sign-writing the company title across the full width of the new garage front, as shown below, Albert Thomas ('Dickie') Ilott also did the work on the coaches for many years, and like Reg he was also a former Wokingham Mayor for the year 1952/3.

After the relocation to Barkham Road. Bill Adams and his wife Edith (nee Brimblecombe) also transferred from No.68 Finchampstead Road to take up residence in the bungalow 'Territon' behind the new garage, though he never was involved with the firm, having been originally a wireless and cycle dealer at No.66 Finchampstead Road by 1936, then later with a shop at No.14 Peach Street by 1952. Also, from at least 1949 Bill Brimblecombe and his wife Diana had been at No.14 Crescent Road in the town centre. Bill would pass away in 1989 aged 70, but her main claim to fame would come in later life, after outliving her husband for many years she started an animal rescue centre locally, her own demise coming in her 94th year in 2013, being awarded an MBE.

This view inside the new garage shows the former Costessey Bedford OB FDL 318, perhaps requiring a caption of 'all our best motors are out'. By it stands the Trojan van also broken up for spares.

There were some notable private hire jobs, one of which involved 5 coaches taking Jehovah's Witnesses to a 10-day event in Scotland, and on that occasion Ted Payton and 2 drivers travelled back by train until their coaches were used for the return run, whilst Bob Hare and Tiny Ducker stayed up with their charges. As previously noted, the latter gained his name by virtue of his size, and at the guest house the landlady had given up her double bed to accommodate the two drivers, but when Tiny got into bed the whole thing just collapsed!

Another task undertaken by John Newman was the re-bodying of a former Trojan van (149 SPB), which went into PSV use after receiving the body taken and repaired from *T.R. Laverick* of Bracknell's VBX 298, which had been involved in a bad smash at the notorious Warren House Crossroads, just north of Wokingham on the Forest Road. This occurred during 1965, and a further Trojan van, originally with Brooke Bond Tea, was also broken up in the garage for spares, and John stayed with the firm until 1974.

Outgoing during 1965 was the Burlingham-bodied Bedford SBO-type YMP 553 in March, followed by the withdrawn former *Costessey* OB-type FDL 318 in November, the latter being far from complete, and indeed both went for scrap after partial stripping.

Apart from the expansion of some local schools and the bussing already referred to above, the County Council opened Braybrooke School, off Kennel Lane in the Priestwood area of Bracknell in the mid-'60's where what were then termed ESN (educationally sub-normal) children would be concentrated, and this lead to a number of contract runs that developed into minibus operations. By the late-1960's Ted Payton, who lived two doors along from the author at No.4 Winchgrove Road in Priestwood, was driving for *Brimblecombes,* and he brought a coach home at night which was parked nearby in Kennel Lane. Apart from the contract run he covered, he spent the rest of the day in the garage, or possibly on taxi work as that had been his trade back in 1962. Ted would also later enter operation in his own right as *Bowler's Coaches* of Crowthorne.

Indeed, changing trends in contracts saw the need to amend the fleet make-up during 1966, with the AEC 'Reliance' 41-seater KMO 939, which had served the firm since 1955, being retired in July, though it passed on nearby for further local use by *Spiers Coaches* of Henley. The intake ready for the new academic year were a pair of Harrington-bodied 12-seater minibuses on Commer LBD-type chassis (ADY 188/9B), new in August 1964 to *McKenzie* of London SE27.

Although there would follow a slant towards minibus contracts, the day of the full-size coach was far from over, so January 1967 saw a trio of identical coaches purchased through Hanworth-based dealer Percy Sleeman formerly in the *Valliant* of Ealing fleet. They were 7197-9 HX on 1960 Ford 570E chassis and with Burlingham 'Seagull 60' 41-seater bodies. However, despite the firm having good experience with other bodies from that coachworks, these soon proved to be an embarrassment, as the hump-roofed style of body was prone to leaks, so an umbrella was advisable!

The outgoing AEC 'Reliance' KMO 939, as seen above at Oxford, had latterly been rebuilt at the front end, so compare it with earlier views on page 29. One of the unfortunate trio of 'Seagull 60'-bodied coaches was 7199 HX, show below with its previous owner.

Only one coach left during 1967, with rebodied AEC 'Regal' FCJ 843 which went for scrap in February.

For 1967 even more pick-ups were requested for excursions, with the Rifle Volunteer (Emmbrook), Three Frogs and The Plough both on (London Road, Wokingham), then later in the year Handpost Corner (junction of Finchampstead and Sandhurst Roads and Ascot (Royal Foresters), all but the last being granted, as it was within *Windsorian's* authorised area.

The Marist Convent route was altered from 1968 to start from Handpost Corner, then via Wokingham (Rose Street) before continuing as before, season tickets now being £11 from Finchampstead or Wokingham, at £9 and everywhere else at £7 5s. From 1972 the route was further extended to start from Crowthorne (Iron Duke), then via Dukes Ride and Sandhurst Road to reach Handpost Corner. Also, for those who like to compare historic costs, the following day return fares applied in August 1968-

Destination	Duration	Adult	Child
Afternoon Tour	Half-day	6s 0d	4s 0d
Bognor Regis	Full-day	15s 0d	10s 0d
Bournemouth	Full-day	17s 6d	11s 6d
Brighton	Full-day	15s 0d	10s 0d
Cheddar Gorge	Full-day	17s 9d	12s 0d
Chessington Zoo	Full-day	7s 6d	5s 3d
Frensham Ponds	Half-day	6s 9d	4s 9d
Hayling Island	Full-day	14s 6d	10s 0d
Kew Gardens	Full-day	7s 0d	4s 9d
Littlehampton	Full-day	15s 0d	10s 0d
London Zoo	Full-day	7s 6d	5s 3d
Southsea	Full-day	14s 6d	10s 0d
Whipsnade Zoo	Full-day	10s 0d	7s 0d
Woburn Abbey	Full-day	10s 0d	7s 0d
Worthing	Full-day	15s 0d	10s 0d

For comparison, the adult fare to Bournemouth in 1949 was 10s 0d and to Whipsnade Zoo was 5s 9d.

March 1968 saw the end for the last of the *Costessey* stock, with the 7ft 6ins-wide Bedford SBG NDF 751 and the SBO-type VPD 488 both sold to Percy Sleeman, though NDF returned to the local area with building contractor Collier & Catley of Reading and was maintained by *Smith's Coaches* of Reading. During August the Trojan 13-seater XBL 477 was also sold. Its replacement was the first new vehicle for some time, with a Commer 2500LB-type carrying a Rootes-built 12-seater body as PBL 362F. Also, at an unrecorded date that year the other rebodied 'Regal' (FCJ 844) was involved in a bad smash, but it then went for further service in Katmandu, Himalayas!

1969 was notable for no planned fleet changes, though certainly the other Trojan minibus (149 SPB) had by then departed. Also, during that period there were some issues with the Traffic Commissioner over the standards of maintenance, and the author recalls seeing coaches with hardboard in place of un-repaired windows, the fleet having been well-maintained prior to that. The effect of a number of Stop Notices was that the Education Authority was reluctant to renew contracts, so it was indeed a dent in the firm's reputation at the time and opened up opportunities for other local operators to emerge on such contracts.

During May 1970 a secondhand Bedford VAL14 6-wheeler with 52-seater Plaxton 'Panorama' body arrived as NJH 814D, being new in May 1970 to the Watford-based *Knightswood Coaches*. During the Christmas school break the pair of Commer minibuses ADY 188/9B were replaced by a 1966 pair of Commer 1500LB-types with Rootes 12-seater bodies as HNJ 182D and JNJ 670D, both new to *Woburn* of London WC2 but arriving via other owners.

June 1971 saw the arrival of the first of many Ford 'Transit'-based minibuses to be operated, with LCM-bodied 12-seater KNM 412G, new in March 1968 to *Holmes* of London SE5. That same month a larger arrival was 895 DBL, a Plaxton 'Embassy'-bodied 41-seater new in 1963 to *Tappins* of Wallingford. 1972 saw the departure of the 'leaky' trio 7197-9 HX during February, September and May respectively. In fact during September there was something of a clear-out of ailing vehicles, with Bedford SBG-type LJB 264, Ford 570E-type 2040 FH and the last Austin to be operated as 12-seater J2VA-type 2652 VF.

Very much a standard type for the fleet was YVN 214, which had several previous owners.

Ford 676E-type GMF 180B with its 'Maurader' body seen <u>above</u> was unique in the fleet, whilst JNK 682C <u>below</u> was a further Bedford SB variety added.

The incoming replacements were again aimed at matching seating capacities to the evolving contract commitments, so they were GMF 180B a 1964 Ford 676E-type with Duple 'Maurader' 52-seater body new to *Finchley Coaches* JNK 682C a Bedford SB5-type of 1965 with Plaxton 'Embassy' 41-seater body from *Hanworth Acorn* of Bedfont, both during July in readiness for the new academic year. November saw a 1961 41-seater Duple 'Super Vega'-bodied Bedford SB1 (VYN 214), latterly with *Tappins* of Wallingford, along with former *Hodge's Coaches* of Sandhurst 53-seater Bedford VAL70 with Duple 'Viceroy 37' body new in 1969 as POT 503G.

1973 saw no incoming vehicles, but those departing were Commer 1500LB-type minibus HNJ 182D in February, followed in December by Ford 676E-type GMF 180B after only 18 months with the firm.

There were no departures from the fleet during 1974, but 3 were acquired, with TXD 696L as a Ford R226-type to replace GMF, being a 53-seater Duple 'Dominant'-bodied coach of April 1973 from *Travel House* of Luton. Further variety came with another 12-seat Dormobile-bodied Ford 'Transit' in May as a new vehicle registered SDP 423M, followed in October by a 29-seater Duple 'Vista 25'-bodied Bedford VAS1-type new in 1967 as JKK 300E with *Davies* of Sevenoaks. These changes in the larger-capacity types would in fact be the final ones, as all subsequent purchases were minibuses, as the nature of operations had now changed so much from those days of regular excursions and private hire of coaches.

Another Ford 'Transit' minibus came in July 1975 as VLY 629M, new elsewhere in February 1974 and carrying a Tricentrol 12-seater body, which replaced Commer JNJ 670D, whilst November saw the departure of 1958 Bedford SB3 RJB 292.

1976 saw another grand clear-out of coaches, which really marked the end of the traditional coach operations by *Brimblecombe's*. During January Ford 570E-type 188 ARX of 1962, Bedford SB5-type 895 DBL of 1963, the 1963 VAL14-type 933 FJB and Commer minibus PBL 362F of 1968 all departed.

In the meantime, *Ronnie Buckland* of Buckland Farm, Broad Common Lane in nearby Hurst had applied to take over certain Road Service Licenses back in late 1975, which was effectively a takeover of the school contracts requiring vehicles larger than minibuses, and the remaining excursions and tours. *Brimblecombe's* in turn surrendered the licenses in their name for the Marist Convent, the excursions and football journeys to Reading FC at Elm Park. That resulted in the transfer of the following vehicles in February 1976 to *Buckland Coaches*, with Bedford SB1-type VYN 214,

Another shot of the former Costessey Austin, this time from an elevated point in Brighton, about where the scale-model Harrington-bodied coaches offering rides to children once operated by Mr. Johnston were in action. This coach and the Guy acquired at the same takeover were in use for some years, so were a compliment to Thurgood the small coachbuilder based in Ware - a favourite with independents for several decades, mainly on lightweight chassis types such as Austin and Morris.

Bedford VAS1 JKK 300E, Bedford VAL70 POT 503G and Ford R226-type TXD 696L. It is also evident that at that time several vehicles were out of use, with 1959 Bedford SB1-type WOT 144 and 1966 Bedford VAL14-type NJH 814D both sold during March. That left the firm with only Ford 'Transits' KNM 412G and SDP 342M, which were joined in March 1976 by brand new Dormobile-bodied 12-seater 'Transits' MRO 996/7P. There then followed another pair of similar 'Transits' in March 1977 as SBH 909/10R, after which there were no further incoming vehicles until 1984, when secondhand 12-seater 'Transits' JTF 141W and JNE 837V were acquired, the former with Smith body and the latter by Deansgate and new in 1981 and 1980. In August 1978 SBH 910R left after a bad smash, then VLY 629M in May 1980, followed by none less than 4 during January/February 1983 as MRO 996/7P, KNM 412G and SDP 342M, all 12-seater 'Transits'. The final vehicles are recorded by the PSV Circle as owned to October 1987 as SBH 909R, JTF 141W and JNE 837V, after which the long-associated name of *Brimblecombe's* appeared to pass into history.

Reg Brimblecombe lived for some years opposite the Two Poplars at No.105 Finchampstead Road, passing away at the Sue Ryder Home at Nettlebed in July 1987. His daughter *Rosemary Hearmon* duly revived the *Brimblecombe Coaches* name when she placed a minibus on the road from around October 1987 and for a time provide a worker's shopping link between Molly Millars Lane and the Town Centre, which the author recalls was at one point supported by the Council. According to the PSV Circle records she operated from then until February 1998, taking over JNE 837V and JTF 141W from the family, adding MJH 26X a Mercedes L2070 with Devon Conversions 12-seater body new in 1981, acquired from *Buckland Coaches*, and H726 XYH a Ford 'Transit' with 11-seater Ford body new to her in 1990.

Another chance to look at two stalwarts of the fleet, with the former Lovick Motors Guy 'Arab' MKIII GMO 418 with Thurgood 35-seater bodywork, as seen above at Wembley after a slight prang en route. Below is AEC 'Regal' FCJ 844 with its later Burlingham body, the 8ft width of that on a 7ft 6ins chassis more apparent in this front view on Finchampstead Road and taken by Graham Low, whose work follows on the two gallery pages from around 1960.

Firstly, we see the frontage on Finchampstead Road nearest to the northern end of the Eddystone Garage site and the railway bridge of the line to Waterloo. The several bungalows in family ownership form the background to ex-Lovick Motors Austin GMO 14 with Thurgood body. On is right is the first minibus in the fleet, an all-Trojan XBL 477 with 13 seats. In front of the bungalow used as an office is the petrol pump for use by the firm for its own needs. Also see the map on page 18.

Moving slightly further south on Finchampstead Road, we can still see the office bungalow, plus the main house with its twin bay windows and gabled roof, quite typically of the inter-war period examples locally. On the forecourt we have the Ford 570E 2040 FH, then the rear of the Trojan XBL 477, and Maudslay DRX 489 with its later Strachans body with full-front. The varied application of the colours of the livery to suit the body styles in evident.

To complete this set, we are now seeing the full frontage of the main house and front parking area, and giving us a good rear view of Maudslay DRX 489 and the Eddystone lighthouse logo, along with the upper rear aperture used in this case for a fleetname. At the front the usual practice was to have that in one of the destination apertures, as can be seen on Bedford SBO-type YMP 553 with its Burlingham 'Baby' type version of the 'Seagull'.

We now take another sweep north-to-south along the Finchampstead Road to see other coaches parked at the front of the site, and the first has been left on the road, as parking was by then becoming an issue, with several of the early departures left overnight in the Pin & Bowl pub across the road. AEC 'Regal' FCJ 843 has returned to the site between duties, but such was the traffic then, does not seem to be causing the havoc it now would! The large property behind in now the Warr Clinic.

Now back in front of the house, we see rear of YMP 553, then the other side of Ford 2040 FH, and with the little Trojan between it and Maudslay DRX 489. On the rear of the Bedford are the two phone numbers then in use, one originally having been that of the Peach Street-based coach and taxi operator Herring Bros. This site became a petrol filling station and is still in use as such, though rebuilt several times since the days of the Eddystone Garage.

Standing in front of the petrol pump is one of the family cars, and then we have the Guy 'Arab' with a Meadows engine, recalled as a reliable coach, hence it remaining in use to 1961, though by then the half-cab layout was becoming dated in appearance. Maudslay DRX 489 next to it lasted to that same year, though 4 years older, but the second body was with a full-front. It seems doubtful that any Council would now allow such parking arrangements on a busy road, but no complaints are recorded.

42

Another line up of coaches in Finchampstead Road comes from John Newman, with (left to right) LJB 264 Bedford SBG with Duple Super Vega body, 2040 FH Ford 570-type with Plaxton Embassy body, 188 ARX a Ford 570 but with a Duple Yeoman body, then WOT 144 Bedford SB1 with Duple Super Vega body and RJB 292 a Bedford SB3 with similar bodywork. The photo also shows that the coaches were kept in good order.

The Plaxton Embassy-style bodywork featured on several purchases, one of which was 895 DBL built in 1963 and purchased in 1971 to cover a contract. It had been new to Tappin's Coaches of Wallingford, but no photos of it with Brimblecombe Bros. have come to light, so here we see its twin 896 DBL when with its original owner. The peaked dome was a feature of that design of body which was used on various front-engine chassis types.

Purchased in 1949, when new coaches were in short supply, was a trio of K4-type Austins with Whitson coach bodies seating 29, which were retained for 10 or 11 years. FJB 733 is seen when quite new as part of a private hire which took it to Lincoln's Inn Fields in the legal district of London. It is shown in the company of several AEC Regal coaches from other operators. Note that the Austin has a panel covering the rear wheel, a feature sometimes found on bodies of that era.

The original body on the Maudslay Marathon MkII coach DRX 498 by Whitson as built in 1947 suffered from the use of timber not seasoned, so by 1953 it was found necessary to re-body it, the replacement being by Strachan and to a fully-fronted design to disguise it true age. It was in fact used on some adverts when new, but the original photo has never surfaced, so here we have a restored version taken from the adverts.

The Daimler Freeline EBV 283 which duly came to Gough's Garage had been new to the London operator Cronshaw in 1953 and was acquired in 1963. It had a Duple Ambassador-style body with centre-entrance and seated 41. In this view we see it at The Derby at Epsom, but the registration plate has been moved up to cover the board showing another regular contract. It only stayed at Bracknell for less than a year due to high fuel consumption.

Another Gough's coach seen with its former owner was TOV 268, new in 1957 to Birmingham operator Allenways, seen here on a break at Gloucester Green in Oxford. It was one of several Commer Avenger coaches with Gough's with the TS3 engine. This had a Plaxton Venturer-type body with seats for 41, coming to Bracknell in 1961 and was to see 6 years there. The author rode on this coach a number of times, with a good view from the front.

Alfred Edward Cartlidge
Crimson Rambler Coaching Service,
Teddington, Middlesex and
California-in-England, Berkshire

The inclusion of a Teddington operator in this volume may seem strange, but read on and the significance will be fully revealed……

The area that became known as California-in-England had originally centred a small pond at Long Moor, which became part of the large 19th century estate of John Walter III, the founder of The Times newspaper. Clay was dug in order to produce the 4.5 million bricks needed to construct his mansion a few miles to the northwest at Bearwood, the resultant brickmaking leaving a much enlarged Longmoor Lake. Indeed, Walter's activities led to several notable transport facets locally, with a narrow-gauge railway constructed for the brick works, whilst his influence was such that he persuaded the London & South Western Railway to open Sindlesham & Hurst Halt (now known as Winnersh Station) in order that his carriage could connect with the Reading to Waterloo line about a mile north of his home.

However, the transport ventures under review here came somewhat later, following the break-up of the large estate at auction as a result of deaths in the Great War and mounting death duties. A large plot around Longmoor Lake was purchased by *Alfred Edward Cartlidge*, who had worked as an aeroplane builder throughout the First World War, employed at the Royal Aircraft Factory at Farnborough, just some 10 miles southwards in neighbouring Hampshire, where he honed his considerable engineering skills which would underpin his future ventures.

The Siddeley-Deasy hire car used by Alf Cartlidge.

He had been born at No.32 Hanbury Road, Battersea in South London in 1891, spending his early years living in various nearby addresses. In 1911 we find him as an aeroplane maker and living at No.10 Darley Road in Wandsworth, still close to his origins, and he married

Ellen Towns at Hounslow, Middlesex in 1916. As she unfortunately died in 1920, he duly re-married Edith King at Kingston in Surrey during 1923. His address by 1919 was No.8 Luther Road, Spelthorne, Surrey, from where his initial passenger-carrying involved the use of a car fitted with a 'Silent Knight' Daimler sleeve-valve engine, as seen below. It was a Siddeley-Deasy new about 1914, either the 4-cylinder 18/24hp version of 3306cc, or the 6-cylinder 24/30hp of 4960cc. That firm was primarily an aircraft maker based in Coventry, but also built some ambulances during the Great War.

That address continued to be used when the *Crimson Rambler Coaching Service* makes its appearance in the 1925 Local Directory, though from the 1926 edition an existing garage and workshop at No.99 Waldegrave Road had been taken over as the operational base. As a motor garage, it also offered facilities to the general public, continuing in that role until at least 1931. Under its previous ownership the name 'Brooklands' had been used, so being somewhat appropriate to a former aeroplane constructor it was retained.

No local newspaper adverts for the *Crimson Rambler* were found for the 1925 and 1926 seasons, and the first known dates from 11th June 1927, with Brighton and Worthing daily, Bognor Regis on stated dates, along with the Ascot Races and Aldershot Tattoo held in the daytime and evening during the third week of June.

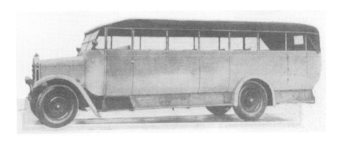

This 32-seater all-weather coach appeared in an advert for the Crimson Rambler Coaches, and it would seem to be based on a Great War era Daimler chassis that had been lengthened and re-bodied.

For the advert of 16th July 1927 a Windsor & Virginia Water tour and a day trip to Southend-on-Sea were offered in addition to the same coastal destinations as above. On 23rd July the advert offered a full day tour of Windsor and the east Sussex resort of Hastings, whilst the 30th July was the first to offer a 50-mile circular tour on Wednesday afternoons, the local shop early-closing day, plus Brighton Races. August 1927 saw T. Sibley of York Street in Twickenham as a booking agent, plus a Surrey Hills tour taking in the popular viewpoint and tea-stop of Boxhill.

Advertising for the 1928 season was quite late in starting, so maybe he relied on local window displays, but for the Henley Regatta on Thursday and Friday 5th and 6th July there were outings, whilst daily runs to Brighton and Worthing, Bognor and Littlehampton were joined by Southend on Mondays, Broadstairs, Ramsgate and Margate on Saturdays, Bournemouth on Wednesdays and Southsea on Thursdays, which represented the peak season operations. More booking agents were added as Curtin & Co., Heath Road in Twickenham, and J. Wade, No.25 Winchester Road at St. Margarets. The advert for 28th August added Hastings every Friday and Saturday, plus a tour based on Hindhead in Surrey and to Goodwood Races.

An excursions newspaper advert for June/July 1927.

September 1928 continued the aforementioned coastal operations, but added Eastbourne on Mondays, along with a Tunbridge Wells excursion, that season proving to be a the most diverse range on offer. However, Alf was coming to the conclusion that such distances were a relatively hard way to earn a living, so his thoughts turned to how he might develop the property he had purchased in Berkshire to form an 'Inland Leisure Resort' at Longmoor Lake, initially as a destination for day-trippers. At first there were canoes and boats for hire, plus children's amusements, a paddling pool and the 'Everglades' train ride for passengers, having been adapted from the old narrow-gauge line.

In respect of the vehicles used, Alf's daughter Vera (born 1917) recalled that her father had 'constructed his own Crimson Rambler coaches, the first being 14-seaters.'. Although several photographs exist, they show the later 26/32-seaters, so the identity of the smaller initial charas has alluded detection. Given the period when they were 'constructed' it seems most likely they were based on the lighter ex-WD types or other large car chassis. Credence to the 'Crimson Rambler' chassis construction is, however, borne out by the later vehicles, as we shall see. In May 1930 he registered the *Crimson Rambler Coaching Service* with an address at No.28 Basinghall Street, London EC2, which may represent a new partnership?

Although not all vehicles are known, it is understood that at its maximum the fleet comprised 6 charabanc or all-weather types. Piecing together from surviving motor tax records and known photos, the following can be confirmed –

LX 8521- an ex-WD 1915 Daimler Y-type which had been a goods vehicle, but became a 26-seater chara with Alf in July 1928, by which time he had The Garage, Waldegrave Road, Teddington, Middlesex,
MT 8204- a Maudslay new to him in February 1928. There are some queries as to whether it was in fact a Maudslay, though such a type apparently existed and was used on a brochure – perhaps a reconstruction?
MY 6105- a 'CR Coach' no chassis number, though the 24hp engine might indicate a WW1 Daimler origin, and with a body for 26 seats new April 1930.
HX 9545- Crimson Rambler chassis no.CR6 and 26-seater body new January 1931, again with an engine number suggesting a 1914-8 build date.

The known photo of a 'Crimson Rambler Coach' shows what is undoubtably a Great War-pattern Daimler chassis, but lengthened to take a London Lorries all-weather body, possibly one of the above? From Vera's recollections, it seems we currently lack several 14-seaters to complete the fleet details.

Alf also managed to get Commercial Motor to insert a piece in March 1931, which extolled the attractions and adequate parking for coaches, which brought even more visitors. It also noted that *Crimson Rambler* had operated day excursions there the previous season, but now refreshment facilities had been added. That also marked the final season of the more general operations as the focus turned to serving California.

In August 1931, under the 1930 Road Traffic Act, his application shows him applying for excursions at fully inclusive prices from The Garage in Waldegrave Road to the site and routed via Hanworth – Sunbury – Staines – Egham – Virginia Water – Ascot – Bracknell – Wokingham – Handpost Corner – Nine Mile Ride. By then the site had been christened 'California-in-England', and indeed the name California can be found on the 1871 Ordnance Survey map, apparently being derived from the extensive stands of tall pine trees and the lakeside setting which evoked such a comparison. Pine trees were also regarded as an attractive alternative to the London smog, as also at the time there was a high incidence of TB, and the smell of the resin from such trees was seen as beneficial, with the Pinewood Sanatorium being situated only about 4 miles further east along the Nine Mile Ride for the same reason.

There is little doubt that the venture was a success, the day-trippers happy to leave 'The Smoke' behind for the clean air and freedom of the large site, and as the 1930's wore on a large ballroom and a number of wooden chalets were constructed to build on the trade. The ballroom offered regular dinner dances, and the venue soon featured on the excursions offered by most coach operators within striking distance, whilst the addition of a speedway track also attracted regular excursions in the evenings, running from 1933-1939 and again from 1948-1958.

However, in a strange twist of fate, the pride that had come with constructing his own chassis became his downfall, when under the provisions of the Construction & Use Regulations introduced in tandem with the 1930 Act, all his were found to be TOO WIDE! That ended direct operation from September 1931, when any such temporary exemptions expired, and according to Vera Cartlidge 'all were sold to an operator based on Jersey'!

The construction of the chalets took the venture to a new phase, being an early example of the Holiday Camp, which brought with it the need for additional transport. Presumably some passengers coming on his coaches could have got period return tickets, but such was the advertising that he soon found many others setting out by rail to Wokingham. As this became apparent Alf approached the *Thames Valley Traction Co. Ltd.* to ask if special buses could be laid on at set times to link Wokingham Station with the camp, making several attempts during 1932/3. At that time *Thames Valley* had two bus services in that area, with Route 3 (Reading – Wokingham – Crowthorne – Camberley) running out of Wokingham by way of Denmark Street – Finchampstead Road – California Crossroads, where it turned towards Crowthorne, whilst the 3a (Wokingham – Barkham – Finchampstead) also only went as close as California Crossroads. Both left passengers a good mile short of their intended destination, armed as they would likely be with luggage and children. Indeed, rather ironically, in the couple of years prior to Alf's approach *TV* had tried all sorts of local route changes to make what was then two services (as 3a/3b) pay, so its refusal to consider his proposal seems rather short-sighted.

Alf also approached the Southern Railway, who now held shares in *Thames Valley*, and asked them to consider issuing through tickets on a service which

would include *TV* laying on the bus link, but even the railway failed to pressurize the bus operator. What exactly occurred over the next year or so is currently unclear, but frustrated by the above *Alf Cartlidge* purchased a pair of rather large double-deckers during 1935 in order to operate a free service for those booked at the camp. This was noted by the Southern Railway, though *Thames Valley* had no comment to make. These buses were old Leyland LB-types which had been reconstructed by their owner, *City Motor Omnibus Co. Ltd.* of London to form 3-axle 'City Sixes' and re-bodied as 60-seaters to become Nos.CS1 (XX 9060) and CS2 (GN 5819), duly passing into London Transport hands for a short time. As such, these were the largest buses in the area and, as double-deckers would have had to reach the camp from Wokingham Station by way of Barkham Road and Arborfield Garrison in order to avoid the low bridge on the Finchampstead Road. Quite how long this arrangement continued is not known, presumably ending with the outbreak of war.

City Six XX 9060 is seen with its original owner.

With the start of WW2 the camp was immediately taken over with the arrival of the Cameron Highlanders, whilst Alf resumed his previous role as an aircraft engineer, converting the restaurant area to a factory. At that point, he and wife Edith, along with daughter Vera and son Norman were residing at The Bungalow, Long Moor Lake, the latter now as an aircraft engineering apprentice. Vera had by then been the Manageress of the Confectionery Shop, but now donned overalls and joined her father building aircraft, often wielding an acetylene torch for the duration. The other son Howard joined the Terriers and went to France. Although he was successfully returned from Dunkirk, he sadly died not long afterwards in Devon, when the vehicle he was driving on manoeuvres overturned. Also on the site in 1939 was the grandfather Arthur Cartlidge, living at The Stores, Long Moor Lake in retirement.

After peace returned a similar contract service was operated by local coach operator *Brimblecombe Bros.*, but only in a fairly limited fashion, and details will be found elsewhere. It is not clear if that was arranged jointly with Alf Cartlidge, but ownership of the site passed from him several years later.

Then, in March 1953 the new *California-in-England Ltd.* applied to operate its own stage carriage route, though it at the time had no known vehicles. It would run from Wokingham (Station) hourly from 8.05am to 10.05pm and then at 11.15pm, taking a circular route as Finchampstead Road – Kingsmere Crossroads – Wick Hill – California Crossroads – Gorse Ride – California-in-England, the return leg as Arborfield Garrison (Theatre) – Langley Common (Cash Stores) – Barkham Road – Wokingham (Station), where arrivals were 43 minutes later. As the initial journey of the day saw a 7.25am short-working from the California site to form the first full journey out, it implied that the service was indeed rather more than a means to transfer visitors to there. It should also be noted that in addition to the objection by *Thames Valley*, there was one from *Brimblecombe Bros.,* which rules out any collaboration on their part, but when the application was heard at Farnham on 28th July it was refused, partly on the advice of the County Surveyor over some of the route.

Although that transport did not progress, the venue continued throughout the 1950's, with regular parties coming down from London, even on double-deckers, with coaches making regular stops for teas, or at other times for evening dances and speedway racing, until the activities on the site were brought to an abrupt end by a large fire in the early '60's. Most photos of the site for the '50's include half-a-dozen coaches and buses.

As a postscript, the author recalls exploring the site in the early 1960's with some friends, and we found a huge 6-wheeler chassis in the undergrowth, which in hindsight I think was actually one of the ex-*City* buses, but sadly it is no longer there. Alf sold up after WW2 and the camp continued for some years in other hands, though latterly rather in decline, until the fire saw the end of the ballroom and other buildings. Most of the area is now a Council-managed Country Park, though there are still residents, albeit in caravans now. Not that the sale marked the end of his enterprises, as he ran the Carr Mill Entertainment Park in St. Helens, Lancashire, where he died in 1954.

Also, the modern-day Drayton Manor Theme Park near Tamworth was actually started by Alf's daughter Vera and her husband George Bryan in 1950, there being a number of parallels with the old California site which she had grown up with, including a land-train and boats, but also adding fairground-style rides which developed into their modern counterpart of fixed white-knuckle rides and other entertainments. Indeed, Alf's Grandson Colin Bryan now heads the enterprise, which is still developing further with a new hotel added.

Young Norman Cartlidge features in both these photos, one advertising half-fares for children, whilst the other cheeky studio portrait shows him about to service the Crimson Ramblers!

Clover & Peacock
Peacock Bros.
Bullbrook, Bracknell and Chavey Down

Charles Edward Clover and *William John ('John') Peacock* were primarily carriers but are included as for some years they provided the only passenger links between various scattered communities into Reading.

Charles had been born in 1880 at Ipswich in Suffolk and married Maude Louisa Hagger there in 1905. However, the births of their children indicate they were at Horsington in Somerset in 1906-8, then at Wargrave in Berkshire by 1910. On the 1911 census they were in Waltham Road at nearby Twyford, with him as an engineer with an agricultural engineering firm. His military records show he had served in the Boer War in South Africa, and when those medals were sent to him his address was 'Brookdale' in Victoria Road at Wargrave. He also re-joined for the Great War as a Driver in the Royal Engineers but no dates are known.

John was born in 1890 in the parish of Warfield, which included much of the town of Bracknell, split as it was between that parish and Easthampstead and Winkfield. He is found in 1901 living at Searle Street in Bracknell, but by 1911 was residing at Wood Green in North London as a laboratory porter. His war service has not been traceable, but he married Annie S. Gray in 1916, the couple having son William John in 1924.

We first hear of *Clover & Peacock* in the transport sense in July 1922, when the pair registered a Ford T-type ton-truck as MO 278. The vehicle was described as a lorry painted dark blue with a khaki-coloured top cover, fitted with seats for 14 passengers. The Windsor area directory includes them as carriers from 1922, as do the Reading directories from 1923. Their address was Bay Road in Bullbrook, on the eastern side of Bracknell, and they took goods and passengers from there, along with the nearby Chavey Down to Reading. The service ran daily (Wednesday excluded) and used the Boars Head Inn in Friar Street as its base in the town and had a return timing of 3.30pm. It is further known that the Clovers lived at No.3 Hampton Villas in Bay Road, the Peacocks were close by at 'Jessie Cottage'. Although they appeared in the Windsor directory there is no evidence they ran there also.

The partners were still evident for 1924, but by the 1925 directory only *Clover* is shown in the list of carriers, but is also noted as serving Warfield (which may have been so from the outset) and also extending eastwards to Ascot and Sunningdale.

Local interviews show that *Peacock* in particular catered for Chavey Down, whilst his brother *Frank* (born 1897) lived very close at 'Forest View' on Long Hill Road. In March 1928 Frank placed a new Morris-Commercial 1-ton truck on the road as RX 1819, with 14 seats in its blue-painted body and a green hood. It was kept a sort way from Bay Road in Park Road at the garage adjacent to The Boot pub. From then onwards the name *Peacock Bros.* appears under carriers from Bracknell and surrounding areas as outlined above, operating over the original route to and from The Boars Head in Reading and at the same frequency and return timing.

At that same time we find *Charles Clover* now as a motor car proprietor, and indeed other sources note he provided a taxi service from his Bay Road address, and in fact it cannot be completely ruled out that these various elements were not part of a joint enterprise by that point in time.

So, whatever, the exact arrangements after 1928, the daily carriers service did continue through to the WW2 and beyond, though not with passengers after the 1930 Act, with the addition of a removals van as well. The family still residing at 'Jessie Cottage' and after John passed away his wife continued the service until shortly before her death in late 1948 aged 58. Indeed, Peter Pribik recalls that their van called into Frank's Café, run by his parents, on an almost daily basis, situated where the large Loddon Bridge roundabout now stands, as well as seeing their furniture van frequently.

Frank Peacock was still supplying a carriers service from his base at Long Hill Road and nearby Chavey Down at 1939, but he did so in his right by then.

Little is recorded of *Charles Clover's* later years other than that he died locally in 1951, but perhaps it is no coincidence that *William John Peacock* is duly found operating a taxi service, which included a school run taking children from outlying districts into Bullbrook School on the London Road, with himself still based at 'Jessie Cottage'.

So, all-in-all, these two families provided transport links of various kinds for several decades, being recalled by several older residents in early interviews with the author.

Now we will look at two local businessmen, each already familiar with motor vehicles, who it seems were keen to enter bus operation at some point.

These events took place in different decades, but for various reasons, neither actually got to operate bus services after all, these matters being one of the interesting aspects that can arise during such historical research.

Frederick Field
Winnersh, Berkshire

Frederick Daniel Field may in fact never have run his proposed bus service, but the events surrounding his story are nonetheless interesting for the insight they also afford into the effects of the variable values of the then system of Hackney Carriage Licensing by Local Authorities.

He had been born at Maidenhead, Berkshire in 1879, though the family were at Windsor in 1881 and at Winkfield Row by 1891, where he was assisting his father as a farmer. However, his elder brother Ernest was a coachbuilder's apprentice, and it is with that trade that we next find Fred in 1901 and residing at 'Woodside Villa' at Yorktown, on the fringes of Camberley and the Berkshire/Surrey border. There he marries Dorothy Elizabeth Alexander in 1902 and the couple had 4 children by 1911, by which time they were at the Norfolk House Carriage Works, just around the corner in Frimley Road, and with Fred now described as a coach body maker.

Whether the events of the Great War had any bearing on post-war developments are not know, as a service record for him (if applicable) does not survive, but an advert of April 1920 in the Reading Mercury advises that motor haulage of all descriptions was undertaken by 2-3ton lorries, apply Field, Murrell Green, given as Wokingham, though corrected in the next advert as being under Hurst. In May 1920 a box-body to suit Ford or other light chassis was for sale, and it should be noted that the location was in fact a local corruption of Merryhill Green, the area north of Watmore Lane in the parish of St. Nicholas Hurst. By 1922 the family has relocated some three-quarters of a mile south across the A329 to 'Holly Bank' on King Street in Sindlesham. During January of that year he put a lorry of unknown make (BL 9447) on the road, and followed that up with another (BL 9661) in March, both of which he used for general haulage work.

The haulage business continued throughout the 1920's, though several further very local relocations are evident from electoral registers, showing that for 1924 they were on the main Reading Road in Winnersh, but by 1925 were noted as Arborfield Road, Winnersh. There is in fact no such road name as the latter, which was doubtless being used for the continuation of King Street onto Mole Road, which, as Sindlesham Road emerges at Arborfield Cross.

However, later in 1925 his address is confirmed by motor tax files as 'The Homestead' at Winnersh, as on 21st November he registered a Ford 1-tonner with a 14-seater green-liveried bus body as MO 6659. This was evidently supplied by the Maidenhead-based Ford main agent Gowrings, and the declaration noted it as kept at his home. Just one week later it was followed by an identical vehicle as MO 6708, though this was noted as being kept at The Tannery, a short turning off the Barkham Road in Wokingham, just north of the bridge over the Emmbrook. Such a location implies there was a partnership of some kind, either with another investor, or at least a hired driver, and the 1924 resident there was Thomas Goodwin, formerly in business at that location under Thomas Goodwin & H. Grace Ltd., though no trade is specified.

Whatever the business arrangements it is evident that *Fred Field* had been tempted into providing a bus service, perhaps inspired by the *Progressive Bus Service* he noted as competing very successfully with the *Thames Valley* along the main road. However, his inspiration may have also come from local contacts, as his proposed Reading to Crowthorne service was intended to serve the communities then without buses at Sindlesham, Bearwood, Barkham and along the Nine Mile Ride. This would also provide those residents with a link to the Reading – Tonbridge train service at Wellington College (Crowthorne) Station.

In order to operate this he sought hackney carriage licenses from Reading BC, who initially refused them at the meeting of 22nd December 1925, on the basis that there were already enough buses between Reading, Wokingham and Crowthorne, as the *Progressive* buses of *Tom Spragg* of Bracknell and its Reading – Wokingham – Camberley service had recently passed to *Thames Valley*. However, as the Council had missed the point that *Field's* service would serve other areas, he appealed against that refusal.

With his service not being able to start, finance seems to have caused him to surrender the first Ford back to Gowrings 4 days after the Reading BC decision, nothing more being heard of that vehicle! Whilst he awaited the appeal decision he also applied to Wokingham BC, though his original route did not enter its area, so maybe he was considering a link with that town, probably also from the rural areas he had previously identified as requiring a bus service. The Borough asked him to submit his vehicles for inspection by Sergeant Goddard prior to considering his (unrecorded) licensing request.

In the next twist to this relatively complicated short sequence of events, Reading BC informed him that at its meeting of 19th January 1926 the earlier refusal had been rescinded providing that the buses ran via Bearwood and Barkham, just as he had intended to do in the first place! Indeed, the need for such small buses had been partly dictated by the very narrow roads in places, along with the narrow and weak hump-backed bridge over the River Loddon at Sindlesham Mill, though there is no evidence that the service even started with the one remaining Ford. As it was, before Wokingham B C came to consider his application, the

Clerk informed the meeting that Mr. Field has withdrawn his request, that taking place on 4th February 1926.

Notwithstanding the above action, on 13th April 1926 he registered a blue-liveried Fiat with a 14-seater bus body as MO 7567. As this vehicle had no declared chassis number it is very likely to be one of a number of that type then appearing on the market from War Department sources, whilst the different livery suggests it came from showroom stock rather than being completed to order, also presumably due to the changing decisions regarding his proposed operation.

However, despite acquiring the Fiat, there remains no hard evidence that any service actually started, and on 24th July 1926 the Fiat was re-sold. What became of the second Ford is less well documented, though it was later a lorry elsewhere, and certainly no such bus service gets a mention in local directories.

And so *Fred Field's* involvement with passenger transport, assuming it ever happened, came to a close. The good's haulage business continued, and by the late 1930's was in the hands of son Frederick E.D. Field (born 1910), also acting as nurseryman at Barkham Oak, Arborfield Cross. It would seem that the proposals had been noted by others locally, as a very similar route would soon be covered by *Bayliss & Poat,* which will be found on page 7.

Charles Henry Victor Fry
Priestwood Garage, Bracknell

Some mystery remains regarding the status of *Charlie Fry* as an operator, though reference to the situation in the Summer of 1948 when *Gough's Garage* was planning its bus service, does show that at that point he was certainly considering doing the same.

What is known is that he was the proprietor of the Priestwood Garage at No.80 Binfield Road by 1935, and his widowed mother had the shop and post office next door, all opposite the old Priestwood School. Although he had in fact been born in Bracknell in 1908, some three years later his parents had a pub in the High Street in Egham, about 12 miles to the east by 1911, but duly returned to the area.

His first known connection with our main topic came in September 1948 with the acquisition of a third-hand former *City of Oxford* Leyland 'Cub' KP3-type 20-seater bus registered BFC 31 and new with Park Royal body in May 1935. That was joined by a Dodge SBF-type with unknown 26-seater coach body (DAA 39), which had been new to *Glider & Blue* of Bishops Waltham in July 1938, coming to him via *Lovegrove* of Silchester in March 1949.

As indicated under the *Gough* story, Charlie had presented the Council with a proposal for a local bus service, though it did not come to fruition. Nor has any evidence come to light of any hire work or attempts to get licensed for excursions, though a contract or some private hire cannot be ruled out. Whatever use, if any, the pair of vehicles saw, what is known is that BFC was licensed to the end of 1951 and DAA until May 1953.

After sale by Charlie Fry the Dodge had another career as a showman's living van, as did many old buses in those days, in which guise it is shown here.

As it was, the author lived quite near to that location and his Father knew Charlie well, but only as a garage proprietor and motor/motor-cycle mechanic. Now Dad was a good storeman in the local motor trade, but one day on his way home from Gough's Garage he called in to chat to Charlie, whose stores was as chaotic as his forecourt was deeply rutted in December 1964. The two agreed that if Dad went there and got it all sorted out the business might benefit, but Charlie got cold feet as the weekly wage sought was actually more than he made, plus Dad also sought the use of a car, as at that time our growing family lacked such transport. They both said they would think about it overnight, but later that night poor old Charlie was found dead in the same chair!

The other PSV purchased when a bus service was in consideration was this Leyland 'Cub', one of a pair new to City of Oxford Motor Services and used on lightly-trafficked country services. Ideal for one-man operation, the body also had a large roof-rack.

Fuller & Pomroy
Beta Bus Services
Maidenhead, Berkshire

Charles Thomas Fuller and *Alfred William Pomroy* were based at Maidenhead, so a full appraisal of their transport ventures will be dealt with under the volume dedicated to that area.

Having started out as charabanc operators in the Spring of 1925, they duly developed a small network of bus services, but here we will concern ourselves only with the route out to Binfield.

The exact date of its commencement has eluded many years of research, but has been narrowed down to the early months of 1930, whilst it is understood that the incentive for opening up that link came from persons who had patronised the charabancs from points in the area between Maidenhead and where the route would emerge on the A329 at the Popeswood end of Binfield, via Boyne Hill (The Crown) – Tittle Row – Heywood Park corner – White Waltham (PO) – Waltham St. Lawrence (The Bell) – Shurlock Row (Royal Oak) – Allanby Park corner – Binfield (Church) – Binfield (Standard of England and Shoulder of Mutton).

It is not clear if Wokingham was an objective from the outset, but certainly in late 1930 the operator did apply to Wokingham BC for a license to cover the 2 miles to bring its buses to that town, perhaps also to become the established route before the 1930 Act took effect? The Police Sargent responsible for vehicle approvals was not happy with them, so in the end the extension was not pursued, passengers being able to transfer to the *Thames Valley* main Windsor – Reading service at the stop near the Popeswood terminus.

In respect of the bus services, the other of which went to Burchetts Green from April 1930, later extended onto Hurley, a pair of 14-seater Chevrolet buses were in use by 1933, one being a 1928 LP-type (VW 6831) and the other a LQ-type of 1930 (RX 5946), and both were secondhand acquisitions.

The service did in fact fill in an area so far ignored by the *Thames Valley* company, but during 1933 that firm started to consider how it might re-organise services around the Binfield area, not only in respect of the *Beta Bus Service*, but also *Cody Bus,* which of course had its garage just yards from the Shoulder of Mutton on the London Road towards Wokingham, operating a Binfield to Reading service via the rural route taking in Shurlock Row and Hurst, originally a carrier's route. And, so it was that the *'Valley*, now armed with a chequebook underwritten by Railway shareholdings made offers to both operators. *Fuller & Pomroy* were offered £850 for just the license, no vehicles included.

Thames Valley duly re-arranged various services in the area after those acquisitions, along with absorbing its *Marlow & District* subsidiary, though most of the experimental routes were over-long and not too successful. That led to The Walthams, Shurlock Row and Hurst becoming part of a Reading to Maidenhead route, which no longer touched Binfield at all.

Fuller & Pomroy retained their service to Hurley and continued until deciding to give up in March 1935, when it passed with their coach operations to *Albert Warwick*, who will also be covered by the volume on the Maidenhead area.

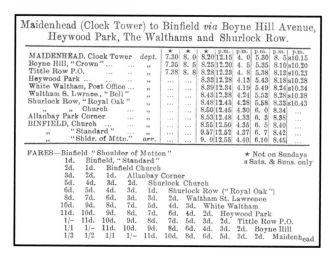

The timetable for September 1932 shows the route and timings as they were at the sale to Thames Valley.

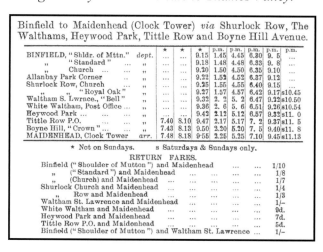

Charlie Fuller is seen as the centre driver on a 1920's charabanc outing when employed by Thames Valley.

Jealotts Hill – A Perspective

Before we examine the need, and various phases of provision, for transport to the rather isolated area of Jealotts Hill, we must appreciate the changes which occurred there during the 1920's onwards. In that respect we shall also encounter some operators based in the Maidenhead area, so the fuller account of their activities will appear in the volume dedicated to that area in due course.

Up to the latter 1920's the area consisted of farms and small groups of scattered cottages, not even warranting the status of hamlet. Situated on the Maidenhead to Bracknell Road, it was some 6 miles from the former and 3 from the latter. Further north the road passed through Hawthorn Hill and Holyport, whilst in the southerly direction it passed through Moss End and Warfield Street, passing the large estate of Warfield Hall, the whole area being largely dominated by large estates in those days.

On the hill itself stood The New Leathern Bottel, the 'new', indicating that it had replaced the older Windsor Forest inn The Leathern Bottel back in the 17th century. Around that hill were farms, a trio of which had been taken over during 1927 by Messrs. Nitrams to form a working trial-ground for the testing of nitrogen-based additives for soil improvement, those being Hawthorn, Jealotts Hill and Nuptown Farms.

Prior to that the *Yellow Bus Service* of Robert Tuck had operated between Maidenhead and Bracknell via Holyport - Touchen End – Hawthorn Hill – Jealotts Hill – Warfield, commencing by February 1924. That was the sole service past the Hill, so when the Road Motors of the *Great Western Railway* returned to operations at Maidenhead from April 1928, the subject of that route was raised. The result was that the *GWR* did not wish to run through to Bracknell, which was Southern Railway territory, but it bought Bob Tuck out all the same in the first half of 1928, operating as Maidenhead – Bray – Holyport – Touchen End – Hawthorn Hill – Jealotts Hill, forsaking the section onto Bracknell.

In the meantime, Messrs. Nitrams had approached the *Thames Valley Company* about providing a service to assist its recruitment to the new research station being developed. Whilst the two concerns were discussing the matter, which the 'Valley was quite uninterested in, Nitrams had been absorbed into Imperial Chemical Industries, though the latter did do so in order to further develop the site.

All of that should have encouraged the *GWR* to expand the service, but it remained at a low level through to September 1931, when the already reluctant *Thames Valley* inherited the route due to a new share-holding

by the railway. As the Road Motors had struggled to make the route pay with a one-man-operated 14-seater bus, there was little prospect of the 'Valley fairing better when fielding a crew-operated 32-seater Tilling-Stevens.

These prolonged discussions and events had, in the meantime, convinced ICI that it would need to address the issue directly, particularly as numbers employed were now building up beyond local resources, along with a guest house added to the site for visitors and other specialists to the location. They therefore ordered a pair of normal-control Guy OND-type chassis fitted with 20-seater bus bodies by Hoyal of Weybridge. The pair was listed as owned by ICI of Millbank in London, but registered locally as RX 6849/50 on the last day of May 1930. One would run in from each of the stations at Maidenhead and Bracknell for work times, plus also being used when required for other duties which, in due course sometimes included trips down to another research site at Fernhurst, north of Midhurst in Sussex. It is also known that they were occasionally used for Social Club outings for the workers and families.

That situation continued through to about the close of 1937, when the buses came up for withdrawal, after it was decided to continue the operations using hired-in vehicles from local concerns. Perhaps unsurprisingly, RX 6850 went locally to Carter of Maidenhead (Alpha Coaches), though the other ended up via dealers with an operator in Ayr, though probably not actually used.

When the *GWR* service had started it had annoyed *West Bros.* of Bray, whose *Blue Bus Service* had run between their base village and Maidenhead Station, so they felt the Railway was seeking to run them off the road. In response they had extended their route onwards to Bracknell from Wednesday 25th April 1928, so can be considered as the true successor to *Yellow Bus*, despite Bob Tuck taking the *GWR's* money! That service ran about 5 times daily throughout the 1930's, though the family recalls that part of the route was never a paying proposition. It also convinced *Thames Valley* to give up its Maidenhead to Jealotts Hill service, which it hoped *West Bros.* might purchase, though the latter told them no when approached, so that last operated on 18th September 1932.

Blue Bus would duly become *Bray Transport*, who would continue the operation through to the 1960's, whilst others would become interested post-war in that area, there having been an estate of houses built for the agricultural workers at Jealotts Hill, along with the development of a 'model farm' at nearby Moss End, though not in fact related to the ICI site. Such developments will be found under the narrative for *S.R. Gough (Gough's Garage Bus Service)* in the following section.

Stanley Richard Gough
Gough's Garage Bus Service
East Berks Services
Bracknell, Berkshire

Business background

Firstly, we must acknowledge the long-standing existence of this family concern, as the bus service and coach operation represented only a fraction of the nigh on 200 years the Gough family has been in business in connection with wheeled transport. Now located over at Billingbear, in Binfield, it was formerly at Warfield, but prior to that in Bracknell. Still in family hands, it is run by Richard Gough, the 5th generation.

The story begins with the birth of William Gough at Holborn in London in 1796 who, after serving as a coachbuilder's apprentice, could be found in Windsor, where he set up in business in 1827. Indeed, he had married Mary from nearby Langley and their first child was also William, born in Windsor in 1833. By 1841 he had premises in Peascod Street, down the hill from the Castle. One account refers to patronage by King George IV (1820-1830), though that is unconfirmed, but the Royal Warrant certainly came with a dog-cart built for Queen Victoria – a fact he and the family was most justifiably proud of.

However, despite that, he had relocated to Bracknell by 1850, with a coachbuilding shop on the London Road to the Ascot side, adjacent to the Royal Oak pub, which was also in his control, now with sons William and Henry. Quite when William senior passed away is not found, but it was between 1851 and 1861, by which time his son William was fully able to continue the business. He married Harriet White from Binfield and they had a son Richard Henry in 1860, followed by Frank Ernest in 1864. Both the businesses continued and William lived through to 1897, certainly as head of the business until at least 1887, though the pub was no longer part of the business from around 1877.

Once the pub was vacated, the original coachbuilding shed was transferred about 200 yards westwards closer to the centre of Bracknell, still on the north side of the London Road, where a large additional shed was built abutting the line of New Road, which will assume its own importance later in our story.

By 1881 Frank was assisting his father, so was another generation taught the many skills of coachbuilding, and by 1891 he was certainly running that business, still a single man, but by 1901 he had married Florence, and they had two children, now with premises also in the High Street, which feature in directories from 1895 to

1903, perhaps an indication of when the new shed was added? See location plan on page 61.

The relocated coachbuilding premises on the left, plus new shed to the right on London Road.

The next future generation arrived with the birth of Stanley Richard in December 1905, who would duly join his father at a time when motor vehicles were also receiving coachwork and repairs. In respect of the Royal Warrant, Frank had been given dispensation to use the phrase 'By Appointment to the Late Queen' after Victoria's death in 1901, and the signboard outside the relocated premises include such wording and the name Royal Coach Works.

In 1935 the directory notes the business still as Frank Ernest Gough, now with telephone number 146, but in 1936 Frank passed away, after which Stanley (always known as Dick or Dicker) took over under the title of Gough & Son, Motor Engineers, though coachbuilding did continue in appropriate fashion, and in due course would in fact witness a return to traditional skills.

Dick married Vera Smith in 1936, followed by their children Richard (1937), Marcus (1940), twins Peter and Janet (1943), all but their other daughter Valerie duly featuring in the business.

A bus service proposed

It seems the idea of a bus service came from contacts in several areas which, in due course would be linked for the first time. The chequered history of bus routes between Jealotts Hill and Bracknell has been outlined in the summary on that unique location, but it was one focus for attention, particularly with the increase in the populations at that point and nearby Moss End, leaving many of what were then stay-at-home wives requiring shopping journeys. There were also several locations in the local area where caravan or park-home sites had developed in response to the London Blitz or other housing shortages.

One of the latter areas was situated on the southern edge of Easthampstead Park in the old Army Camp and not served by any buses whatsoever. It was also opposite the Pinewood Sanatorium, a TB hospital, served only infrequently by *Thames Valley* as an express service, despite that Company having a Dormy Shed at Crowthorne since 1926!

The original concept was to operate from Hawthorn Hill, where a collection of cottages and a few larger houses were set around a triangular junction where the roads to Maidenhead and Winkfield met, which also provided a convenient point to turn the bus. It then ran past the growing ICI Research Station, with its estate of houses, down the hill to Moss End (The Shepherds House), before turning left at the New Inn (later the Three-legged Cross, now an Indian restaurant) at Battle Bridge and along Warfield Street past the Post Office, another area with recent building of private dwellings, to turn right at Fiveways junction to pass the western entrance of Warfield Park Camp. From there it went up Jigs Lane and Park Road to the crossroads of the High Street and Church Road in Bracknell, stopping by the Hinds Head and where the cattle market was still then situated, the High Street and London Road still linked as a through road prior to the diversion via the roundabout.

The southern section of the route, for its seems that from the beginning the Gough's did regard it as two co-joined routes, started from the Hinds Head and along Church Road to the Bagshot Road, where it passed the Horse & Groom pub, with another caravan settlement to its rear, a number of them being interesting old buses, before turning right at the crossroads with Harmans Water Road into South Hill Road, then right again up Reeds Hill, past Easthampstead Church and the Union (where the *Thames Valley* bus on Route 2b from Windsor then terminated), to cover new ground onto Crowthorne Road, turn right at Nine Mile Ride crossroads to reach the next junction by Easthampstead Park Camp and Pinewood Hospital, before turning left for the final stretch into Crowthorne (Dukes Head), with a journey time of 45 minutes overall.

The original application only had a service on Tuesday, Thursday and Saturday, which, in those days before all had refrigerators, was obviously intended primarily for shopping trips, the first bus not leaving Hawthorn Hill until 9am, with only further runs at 12noon and 4.55pm, that last one only working back to the Hinds Head from Crowthorne.

It should be noted that the Easthampstead Park Camp buildings were Nissen huts vacated by the Army and pressed into service as temporary accommodation for some 500 people there awaiting re-housing, including Andy Goddard's parents amongst those placed in that not ideal situation, so perhaps ironic he would duly become the long-term Manager at Gough's Garage! Both Andy, myself and David Nicholls also worked there as Saturday boys in the Motor Factors.

Alternative services?

At this point it is necessary to acknowledge that during the time Gough's were considering starting a service, two other local men came forward with apparently similar plans, as noted by the ERDC at its meeting on 27th May 1948. *Alexander Ronald Clarke* of The White Bungalow, The Warren was an established taxi driver and car hire operator, now offering towing of caravans put forward a proposal for a Maidenhead – Bracknell – Crowthorne route, but no details were recorded at that point. Also, *Charlie Fry*, proprietor of the Priestwood Garage also sought Council support for his proposed service, more about him under his own heading.

Out of the three contenders, the Council favoured *Gough's* proposal, so the application went to the Traffic Commissioner in late October 1948. Although largely welcomed by the Local Councils, it fell foul of an objection from *Bray Transport*, which already operated Maidenhead to Bracknell via Hawthorn Hill, so that section was turned down at the Hearing, sending the *Gough's* away to re-think their plans. Indeed, correspondence in the local paper voiced the need for better links for the points highlighted, not all served by either the *Bray Transport* service or the *Thames Valley* one through Winkfield and Chavey Down – the latter essentially conceived because the Parishes of Easthampstead, Winkfield and Warfield had jointly operated the Union Workhouse mentioned earlier.

The other point made locally was the need for a daily operation, and indeed for *Bray Transport* to run on a Sunday, as Taplow Hospital was noted as a particularly torturous journey those visiting from Bracknell, or indeed to 'allow Mr. Gough to provide such a link'.

Gough's returned to the Traffic Commissioners with a modified application on 12th February 1949 on a daily basis, but bruised from the objection, it would operate only between Bracknell (Police Station) on the previous route to Crowthorne. The Police Station was in those days situated at the western end of the High Street, where the Wokingham Road and Skimped Hill Lane met, which again provided somewhere to turn the bus easily. The revised timetable still had 3 journeys on Monday to Friday, the first leaving Bracknell at 8.10am, which returned from Crowthorne at 8.33am, making its use by workers and children at the junior school in Easthampstead or Ranelagh School practical. The other journeys left Bracknell at 10.10am and 3.50pm, returning from Crowthorne at 11.10am and 5.10pm. On Saturdays there were 4 journeys, the first from Bracknell at 9.10am, followed by 12.10pm, 4.10pm and 10pm, returning from Crowthorne at 10.10am, 12.50pm, 5.10pm and 10.23pm.

The revised service was indeed approved, but straightaway correspondence reached the Council and in the local press from those who had hoped to have transport from the Warfield area, and in fact a number of nearby points not in the original routing, again most of them being caravan settlements or unserved areas. It should also be appreciated that the revised service as approved was soon found not much of a paying concern, so *Gough's* returned to the licensing process on 30th July 1949 with a modified southern section to which was added a 'Warfield circular', which also widened its use by various groups of passengers. The Monday to Friday Crowthorne runs from Bracknell were at 8.03am, 10.10am, 1.10pm and 3.10pm, returning at 8.31am, 11.10am, 1.40pm and 4.10pm. Those journeys reaching Bracknell at 8.55am and 4.34pm would then take the loop out to Warfield and back. On Saturdays there were 4 journeys out from Bracknell to Crowthorne at 9.10am, 12.30pm, 4.10pm and 8.03pm, turning at Crowthorne to reach Bracknell to form the Warfield departures at 10.35am, 1.55pm, 5.35pm and 8.53pm.

turned right back onto the Forest Road towards Warfield, past the northern entrance to Warfield Park Camp, then up Jigs Lane and back into Bracknell. By the time the revised route started on Monday 28th November 1949, another small modification saw the bus now using Station Road in Bracknell as a more convenient standing point than the Police Station.

The final route changes came from 6th August 1951, with an overall increase in journeys, though several now only ran between Bracknell (Station Road) and Easthampstead Park Camp on Monday to Friday only, plus a Saturday evening Warfield loop leaving Bracknell at 9pm. However, only 2 of the 4 Saturday journeys were now projected onto Warfield, suggesting the others were poorly patronised. In those days the Road Service Licenses were issued for 3 years, so it was due for renewal from September 1954, but although Gough's did submit a slightly modified application in due time, they subsequently withdrew it, resulting in a cessation of the service on a date not so far discovered, though a letter in the local paper on 30th July 1954 bemoans the 'recent loss', which had ceased with the end of the Summer Term that month.

Thames Valley to cover?

Indeed, the withdrawal led to a further round of local correspondence and Council activity, as the assumption that *Thames Valley* might step in was initially dismissed by that Company on the grounds it had insufficient buses or crews, so even when it finally agreed to extend the 2b to Crowthorne from 21st May 1955, it had to further postpone that. Much of the issue lay over the many people at Easthampstead Park Camp, which now included some 50 children with places allocated to St. Michael's School at Easthampstead and therefore entitled to assisted transport. Although the Council subsequently decided to close the camp as soon as practical, a similar concern was raised by Dr. Moon at Pinewood, whose staff relied on the bus link. However, despite the *'Valley'* duly reaching Crowthorne, the Warfield area remained unserved.

The fleet

We will now turn our attention to the vehicles used by *Gough's Garage Bus Service*, and the initial purchase in April 1948 had been a rather stylish Leyland-bodied Leyland 'Lion' LT5A-type new in August 1934 (VD 3503), part of a batch of 110 delivered to *Central Scottish Motor Traction* and its associated *Lanarkshire* fleet. Its 32-seater bus body had a cutaway rear platform entrance of the type usually only found on saloons north of the border, but its half-cab layout was perhaps an odd choice for a small rural operation. Indeed, in due course Vera Gough obtained her PSV Driver's License, but with the then common restriction

TIME TABLE
Commencing Monday, April 25th 1949

BRACKNELL—EASTHAMPSTEAD—CROWTHORNE

	a.m.	a.m.	p.m.
Bracknell Police Station	8.10	10.10	3.50
Bracknell Station	8.13	10.13	3.53
Horse and Groom Public House	8.16	10.16	3.56
Harmans Water Cross Road	8.19	10.19	3.59
Church Hill House	8.23	10.23	4. 3
Easthampstead Park Camp	8.28	10.28	4. 8
Crowthorne	8.32	10.32	4.12

Monday to Friday

CROWTHORNE—EASTHAMPSTEAD—BRACKNELL

	a.m.	a.m.	p.m.
Crowthorne	8.33	11.10	5.10
Easthampstead Park Camp	8.37	11.14	5.14
Church Hill house	8.42	11.19	5.19
Harmans Water Cross Road	8.45	11.24	5.24
Horse and Groom Public House	8.48	11.27	5.27
Bracknell Station	8.51	11.30	5.30
Bracknell Police Station	8.54	11.34	5.34

Monday to Friday

BRACKNELL—EASTHAMPSTEAD—CROWTHORNE

	a.m.	p.m.	p.m.	p.m.
Bracknell Police Station	9.10	12.10	4.10	10.00
Bracknell Station	9.13	12.13	4.13	10. 3
Horse and Groom Public House	9.16	12.16	4.16	10. 6
Harmans Water Cross Road	9.19	12.19	4.19	10. 9
Church Hill House	9.23	12.23	4.23	10.13
Easthampstead Park Camp	9.28	12.28	4.28	10.18
Crowthorne	9.32	12.32	4.32	10.22

Saturdays only

CROWTHORNE—EASTHAMPSTEAD—BRACKNELL

	a.m.	p.m.	p.m.	p.m.
Crowthorne	10.10	12.50	5.10	10.23
Easthampstead Park Camp	10.14	12.54	5.14	10.27
Church Hill House	10.19	12.59	5.19	10.32
Harmans Water Cross Road	10.24	1. 4	5.24	10.36
Horse and Groom Public House	10.27	1. 7	5.27	10.39
Bracknell Station	10.30	1.10	5.30	10.42
Bracknell Police Station	10.34	1.13	5.34	10.45

Saturdays only

GOUGH'S GARAGE BUS SERVICE
Telephone: BRACKNELL 146   A.22.4

The northern section saw the bus run up the High Street once again to pass the Hinds Head, then down Park Road and Jigs Lane to pass the Warfield Park Camp western entrance. At the Fiveways crossroads it took the Forest Road eastwards to Hayley Green (Goose Corner), turning left again for Warfield School, then onto Brock Hill and on Winkfield Road, before it

to a maximum of 29 seats, so VD must have been crew-operated, as it remained with the firm until May 1952.

No photos of the 'Lion' in service with Gough's has survived, but here is one of that batch seen when new.

The 'Lion' was indeed followed during December 1948 by a smaller vehicle in the shape of Bedford WLB-type which carried a 20-seater front-entrance coach body by Wilmott's (GW 724), with whom it was initially a demonstrator in December 1931 before sale to *Fullbrook* of Yateley in Hampshire. However, as it was declared as scrapped in May 1949 it may not have actually seen much use?

It seems that a conscious decision had been made to run the service as one-person-operated, as in June 1949 two suitable vehicles were acquired. One was a Commer PN3-type (NV 8218) of November 1936, and new to *Belgrove* of Cold Higham. As it had been supplied by the Northampton-based Commer agent and coach-builder Grose, it is very likely that its 20-seater front-entrance coach body was built by that firm. It also had a 'sun-saloon' roof, a common arrangement then with smaller operators, who used vehicles on both bus services and for other work, and as new it was painted red, cream and black.

This is a similar Grose-bodied Commer as shown at the Commercial Motor Show of 1936.

The other purchase was a Bedford WTB-type of February 1938 (UD 9831), fitted with a 26-seater front-entrance coach body by Thurgood of Ware, previously with *Surman's* of Chinnor. Unfortunately, there are no surviving photos of those earlier vehicles within the family, so whether a standard livery was then in effect is not known.

Garaging for the vehicles was provided in the former coach-building shop at the London Road premises and was entered via the yard entrance in New Road. Indeed, that shed continued in use for at least some of the PSV's throughout, though as the motor garage and dealership for Ford had expanded, a new showroom was built on its western flank. Also on the site was the Gough home at 'Cumnock', whilst to the east across the New Road entrance stood No.1 South View, when Johnny Groves lived, known to have undertaken sign-writing for the fleet. John Thomas ('Jack') Macro and his dog-breeder wife Dorothy lived just into New Road at 'Garage Cottage'.

Whether it had been the intention from the outset to also undertake private hire work is not known, but the fleet was certainly increased beyond daily requirements from May 1951. The addition was another Bedford, but of the wartime OWB-type, fitted with the utility-style Duple front-entrance saloon body, new in August 1942 to *S. Grainge* of Westbury, then in Northamptonshire as VV 8771. That it by then had seats for 29 most likely indicates that the original wooden slatted seating had been replaced by upholstered seats.

That was followed by the first postwar Bedford OB-type in May 1952 as CFV 677, new in February 1948 to *Whittaker* of Blackpool and carrying a standard 29-seater Duple 'Vista' front-entrance coach body. That same month saw the 'Lion' departing, whilst November 1952 saw the withdrawal of NV 8218, though it languished through to about a year later.

In respect of the origins of these vehicles, and ongoing, my Dad (who later worked for Gough's Garage) told me that the firm used a dealer based in Northampton for sourcing secondhand stock.

It was found necessary to withdraw VV 8771 at the close of July 1954, so another Bedford OB with 'Vista' coach body (BNL 676) arrived in its place, new in January 1946 to *Bedlington & District*, before that Northumberland operator was merged with others to form *Crown Coaches* of Newcastle, though it came to Bracknell after use by *Creamline* of Bordon.

The next fleet change saw another straight replacement, but quite a different type of vehicle, with a return to the half-cab format. Outgoing in June 1956 was Bedford WTB-type UD 9831, replaced by HDG 473, an AEC 'Regal' 9621E chassis carrying a 33-seater front-entrance Duple A-type coach body. New in October 1948 to *Neale* of Berkeley, but coming via *Invicta* of Southend, it was the first vehicle known to have worn the cream with red trim which would become the fleet standard. With its 9.6-litre engine it was quite a flier and was popular with the drivers.

The stylish 'Regal' is seen on an excursion to the races at Goodwood, where the coach park high on the South Downs was a great venue for my early bus-spotting!

The disposal of UD brings us to the first amusing episode connected with the Gough fleet, as it was sold to Rank Studios at their Pinewood Studios, so its 15 minutes of fame came in Blue Murder at St. Trinian's in 1957. For those not familiar with the story, the infamous girls' school won the chance to represent the UK in a UNESCO competition trip to Italy, but none of the local coach operators would touch them. Desperate, the Man from the Ministry approaches 'that chap up on The Ridgeway', which must surely have been based on the premises of *Reliance Motor Services* of Brightwalton, in whose adjacent orchard the older vehicles slowly faded away! Captain Romney Carlton-Ricketts is played by Terry Thomas, whose 'Dreadnout Motor Traction' office is an old London General bus body, where he tells them 'all my best motors are out' before agreeing to tidy up the 'reserve fleet', and cue UD shown full of straw and chickens!

The next vehicle to arrive again increased the fleet size from what had generally been a trio of active vehicles. It was another standard Duple-bodied Bedford OB 29-seater (DVH 531), new in March 1948 to *Hanson's* of Huddersfield in April 1958 coming via other owners. It stayed until March 1963 when, like a number of other smaller coaches of that period, it was converted to a mobile shop and seen in the Reading area.

As already noted, *Gough's Garage* had been a Ford Main Dealer for some years, and of course vehicles of that make had often been the basis for many post-Great war passenger enterprises, but that firm had ceased to produce larger specific chassis by WW2. It then returned to that market from May 1957, and indeed *Gough's* took a 'Thames Trader' 510E model with a 41-seater front-entrance Duple 'Yeoman' coach body as new in July 1959, though registered in Coventry as XKV 121.

In another Ford-related episode, although Dick was known to be 'careful' with money, he was also kind-hearted. It had come to his attention after a particularly harsh Winter that the local District Nurse was still undertaking her duties by bicycle, so he donated for her a car he had left in the showroom, but it transpired she couldn't actually drive! As it was, the garage did have a Driving School arrangement with another, so lessons were soon provided free of charge as well.

The firm had also for many years had a car or two for local private hires, but by the time my Dad was there it was a rather impressively long Humber 'Imperial', a black-painted limousine popular for weddings and also hired to local funeral directors. We would occasionally borrow a car from the yard for seaside trips, as we did not have our own at that time, so one day it turned out to be the above beast. However, when we reached our destination of West Wittering it was raining and windy, so the picnic was instead laid out in the capacious rear of the 'Imperial', with the extra row of seats in the upright position, us 3 kids sitting on the floor!

It is worth noting at this point that *Gough's* never did apply for Road Service Licenses for advertised excursions, though they did a fair amount of local private hire. The other activities centred on work's and school contracts, of which a regular daily run to Mytchett was driven by Ted Waterman's son-in-law, who also worked at that factory, whilst no details are known of the various school contracts over the years. The only applications put before the Traffic Commissioner both concerned serving ICI at Jealott's Hill, a job which seemed to alternate between *Gough's* and *Bray Transport* over the 1960's. The 1961 route was from the Bracknell (Station) – Bracknell (Cinema) – ICI Jealotts Hill, granted in October 1961 and extended through to February 1964. A license from East Berks Service Station (London Road) in Bracknell was issued from January 1970, again for the sole use of ICI employees, and that expired in April 1971.

The Ford coach XKV 121 was fitted with a variety of Duple body designed for that chassis, and it is seen when newly delivered in the hands of Senior Driver Jack Macro on the approach to Wembley coach park.

1961 was another busy year for fleet changes, though that sadly saw the sale of the 'Regal' during April to *Jeff's* of Helmdon. Incoming was the first of what would become a trio of Commers, and TOV 268 was of the 'Avenger' MkIII-type, fitted with the unusual 3-cylinder TS3 engine that used opposed cylinders with a piston at either end of the cylinder, with all 6 acting on the single crankshaft, and the 3.261-litre diesel engine had a very distinctive sound. It carried a 41-seat front-entrance coach body of the Plaxton 'Venturer' MkIII style and had been new in March 1957 to *Allenways* of Birmingham.

Also a Commer, but of the 44A-type and fitted with the same engine, KET 888 was acquired in July 1961. It had the same style of body as TOV but only seated 37, being new in March 1954 to Rotherham-based *Smart & Riley*. It was invariably known as 'Katie', and from that point the fleet was maintained at 6 coaches. The third of the modern Commers to be acquired was in July 1962 as SWK 971, another 'Avenger' MkIII, but carrying a Duple 39-seater of a body style developed for that chassis type. It had been new in June 1956 to *RHMS* of Coventry.

Commer TOV 268 is seen later when with East Berks, parked on the land between Station Road and Drake & Mount's Garage after it too was acquired by Compton.

It was at that time I became more familiar with the London Road-based fleet, as my Dad joined them as Stores Manager just as the *Gough's* sold the Bracknell garage to Compton-Burnett as *East Berks Services*, the new title also going onto the coaches as well. Indeed, Dad recalled ordering the new EBS-monogramed headrest covers soon after starting there.

It was also around that point, with 'Dicker' Gough now supposedly retired, that his family finally persuaded their parents to take the first proper holiday ever! The arrangements were made for a week at Littlehampton, and Mr. Gough appeared with a new cap and sports jacket, whilst their small case was loaded into the Ford 'Squire' he ran, an estate version of the 100E of about

1959. The whole family was present for the departure at 9.30am, along with Garage Foreman Alan Roberts, who had been with them since leaving school and thought he'd never see the day. Despite having sold the business, the Gough's still were awaiting completion of their new house at the Warfield Garage, so by being on site he still tended to 'keep an eye on things'. And off they went, only to phone about 2.30 that day to check all was OK, and in fact they returned on the Thursday!

Despite a number of Duple-bodied Bedford OB's used, no photos have come down, assuming any were taken, so here is the batch-mate for BNL 676.

However, I had one encounter with that fleet previously and recall my day out on the 'Regal' for reasons not of a transport nature. As an occasional attendee at the 'tin tabanacle' church Sunday School off Binfield Road, I was allowed to go on the seaside outing, which that year was to Worthing. As it was organised by (the what seemed to me to be ancient) Mrs. Hobley, the venue was not a great one for children, so I decided to explore the breakwater area for crabs etc., though I was fully clothed at the time. On the western side was some sand with about 2 inches of water, so my bare feet were fine, but when I stepped on the breakwater I slipped on some seaweed, landing in a good foot of water on the other side! Soaked to the skin, all I had left was my duffle-coat and my swimming trunks, so Mrs. H took me to the St. John Ambulance hut, where much to my horror 2 old ladies dried and re-dressed me in the dry items!

Once Dad settled in at East Berks and I developed my interest in PSV's, he would sometimes arrange for me to accompany one of the drivers on a trip where I could go coach-spotting, such as to Goodwood Races. As I joined the coach at the garage, I always got the front seat, whilst drivers Jack Macro, Norman Lovejoy (ex-*Thames Valley* at Ascot and Bracknell), or Ted

Waterman would chat to me about their driving experiences, which got me out of the house for the day.

At other times I would go out with Dad's friend George Stimpson, a one-time heavy lorry-driver, who also told me of the old types he had known and adventures on the road. He was then driving a small truck for Wayne Pumps, so we went mainly to food factories, and on the trip to the Epicure plant I returned home with a carton full of pickles, red cabbage and other things I had only ever seen at Christmas prior to that, all with wonky labels, so my Mum was most pleased by that visit!

The next coach to come to *East Berks Services* was in fact my favourite, and also the only under-floor engine type owned. Coming in June 1963, it was a fairly rare Daimler 'Freeline' D650H-type chassis, which featured a 10.5-litre diesel engine and 5-speed gearbox of the pre-selective type. EBV 283 had been new in April 1953 to *Cronshaw* of Hendon, and carried a 41-seater Duple 'Ambassador' centre-entrance body. It was a powerful coach and popular with drivers, so smooth on the road, with a splendid view from my usual front perch. It was maybe a bit too thirsty for its own good, as it was sold on after only a year or so.

The 'Freeline' seen with its original owner, its cream livery at Gough's being retained due to its good order.

The replacement in February 1964 for the exotic Daimler was a rather more mundane Bedford SB5-type (4019 AW), which carried a 41-seater front-entrance Duple coach body. It had been new only in March 1963 with the Highley-based *Whittle* fleet. A similar coach arrived in July 1965 as 1212 MG, new in April 1962 to *Grundon's* of London SW9.

May 1966 saw a further Bedford, but of the SB8-type, and bearing a Plaxton 'Embassy' 41-seater front-door coach body (294 BLB), which came from *St. Valentine Coaches* of Shalbourne and was new in April 1962.

The final purchase of coaches came with a pair in March 1967, consisting of Ford 570E-type chassis with Plaxton 'Consort' MkIV 40-seater front-entrance coach bodies. 1316/7 WA had been new to Sheffield United Tours in January 1961 and, typically of the operator, their bodies carried additional side beading.

Both were in very good condition, and in general the fleet at *East Berks* was kept in fine form.

Another race-day photo shows the pair of ex-Sheffield United Transport Fords, headed by 1316 WA. The side embellishments were typical specification for SUT.

Despite a reasonably steady amount of local contracts and private hire, as the new owners developed the business it became apparent that there would be no room for the coaches once the new showroom was constructed in line with becoming a Rootes Main Agent. Indeed, it was quite usual to find several coaches parked on a rough yard as part of the former Drake & Mount Garage off Station Road, now also under the same ownership.

And so it was that in March 1970 *East Berks Services* announced it was cease coach operation at the end of that month, Manager Peter Seed noting the impending rebuilding of the showroom and other site changes. As it was, another local operator upon which the County Education Committee relied on for school transport, *Ted Payton's Bowler's Coaches*, had just been forced out of its parking spot on Station Road by Bracknell Development Corporation enforcement action, thereby precipitating another crisis in school transport locally!

Following that decision to end such work the remaining fleet of 6 coaches, Bedfords 4019 AW, 1212 MG, 294 BLB, and Fords XKV 121 and 1316/7 WA were all put up for sale, and all found further operators.

The Warfield Garage

The new Gough premises at Warfield already had a long history of coachbuilding, a nice twist to the tale of the family given its own origins. It had been the former premises of Thomas Bowyer, wheelwright and coach-builder, who had died in 1948 aged 82. In fact, that family can claim the earliest entry in the Parish Register for Warfield back to the time of Queen Elizabeth I. His widow and daughters continued to live in the Queen Anne-style house between the site and the Three-legged Cross pub, whilst the Goughs had a new house built to the eastern edge. In the yard there was still the

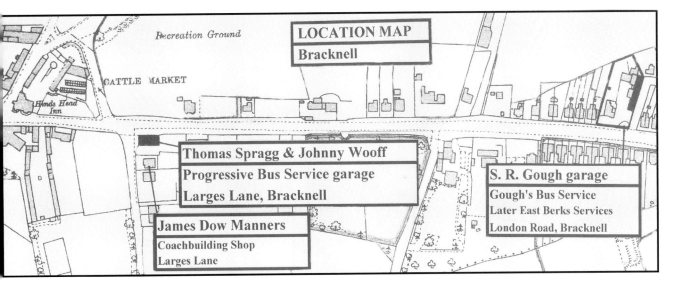

LOCATION MAP
Bracknell

Recreation Ground

CATTLE MARKET

Hinds Head Inn

Thomas Spragg & Johnny Wooff
Progressive Bus Service garage
Larges Lane, Bracknell

S. R. Gough garage
Gough's Bus Service
Later East Berks Services
London Road, Bracknell

James Dow Manners
Coachbuilding Shop
Larges Lane

This location map shows where the coachbuilder's business was relocated by Gough's, the motor coach shed shown in solid black. As the site developed into the motor garage, other sheds and a workshop were added, plus the house to the left of the site for the family. In due course further extensions took place to provide a large showroom under the investment by the Rootes Group. Further left we see the properties in Larges Lane, with the bus garage of the Progressive Bus Service, with Tom Spragg's bungalow behind that on the London Road. Next in Larges Lane comes the coachbuilding shop of James Manners, rented from Spragg, and also contributing to events in his fleet.

iron 'plate' used for constructing cart wheels. His daughter Alice Bowyer was one of my teachers when I first came to Sandy Lane School in 1957, whilst the coachbuilding business can be traced back to at least 1735, almost a century before the Gough's!

My Dad continued to work at East Berks, also sometimes within the other local garages added to the fold, but in March 1965 he went over to see Dick at Warfield with a proposal to start a Motor Factors business. The garage was now being run by the three sons, Richard, Peter and Marcus, with assistance from their sister Janet, and Mrs. Gough still going the books, so Dick didn't want to upset that transition, but said he would think about it. However, a few days later on 8th March he passed away from a heart attack aged just 59, though in due course Dad and the Gough's did start Warfield Motor Factors in the old coachbuilding that had previously been used by Thomas Bowyer.

Old skills live on

In a fitting postscript to the early origins of Gough's, 2 interesting items duly highlighted that the old skills had not disappeared. The first concerned an item in the Local paper in August 1962, which after noting the Royal Warrants issued by King George IV and Queen Victoria, showed the recent coachwork undertaken at Warfield on behalf of the show-piece collection of

horse-drawn vehicles owned by Mr. A. Gilbey, head of that Gin-making firm who lived nearby. Dick and his son Marcus said they were proud to keep the traditional skills alive, whilst the reporter commented on the fine finish achieved, Dick adding 'it was all done by hand'. During my visits to Warfield Garage I often saw that work in progress, kept in a separate shed away from the grime of the day-to-day servicing, and there were a number of examples to be seen locally, including an old stage-coach outside the Jolly Gardener pub at Maidens Green. Indeed, the second press item of 1966 refers to the discovery by local builder Jimmy Moss of 'Grandad Gough's Old Bus', which he rescued after it had been used as a chicken house nearby. According to the item, Mr. Gough, which I take to mean Frank, had used it for trips to Ascot Races for some years, but after that it became the staff bus for Warfield Hall, though now re-discovered it was restored to its former glory.

The Warfield Garage relocated a while back to Billingbear just a few years short of 200 still as a family concern in continuous business, adapted to the times.

David Nicholls, Andy Goddard and the author seen outside Bowyer's old coachbuilding shop as Saturday boys in the mid 1960's for Warfield Motor Factors.

Above - The final style of letterhead from Gough's Garage at the London Road site, red lettering on cream quarto.
Below - The relevant locations in the Popeswood area of Binfield, with the London Road Bungalow built for Mr. & Mrs. Keene, and where the Cody Garage was developed. To the east was Popeswood Garage, base for Hinman.

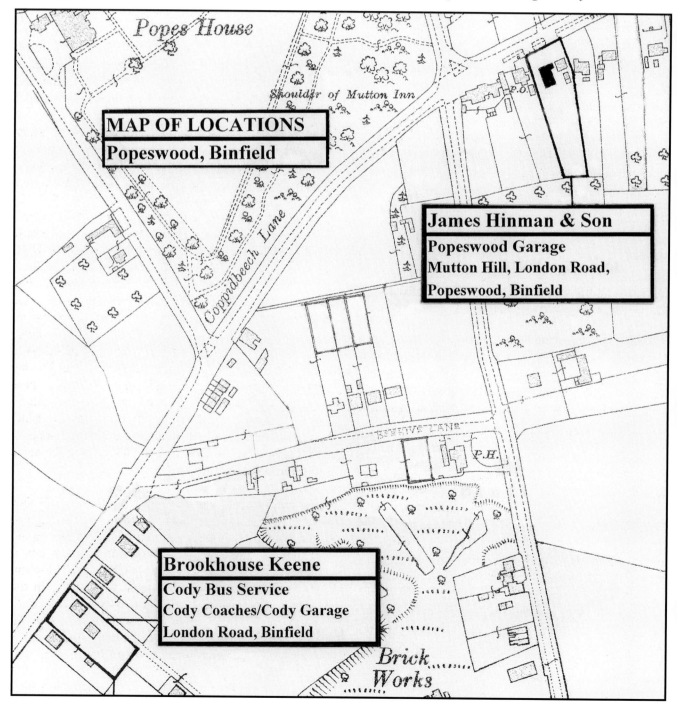

Richard Herring & Sons
Herring Bros.
Wokingham, Berkshire

The Herring family featured in the daily lives of the inhabitants of the then relatively small market town of Wokingham, Berkshire for over a century, providing them with a diverse range of services and goods which included beer, oil, petrol, glass and china, household requisites, furniture, bedding and groceries, along with various forms of transport. In fact, such were the wide interests of the family that this may seem like a commercial history of Wokingham!

The latter aspect of the business grew to encompass a wide range of horse-drawn vehicles, including pair and single-horse buses, brakes and broughams, pony traps, landaus, victorias, and a 4-wheeled dog-cart with rubber tyres. Apart from this range of wheeled vehicles, all 'ready at short notice', a brougham could be summoned to meet any train on the two lines running through Wokingham, something the more well-off who did not maintain their own carriage might do. Stables were also kept for horses taken on livery terms, whilst a pair of horses was kept ready to rush round to the Wokingham Fire Brigade's appliance, which was activated by a special bell connection from the station situated within the arches of the Town Hall.

With this range of transport facilities, they provided transport for a wide spectrum of the local populace, as even those who could not afford such a luxury on a daily basis usually might avail themselves of the rubber-tyred wedding carriage or failing all else ride in the hearse for their final journey. To power these a stable of around 14 horses was generally maintained.

However, firstly we must examine how the family became involved in the locality, as William Herring was not a local man. Born in March 1811 he had originated from Finsbury, then in Middlesex, marrying Betsey Lawrence a few miles east of Wokingham at Binfield, Berkshire in 1831. The couple evidently remained at Terrace Road in Binfield until sometime between 1843 and 1846, when they relocated to Wokingham. William's role is unclear on the 1841 census, but that of 1851 clearly shows him as Chief Constable, then residing at No.80 Rose Street, by then with seven children, William 19, a butcher, James, 17 and working with his brother, Betsey 14, Ann 11, Maynard 8, Tom 5 and Richard at just 8 months old.

In those days the Wokingham police were a borough force, which operated only within the relatively local boundaries of that town. William had retired from that post by 1861, by which time he was 50 years old and now living in the town end of Star Lane (today's Easthampstead Road), by which time daughter Alice, aged 7, had been added. His son Maynard was now a brick-layer, whilst Tom was a steam-sawyer. Richard, now aged 10, was a scholar, no doubt receiving an education that would set him in good stead for future business enterprises.

Although William had retired from his former post, he had by 1868 taken up a new role as the landlord of the Welcome Inn (sometimes also known as the Welcome-to-Town) situated at No.33 Peach Street, on the east side of the road and just a short way from the junction with Star Lane. He remained there, aided by wife Bestsey and later also by daughter Alice, until about 1877, when that pub passed onto his son Richard, who had in 1871 been working as a blacksmith, a trade likely to have had in influence on the involvement of horse-drawn wheeled transport in due course.

William stayed in the pub trade and moved to the Dukes Head, at the southern end of Denmark Street and by the junction with Langborough Road, where he continued through to his death in 1887, aided by Betsey until her death in 1885 and throughout by daughter Alice. Wokingham at the time of the 1881 census had just a population of 5043.

In the meantime, another significant son in the story, Maynard, who was now married to Sarah Annie and with children Betsey Alice aged 8 and William aged 6, had relocated to Cockpits on the east side of the Market Place, though he was still a brick-layer at 1871. By 1881 they had relocated a short distance to The Clock House in Peach Street, which was actually next door to The Welcome Inn and known as No.31 by 1891. Between 1881 and then Maynard added the role of General Shopkeeper to his established brick-laying, presumably in the daily care of Sarah. The significance to the general development of the family enterprises comes from the addition of glass and china to his range of goods, along with the fact that he died in 1900, thereby creating an opportunity for his brother Richard to encompass that class of goods. Despite these enterprises, Maynard also found time to be the landlord of The Anchor (sometimes referred to as the Little Anchor to distinguish it from the nearby Hope & Anchor), which was at No.37 The Terrace for some time around 1887.

Richard Herring married Henrietta in 1877, and they ran The Welcome-to-Town public house through to 1891, by which time he had also become an oil merchant. Gotelee's Compendium of Wokingham of 1888 shows that he was also supplying Wokingham Borough Council with Tea Rose Oil for use in the town's street lights. He could supply a barrel of 40 gallons at 7.5d per gallon, or 5 or more gallons at 8d, or a single gallon for 9d, all delivered for free locally, which also confirms the existence of a cart.

Also on offer there was china and glass, along with a general stores selling bassionettes, perambulators, brooms and brushes, baskets, ironmongery, and tinware. In addition, he advertised the 'Herring's Improved Wringer & Mangle' at 45 shillings! No other address is given at that time other than 'the middle of Peach Street', but by the 1891 census the latter certainly refers to the shop premises at No.48 Peach Street, which would now formed the basis of his business, the pub being in other hands by 1893.

Richard Herring on the left, with daughter Mary seen amongst the extensive range of goods then on offer!

From this new base, with the growing family living overhead, the business soon took in No.50, then in due course the yard behind Nos.54/6, with an entrance from Peach Street into the yard. It is difficult to be precise on the origins of the provision of transport, but the yard included a forge, perhaps even the same one Richard had worked at in earlier years? By 1899 an '& Son' had been added to Richard Herring as the title of the business and by 1901 Richard was styled grocer and hardware merchant, though that rather belied the full range of goods, which still included glass and china, along with the significant provision of oil for use in household oil-lamps. See location map on page 18.

In the meantime, Richard and Henrietta's family had grown steadily, so that by 1901 it consisted of Dick, 21 and grocer's assistant to his father, Rich aged 16 and no doubt also helping out, Mary 13, Tom 11, Violet 9, Burt 7, Winifred 5 and the last and final arrival Harold, just 7 months old. Needless to say, as the children grew up so their contribution added to the diversity of the business, especially the role the sons played in developing the transport department.

In respect of the shop-based business, adverts in the locally-printed Gotelee's Compendium of 1907 show the range of goods to encompass general storekeepers, furniture, bedding and household requisites, along with a range of oils for home use which featured Tea Rose Test 75, Bear Creek 80, Day Light 120, and White Rose 120, the numbers referring to the light-producing intensity of each brand. Also now included were 'the best brands of American petroleum which could be delivered by the barrel at London prices free within 7 miles'. Also available was paraffin, then widely used for heating stoves, cooking or lamps.

At that time only *John Benham* of No.61 Peach Street was offering horse-drawn carriages for hire in the town, he having become established in 1881 and duly assisted by his son Frank they progressed into the motor age and Frank even later adding a charabanc, their enterprise remained at much the same level, whilst steady expansion took place of that aspect of the *Herring* business.

It seems that transport was added once Dick and Rich could be released from other duties, and it may indeed have had its origins in the need to be able to deliver heavier items purchased through the shop or perhaps delivered by rail, as a sturdy cart was owned. Certainly by 1905 that aspect featured closed and open carriages, along with the link to or from the station available on request. It is also worth noting that amongst Richard's erstwhile neighbours in Star Lane, was the Lush family who, apart from also running The Victoria Arms, provided some three generations of coachbuilders between the 1860's and the early 1900's, so it seems a distinct possibility that Richard was a customer of that firm as his fleet expanded.

Photographic evidence shows a lightweight trap with seats for 4 or so passengers, but by 1912 the whole range of vehicles as described in the second paragraph of this narrative were evident and the '& Sons' had been added to the business name, along with facilities for storage of motor cars. However, the census of 1911 confirms that only sons Tom and Rich were cab drivers, whereas Dick was assisting his father as oil merchant, and the next youngest son Burt was a builder's clerk and would not feature further in the story. The Herring family were also responsible for a wider sphere of goods transport in their role as agents for both Suttons, the nationwide cartage company, as well as Globe Parcels Express for worldwide carriage, which had featured from 1896. The advert below was from 1912.

Dick James Upton Herring had married a Cornish woman Alice Farland in April 1907, and in 1911 they were living at No.47 Denmark Street in Wokingham town centre.

According to family sources the first involvement with the operation of motor vehicles was as early as 1906, though contemporary adverts do not confirm this.

A photo taken during the horse-drawn era shows one of the sons with a single-horse trap posed in the yard.

However, a very early taxi used by them was AA 992, a registration from 1904/5 about which no more has survived. Although Richard was licensed to store the oils he used for re-sale, from August 1902 he was licensed to store petroleum for his own use, initially at 80 gallons, but increased to 130 from 1915.

The next phase of motorisation came with the purchase of a brand-new Renault 14hp car with the characteristic coal-scuttle bonnet and a dark green and black painted landaulette-type body, which was registered as BL 2932 on 25th March 1913. A new Napier 15hp, also with landaulette style body followed on 14th May 1915 with registration BL 4298. A further similar car of about 1911 vintage was obtained secondhand and bore the Reading mark DP 680, whilst a secondhand 1913 Briton 10hp 2-seater (BL 2830) was added in June 1917. Whilst the original Renault had departed by the start of 1921, Napier DP 680 was still in use, whilst little information survives on the other pair. These all came from Vincents of Reading, likely with its bodies.

Another posed view in the yard shows the first Renault (BL 2932) with Tom Herring in the front with his wife apparently driving, whilst in the rear are his brother-in-law Arthur Turner and his wife Mary (nee Herring) and her sister Violet.

Rich and Tom continued to undertake most of the driving duties and the original horse-drawn vehicles were soon phased out. Dick did very little of such work,

being primarily concerned with the shop business. However, even young Harold soon became involved as each of the brothers either volunteered or was called up for military service in the Great War, and that resulted in him doing some driving before he was legally old enough to do so!

Tom was the first to enlist at Reading for the Army Service Corps (Mechanical Transport) on 1st December 1914, though he was placed on the reserve until posted on 4th September 1915, when he was put with the 21st Division Supply Column and shipped to France the following day from Southampton. His posting was to the 273rd MT Company, in which he served with *Alf Smith,* who became a good friend and went onto to form *Smith's Coaches* in Reading after the war, a fact that undoubtably had a bearing on the direction of the *Herrings* business after his safe return in May 1919.

Rich and Alice had their son Patrick in June 1915, who would later head the family business, though Rich volunteered for the army on 9th December 1915, he was not posted for a further year, when he was sent to 2nd Wireless Signals Squadron and trained as a wireless fitter at Worcester. After that he embarked from Devonport for Persia (Iraq), being in Basra in September 1917. Whilst out in what was then known as Mesapotamia he gained even more experience driving motors, especially Ford Model T's and Daimlers. Rich would be the last of the sons to return home, not until January 1920, by which time he had contracted malaria (as did many of his comrades).

Dick was somewhat older than the above brothers, so he was duly drafted in December 1915 when aged 38. Although he gave his trade as shopkeeper, the fact that he had some experience of motors saw him posted to the ASC (MT) at Isleworth for training on heavy lorry driving. It is noted that he passed his learner's course and was regarded as proficient on Peerless, Commer, Pierce-Arrow and Locomobile lorries. He was duly assigned through the Grove Park centre at Lea from barrack-based duties to 348 MT Company at Larkhill near Salisbury. However, he was considered medically unfit for overseas service, so continued on home duties until being demobbed in March 1919.

Following the return of these three, Richard and his sons considered how to shape the future of the business, though Richard passed away in August 1921. The business activities then continued under the name *Herring Bros.*, with the active participation of Dick, Rich, Tom and Harold, whilst by 1924 their mother Henrietta was living close by at No.54 Peach Street.

Rich was the one with the best business acumen, and at his suggestion they bought their first Ford Model T, a type he knew well from his wartime experiences as being both rugged and reliable. This could be used as a lorry, and also was at times fitted with dining chairs as seats for up to 13 passengers, taking to the road as BL 8098 in November 1920. The rather basic seating arrangements sufficed for some local trips for darts teams etc., but when excursions started the following Easter the arrangement was found not particularly successful, as on occasions a sudden stop meant the passengers being spilled out on the floor! In order to overcome this, long side seats with removable cushions, made by the family, were substituted, the modified vehicle remaining in use until September 1923, though still with a centre rear entrance, and is seen below in front of the new garage for motors.

After the end of the First World War all horse-drawn activities had ceased, and indeed they had probably seen the last of their horses requisitioned by the Army Remount Depot a few miles south at Arborfield, as it is sometimes forgotten that the toll on horses was as heavy as it was for the humans in that conflict. The emphasis after the war was on motor hire, and general facilities for the growing number of motorists. The supply of petrol also continued, as separate filling stations were as then virtually unknown. A new motor garage was built across the end of the yard, and in due course the adjoining stables were converted as workshops.

Indeed, there was an advert in the Reading Mercury of 15th March 1919, with a light brougham with 4 seats and rubber tyres for sale, the space being urgently needed. That was followed a fortnight later by one for a first-class pair horse-bus with moveable top, rubber-tyred landau, a victoria and a 2-wheel village dog-cart. A further parcel agency had also been added by January 1919 for *the British Automobile Tranction Co. Ltd.*

With the success of the initial excursions now noted, it was time to more fully commit to such activities, and in July 1921 a brand-new Fiat F2-type with dark blue-painted 14-seater charabanc body was placed on the road as BL 8843, bodied by W.C. Ford of Kings Road in Reading. This proved to be a good purchase, and it remained in use until the end of September 1929, the chassis still with them in March 1931.

The following Summer saw another 14-seater charabanc added, by which time no doubt the Ford BL 8098 had been relieved of passenger duties. The new arrival was a former War Department Crossley 20/25hp-type, one of many used for lighter duties,

particularly by the Royal Flying Corps (later the RAF). This bore the civilian registration number XK 7162, indicating that it started its new life in April 1922. It should be noted that after the war had ended, Tom Herring's old army buddy Alf Smith had gone to work at the Army Disposals based at what would become the Slough Trading Estate on the Bath Road to the west of Slough, but then he set up in a small way in the charabanc business in Reading. From family interviews it is known that Alf rebuilt the chassis on this vehicle, as he done a similar one for himself, procuring the chassis on behalf of Tom. It was then sent, as was Alf's example, to be bodied by W.C. Ford as a 14-seater charabanc.

Indeed, Alf and Tom remained friends for some years, the Smith family album containing photos of daughter Jackie playing on the *Herring* coaches in their yard alongside their own growing family, and indeed the two operators often helped each other out on large jobs.

On the taxi front the earlier types gave way to newer types, though further details are not known for those used in the 1920's, although AA 992 was still with them in May 1921, along with Napier DP 680. The latter had come from William Vincents in Reading, so quite possibly had a body also constructed by them. As seen below.

The very popular British Empire Exhibition held at Wembley during 1924 produced an unprecedented demand for charabancs, so it was decided to purchase another for the season. This was a further Crossley 20/25hp, new in 1916 to the War Department, which had subsequently been re-registered T 8864 as a large touring car in June 1920. Herrings acquired this and sent it to No.191 Kings Road in Reading, where bodybuilders W.C. Ford Ltd. constructed a 14-seater charabanc body on it. Again, this was to last quite a time, being last licensed in May 1933 on goods work.

Although the Fiat was a true charabanc, with a doorway to each row of seats, the Crossleys were not strictly of that layout, having just two nearside doors towards the front. However, as they lacked side windows and had a folding canvas hood, the correct description would be gangway charabancs, the other seats being reached through those doors and gaps between rows.

With the increased fleet size came the need employ a non-family driver, so Tom Wigmore joined them. As it was he had served with both Tom Herring and Alf Smith and had latterly also been at the Slough 'dump' preparing ex-WD vehicles for disposal. He remained with *Herrings* as a driver through to the end.

After the success of the very regular London runs in 1924 Rich suggested that they set up a daily express service between Wokingham and London, particularly as the railway line of that time was still steam-hauled and rather slow. This was actually some three years before the Reading-based *Thames Valley Traction Co. Ltd.* commenced its twice-daily London service, but the idea did not find favour with the other brothers.

The grey-painted Crossley T 8864 is seen on hire to Alf Smith of Reading, one of many such inter-hirings.

At 1924 the family members were distributed about the town, though all within 2 minutes of each other, with Dick and Alice at No.48 Peach Street, Henrietta at No.54 and Tom and Gladys at No.56, whilst Rich and Alice were at No.36 Wescott Road and Harold over at Cockpit Path. Rich had married Alice at Gloucester in 1914 and Tom had married Gladys at Wembley in 1915, reflecting how the war changed their horizons. Harold Herring was still single and decided to leave the business about 1925, so his place was taken by George Ping, who remained as driver-mechanic until 1942. It should of course be noted that charabanc work was still rather seasonal, so during the winter months vehicles were thoroughly overhauled or repainted. In due course a new standard scheme of two-tone gull grey was adopted for the fleet, probably from 1928, whilst one Crossley was painted with a rear end depicting a fish emblem (for *Herring*), though this was not particularly liked and was not continued!

Another driver also duly joined by 1927 in the shape of Alf Pearce, and in his case the connection was that his father and Rich Herring had served together in the Royal Engineers (Signals), such loyalties being important in a post-war Britain with poor job prospects

for those who had returned from serving. Alf stayed with them for some 8 years, leaving to go to drive for *Thames Valley* at Wycombe Marsh from 1935 to 1946, after which he went to *Pilot Coaches* of High Wycombe. He is shown below when the Fiat chara was decorated for the 1927 Wokingham Carnival, complete with a model horses head above the bonnet, a 'fishy' sign for Herrings, along with some family members in various outfits, including 'Ole Bill' representing the soldiers of the Great War!

There was very little local competition for Herrings in the Wokingham area, whilst a lot of business came from the neighbouring town of Bracknell, where a booking agency was set up in the hairdresser's shop of Mr. Bullen in the High Street. Only *Frank Benham* offered his sole charabanc as an alternative in Wokingham from August 1924, so business was good. At slack times vehicles were hired by *Alf Smith*, who would not turn away a hire, no matter how large.

The destinations served for excursions were the usual range of coastal resorts, mainly on the south coast, but in due course a bit farther afield to Weston-super-Mare and Southend-on-Sea, as well as more local beauty spots and places of interest. Royal Ascot Week saw the coaches busy, and in due course an express service was licensed (after the 1930 Road Traffic Act) between Wokingham (Town Hall) and Ascot (Royal Ascot Hotel) for race-goers.

On the passenger front the rather crude charabanc of the early post-war era had developed into the more sophisticated coach, passing through stages of the all-weather type to those with permanent roofs, though sun-roofs remained understandably popular for better weather. More importantly, these changes helped change the perception of such vehicles only being for seasonal use, though the smaller and pneumatic types used by Herrings had seen some use out of season for sports teams and other local events for private parties.

The next new coach was indeed a step up from the older types, being a brand-new Star 'Flyer' VB4-type, with a low-slung chassis and 20-seater body built by Weybridge Motor Bodies, the style of body had entrances at the front and rear on the nearside, along with fixed side windows, though all but the rear dome

Both of the Stars seen at the coach park in Southsea as organised by the Salvation Army, with Captain Thomas Boyd seen centre rear in uniform.

was still covered with a retractable canvas hood. This took to the road as RX 2379 in May 1928 and saw service through to 1940. It is also the first vehicle recorded with the two-tone grey livery, which it most likely introduced, the rear end lettered in gold.

The Star was obviously a good buy, and a second was ordered for the start of June 1930. This was RX 6923, which was also bodied by Star with a 20-seater dual-doorway body, though this featured fixed front and rear domes and a canvas central roof section. The rear dome was also fitted with a luggage pen reached by small folding steps set into the nearside of the rear end. It also carried the two-tone grey scheme, and was lettered out in gold shaded by pale blue with Herring Bros. and the phone number set in a 34-inch oval across the rear panel. The seating of this coach was in an antique maroon finish, making this a fine and popular coach that would outlast the business.

The involvement with onward delivery of parcels trunked nationwide by Suttons had not ended with the horse-drawn era, so a van was active on such duties, along with the firm's own deliveries, so under the new licensing system they held a 'B' license for goods.

The implementation of the Road Traffic Act 1930, effective from 1st January 1931, introduced a new system of Road Service Licenses in respect of both Stage Carriage and Excursions & Tours operations. To many smaller operators this system, which was administrated through Traffic Commissioners and Public Hearings (also known as the Traffic Courts), imposed a burden on their time, which compared with

the larger firms could be ill afforded. However, there were some assurances from this, as it removed the unbridled competition that had seen some dubious tactics employed by those with larger resources. The new licenses therefore gave protection to operators, whilst also forming a readily saleable element should they decided to sell up.

Prior to this system many Local Authorities undertook licensing of vehicles, drivers and conductors under the earlier Town Police Clauses, though Wokingham BC did not undertake anything more than collecting fees for individual licenses. However, during the initial round of licensing applications under the Act, support from the Local Council was taken into consideration, so the *Herrings* good standing in the town certainly helped in the Council objecting to *Thames Valley's* attempts to gain excursions pick-ups in the town, and thereby preserved *Herring Bros.* (and indeed *Frank Benham's*) roles as the local coach operators.

The E&T applications were not heard for up to a year after the implementation of the 1930 Act, as priority was given to sorting out the Stage Carriage applications, so standing operators were effectively granted the status quo in the interim. *Herring Bros.* duly applied for the traditional destinations they had provided excursions to, and these were granted, with approval for the following destinations and types of excursions:

Aldershot Tattoo, during June, evening excursions for leisure activities, dancing or speedway races;
Arborfield Remount Depot, for race meetings;
Bognor Regis, seasonal day excursions;
Bournemouth, seasonal day excursions;
Brighton, seasonal day excursions;
Burnham Beeches, afternoon tour;

California-in-England, afternoons or evenings;
Elm Park, Reading, for matches of Reading FC;
Epsom, for race meetings;
Goodwood, for race meetings;
Hayling Island, seasonal day excursions;
Henley-on-Thames, afternoon excursions;
Sonning, for race meetings;
Southsea, seasonal day excursions;
Sunninghill, evenings on Tuesdays for a whist-drive;
Worthing, seasonal day excursions.

All of these picked up at Wokingham Town Hall, but Wokingham BC also included a request that a pick up should be added at Emmbrook in view of its support for the application and opposition to *Thames Valley*. The popularity of the local afternoon excursions is explained by the then common tradition of shops taking an early-closing day during the week, that in both Bracknell and Wokingham being Wednesday. Some trips started out from Bracknell if appropriate to the direction of travel.

The traditional daily link from Wokingham to Royal Ascot Races in June was also duly licensed, which allowed *Herrings* to run a continuous service towards the racecourse from 10am until 1pm, and then return journeys from 4.30pm until 6pm, which was a busy time for the drivers, who then covered the Aldershot Tattoo during the evenings of that same week. From 1932 they were increased in permitted vehicles to 2 on the Friday and 3 on other racing days.

Just to return to the earlier days for a moment, here we see a nice family gathering around Renault BL 2932 in the yard, with (left to right) Henrietta Herring, Arthur and Mary Turner, unknown, Tom Herring and Gladys, then on the right Richard Herring, the younger ones being some of the grandchildren.

A further Ford T also came to *Herrings* about 1931, when an advert in Commercial Motor of 10th March offered the Fiat chassis (last used September 1929) in exchange for a Ford. This had been a carriers van with Albert Wickens of Bradfield and was registered new in July 1921 as BL 8812. However, with *Herrings* it was used for goods and saw service until March 1936.

During April 1932 they also applied for an Express license in respect of a Saturday and Sunday service to Southsea. The intention was to operate this on the last two weekends of July, all through August and the first two weekends of September, in order to cater for the school holidays to that popular resort, with additional pick-ups at Popeswood (Shoulder of Mutton), Bracknell (High Street), Easthampstead (School Corner, Crowthorne Road), Finchampstead (Greyhound) and Crowthorne (Iron Duke, High Street). Again, Wokingham BC assisted *Herrings* by objecting to *Thames Valley's* proposal to make similar pick ups, which was successful. Despite that, the application by *Herring Bros.* was refused, due to the justifiable prior claim of *Smith's Coaches* of Reading.

During March 1933 a successful application allowed them to additionally pick up at Crowthorne for matches of Reading FC, both home and away league or cup ties, all of which were well supported. The final phase of developments under the 1930 Act came in the Spring of 1934, with the addition of further afternoon and evening circular tours.

Afternoon tours:
Hazeley Heath – Wellington Monument – Stratfield Saye – Swallowfield – Arborfield – Barkham;
Henley-on-Thames – Sonning – Woodley;
Haines Hill – Ruscombe – Marlow – Henley-on-Thames – Sonning;

Evening tours:
California (Nine Mile Ride) – Finchampstead Village – Eversley – Sandhurst;
Bracknell – Easthampstead – Nine Nile Ride – Swinley – Winkfield – Warfield – Binfield.

The evening tours took in many of the local heaths, which could be attractive when the gorse and heathers were in bloom, whilst such excursions invariably included a pub stop (or two), either at the discretion of the driver or by popular request, all of which offered a change of scenery.

For the 1934 season the coach adverts included the slogan 'The Road Is Your's – Use It', variations of which appeared in other operator's ads, including those of *Newbury & District*.

After Alf Pearce left in 1935 his place was taken by Walter Englefield, who had been driving for *Frank Benham*. About then Dick Herring began to suffer with his health and left the business, his place being taken by Rich's son Patrick. By 1939 Dick was at No.23 Morris Road at Farnborough in Hampshire with a small general grocery business.

A secondhand Ford AA-type was obtained sometime between 1933 and 1936, being TK 7376 new in February 1932 to *Tapper Bros.* of Durweston in Dorset, and it carried a 14-seater sun-saloon coach body, now the only vehicle of that capacity in the fleet.

In 1937 Tom Herring decided to leave and set up his own hardware shop at No.9 Church Road at Caversham, leaving Rich and Pat to run the shop and hired drivers to cover the coach work. Rich by then had moved south of the town about a mile-and-a half to No.265 Barkham Road, then a quiet rural road.

The Ascot Race Week service continued to be operated, which also coincided with the evening trips to the popular Aldershot Military Tattoo, and the latter had a return fare of 4 shillings from Wokingham or Bracknell. Also the trip to The Derby on 1st June is noted as leaving from the garage.

In February 1938 a further secondhand coach was obtained, this time a Morris-Commercial 'Leader' with Duple 25-seater front-entrance body, which had been new as DWL 918 to *Aldcorne* of Cowley, near Oxford in November 1936. This is also recorded as a 26-seater, so Herrings probably altered the rear seat to take 5 passengers. The final coach to be purchased was an early example of the once widespread Bedford OB-type, which was given a 26-seater front-entrance body by Thurgood's of Ware and registered as CBL 502 in November 1939. In what became the final application under the 1930 Act, March 1939 had seen the addition of excursions to the zoo at Whipsnade and for the Thame Show.

The 1939 Bedford was one of only a small number built before the war overtook production at Vauxhall. It is seen here later with Brimblecombe Bros. working the service between Arborfield Garrison and Wokingham.

Throughout the 1930's the taxi fleet had been steadily upgraded, and an annual ritual soon developed whereby *Herrings* bought the outgoing Armstrong-Siddeley car owned by Sir Henry Head (1861-1940), the eminent neurologist who lived at Hartley Court, just south of Reading. Sir Henry had delved deeply into the effects of degeneration and regeneration of the nervous system, having crippled himself through self-experimentation. Although the car was only used for a short chauffeur-driven journey daily, he generally ordered a replacement from Vincent's of Reading each

year, so *Herrings* built up a fleet of 5 similar cars in fine condition through to his death in October 1940.

With the outbreak of war in September 1939 normal coaching activities soon wound down. However, the fleet was actually kept very busy due to re-locations and the increase in military activity.

Indeed, the International Stores had relocated some 500 of its head office staff to Bracknell, buying several large houses in the Binfield area for office use. These were provided with a shuttle service between Bracknell and those locations, with *Herrings* running coaches from 8am until 6pm, the staff working, eating and sleeping in relays.

From 6.30pm each evening until midnight a service was laid on to cater for soldiers billeted at Easthampstead Park Camp into Wokingham for free time in the pubs and cinema. There was also a regular contract between Wokingham Station and Arborfield Camp for transfer of soldiers travelling by train.

At the end of March 1940 the original Star (RX 2379) was advertised for sale, leaving the newer Star, the Morris-Commercial and the Bedford still in use. After the 'miracle of Dunkirk' in 1940, *Herrings* were put on a 3-day notice should an invasion require the use of their coaches for troop movements. One interesting item from Aubrey's Guide to Berkshire in 1940 was that the wheelwright F.J. Carter was still renting the former forge premises in Herring's yard.

Indeed, even after the war in Europe had ended, there was little let-up in activity, as the International Stores staff stayed on for a while, and Easthampstead Camp saw a regular throughput of soldiers from Holland being trained for service in the Dutch East Indies. The taxis were also busy throughout the war years, though petrol rationing made life a bit difficult, and after the war 3 Austin 12hp taxis replaced the Armstrong-Siddeleys, as they were more economical on fuel.

However, Rich Herring, who was now living east of the town centre at No.70 London Road, was suffering badly with arthritis and the future of the business was reviewed. Despite the inevitable demand for coaching in post-war Britain, the little fleet would need to be replaced after the very busy wartime years. It was decided that the future lay in developing the opportunities through the shop, and they let it be known that the coach business was for sale, and also that they would cease taxi work. Word soon reached the ears of *Valliant Direct Coaches* of Ealing, who were interested in setting up a depot west of London, there being lots of contract work in the pipeline as the former airfields at Aldermaston and Harwell were earmarked for large-scale re-development as the two Atomic Research Centres, the former for military purposes and the latter for peaceful applications of the new technology.

At the same time, the rather small coach operation of *Brimblecombe Bros.* of Finchampstead Road, Wokingham, was poised for post-war expansion, so the business was offered to them instead, partly because it was felt it better to keep the operation local. Also, the licenses of *Frank Benham* had not seen use since before the war, and he too was interested in disposing of them, so *William Richard Brimblecombe* and *Reginald Hooper Brimblecombe (Brimblecombe Bros.)* bought both operators licenses and duly renewed all of those without modification, thereby greatly expanding their activities.

Some of the taxis also passed to *Brimblecombes*, who continued to base them at the garage at Nos.54-56 Peach Street for a few years, but that had ceased by 1952. Some of the Armstrong-Siddeleys were sold off privately, whilst one Austin retained for personal use. The remaining trio of coaches passed to *Brimblecombe Bros.* in February 1946, these being Star 'Flyer' (RX 6923), Morris-Commercial 'Leader' (DWL 918) and the Bedford OB (CBL 502), all of which ran for the new owners. Also included in the deal was the good's license still held by *Herrings*, along with an unknown van which they replaced in 1949.

However, *Herrings* were not entirely disconnected from transport, as they became the Wokingham booking agent for *Brimblecombe Bros.*, the town centre shop being more convenient than their garage south of the town in Finchampstead Road. No doubt the goodwill that evidently existed between Herrings and their old customers also did much to assist *Brimblecombe's* in their rapid post-war expansion.

With the transport business now disposed of, Rich retired and lived until January 1961, still living at No.70 London Road, just east of the town centre, so son Patrick and his wife Doris operated the shop business, living above at No.50 Peach Street (and later nearby in Rectory Road), and it continued to supply china and glass, furniture and other household items, though of course no longer the oil that once sustained much of the trade. The shop remained open until Patrick took retirement in August 1983, when the closing sale saw numerous bargain clearance items, but sadly, the end of over a century of the *Herring* family enterprises.

J. H. Hinman & Son
Popeswood Garage, Binfield

James Henry Hinman was not a local man and had been born at Oakham in Rutland in 1875. By 1891 he was working as a coach-smith in the black-smithy run by his older brother Robert in Mill Street. He married in that town in early 1896 to Annie Maria Ellingworth, and their son of the same fore-names arrived at the end of that year. By 1901 they were at Braunston Road and James senior was now a house painter. By 1911 his employment had once again changed, reflecting trends of the era as an electrical and mechanical engineer.

Young James went into the Army during the Great War, during which time he too became skilled with motor vehicles. Quite why the family relocated to the Popeswood side of the strung-out village of Binfield is not known, but perhaps around the time of his demob he was familiar with the area? Whatever the precise detail, they family came to that location, where on the south side of London Road, next door to the local post office, they set up a motor garage. That stretch of road was also known as Mutton Hill in those days, with the long-gone Shoulder of Mutton pub very close by at the turn into Beehive Lane, which ran down to a large area of brick-workings, that name reflecting the shape of the kilns rather the honey-bees – see map on page 62.

Apart from catering for the growing number of car owners, they also used their old skills to repair any kind of agricultural implements, tools and other items. But, quite soon after the garage had been established, they added a carrier's service, which was in the daily care of James junior. For that venture a new Ford Model T with dark green-painted open truck body was fitted with seats for 13, registered as MO 250 in July 1922. Also owned from September 1923 was a motor car as MO 2150, but no further details have survived.

The carrier's service ran to Reading daily other than Wednesday (early-closing day) and Sundays, taking in Wokingham and Sindlesham, using the Dukes Head at No.41 Broad Street in Reading as its lay-over point. By 1926 Bearwood and Earley are also listed, though by then the Monday journey had been abandoned. The only other carrier serving Binfield at the time was *Brookhouse Keene*, though at that point he was still based on the northern fringe of the village by the Jack of Newbury pub, plus his route ran out northwards to take in Shurlock Row etc., so no competition ensued.

The same situation existed over excursions, as both operators only had a limited capacity, with most hire work initially being centred on sporting and social events nearby, though each would develop that work. In order to cater for requests for more comfortable outings, the original Ford was replaced by a nice blue-liveried 14-seater Chevrolet LP-type with sun-saloon style body, registered in November 1928 as RX 3130. The Ford could be found elsewhere by March 1929, and that same year young James married Gertrude Hawes at St. Faith's in Norfolk.

The pattern then settled down to the Chevie covering the carrier's route, but hireable at other times, plus a regular excursions programme throughout the relevant months. Indeed, the carrier's service had been reinstated on Mondays, remaining so at 1931. Under the 1930 Act the usual selection of coastal destinations was licensed, along with the Aldershot Military Tattoo and other annual events. Because of their development, the carrier's service ceased from December 1935, but the little Chevie was sold in January 1937.

It was replaced by a new Bedford WTB bought new in October 1936 and dealer registered as DGY 375, carrying a Duple 26-seater coach body. That was the sole coach through to August 1950, when it was replaced by a Mark II WTB-type, with what became the OB-style front end, new in March 1939 as DHO 588 with a Duple 26-seater coach body, though it was acquired after use by *Smith's Coaches* of Reading. Its own replacement also duly came from that fleet during January 1955, being an OB-type Bedford with Duple 29-seater body new to that firm in 1949 as DRD 382.

The senior James had passed away in 1943 and, despite James continuing the coaching aspect of the business in the post-war years, things were becoming harder by the mid-1950's, so the decision was taken to concentrate on the garage side. Despite the recent acquisitions and the fact that vehicles had at times returned to Smith's for painting etc., Hinman actually offered his license and the coach to *Brimblecombe Bros.* of Wokingham instead! The latter were of course happy to extend their pick-ups in the Binfield area, when in October 1958 they made the purchase. DRD 382 stayed with them to January 1960. James retired to Norfolk and passed away at North Walsham in 1979.

Bedford WTB DGY 375 is seen later with Hodge's of Sandhurst on an outing from The Royal Oak pub on Branksome Hill Road in nearby College Town. Such social outings were still a regular feature of coach hire, often financed through raffles to treat local families.

Hodges Coaches,
Deepnell Garage, Sandhurst, Berkshire

The full story of what is now Berkshire's oldest family-run independent coach operator deserves its own book, so here we will merely set the scene on its origins and early development.

As often occurs in those pioneering days, the origins of passenger-carrying came only secondary to the main business of coal merchant *George Edward Hodges*, and his yard was off Yorktown Road, still the same site as the garage for the modern and well-kept fleet wearing its blue and ivory livery. His Overland lorry (MO 5802) came in July 1925, which was fitted when required with a blue-painted 14-seater charabanc body. That body carried the name Venus across its rear panels after the Royal Navy ship his father had served on.

The work proved worthwhile, particularly as the coal trade was largely seasonal, so in April 1926 he bought a dedicated Bean 30cwt with 14-seater chara body also painted blue as MO 7642. With that he continued to develop a selection of excursions and private hires, and adding a further vehicle every couple of years to bring the small fleet up to scratch as coach design 'grew up' from the early open types to the fully enclosed models.

MJ 9818 was a Bedford WTL-type with a Willmott 26-seater coach body new in 1936 but acquired in 1943, remaining in use until 1956. Alan Lambert caught it at Southsea on a day excursion in its latter days.

Once the Second World War came along, there was much activity on Government-directed contracts, also with the nearby Royal Military Academy and various other military establishments in the local area, so the fleet was actually expanded to cope.

Once Peace returned the excursions resumed again, also leading over the years to the development of extended tours reaching all over Britain, which were of a high standard. Local school transport also became an important factor, whilst the nature of its base location in the very corner of Berkshire saw it dealing with the neighbouring Counties of Surrey and Hampshire, the carriage of schoolchildren often involving crossing the nearby borders. Similarly, the take-overs of other local firms in post-war years has included those with bases in those Counties, whilst other earlier competition in Crowthorne or Camberley has disappeared, leaving the firm with a good steady trade in school contracts and private hire, some of the latter from the Crowthorne-based Wellington College, whilst standards of fleet maintenance have been kept by the third generation.

William Joseph & Sarah James Blanche Evangeline Lester
Wellington College Hotel Bus
Crowthorne, Berkshire

This establishment was a private hotel built to the north-west side of the road bridge over the railway at Wellington College (Crowthorne) Station, and some 1.5 miles west of the centre of Crowthorne. Being so positioned by the railway, it no doubt provided lodging for some of the official visitors to Broadmoor Asylum and Wellington College, so having its own transport developed to cater for such onward journeys, perhaps also for those arriving at the station to local estates at a time before local bus services had arrived?

It is also worth noting that this related activity went through several phases of ownership of the hotel, though actually remaining within the same family. We first encounter *William Joseph James* at the Wellington Hotel, as it was generally known, on the 1881 census, by which time he was aged 44 and had originated in Godmanchester in Huntingdonshire. At that time his wife was Ann Conquest James, aged 40 and from St. Ives in that same county, and there were 2 daughters Blanche Evangeline and Grace Violet, plus a son Joe Conquest, their birth dates indicating a relocation from Beenham in west Berkshire to Crowthorne only in the previous year. By 1888 they are also noted as parcel agents for the South Eastern Railway for the Station, the wording of the directory entry indicates operation of a vehicle of some description used for delivery and collection of the same.

Ann James died aged 48 in 1889, but in 1898 William re-married Sarah Coleman from Leatherhead, Surrey, she being about 33. There is no evidence of transport activities connected with the hotel, but as no local licensing would have been required, any that existed prior to the motor age may well have gone unrecorded.

To complete the relevant sequence of family events, it should be noted that daughter Blanche married Claude Dallas Lester in 1901 locally. He had an interesting history as born in 1867 at Truro in Cornwall and served with the Indian Staff Corps as a Captain, and indeed his father had been a Major-General born on that sub-continent at Poona. They returned to India, where he rose to Major, but passed away in late 1907. 4 years later she is found as a widow and living in Reading, along with their 8-year old son Norman who had been born in Bombay. It is believed that not long after that she joined her mother running the hotel, whilst her father was also a farmer at Heath House on land between the hotel and the town of Wokingham and just off the Finchampstead Road, by then aged 73. It should

also be noted that son Joseph re-appears by 1914 at the Wellington Hotel, by which time his step-mother is running the nearby Waverley Hotel in Ravenswood Avenue. The hotel and station area are shown below.

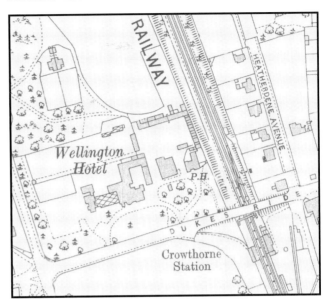

Also adjacent to the main hotel was the Wellington Tap, operating as a public house from at least 1899, though never noted with a family member as licensee.

The story in respect of motor vehicles appears to start in December 1921, with the arrival of a Ford 1-tonner registered as BL 9422, which had seating for 12. It was licensed to William, but after he passed away in 1922, it was changed to Sarah's ownership on 13th January 1923. A second similar type with 14-seater royal blue-painted saloon body joined it on 9th October 1923 as MO 2206. The appearance of a second vehicle adds greater weight to provision of a regular service linking the station, the hotel and Crowthorne, but no documentary evidence has been found.

The original Ford changed ownership to Blanche with effect from 25th March 1924, when noted as in a green livery, and that might be when she took over the running of the hotel as well? The second Ford also went to her ownership by its next log book starting January 1925. However, as Sarah James did not pass away until 1950, she may have still resided there at that point. Blanche was fully the proprietor of the hotel by 1939, by then aided by her son Norman and his wife Helen. Never re-marrying, Blanche passed away in her 96th year at Redruth in Cornwall.

The next significant factor occurred in October 1925, when Bracknell-based *Thomas Spragg* added to his *Progressive Bus Services* with a Reading–Wokingham-Crowthorne-Camberley service, started right under the noses of both *Thames Valley* and *Aldershot & District*! That provided for the first time a regular bus link over those points, also passing the Wellington Hotel and the Railway Station. *Thames Valley* acquired *Spragg's* operations on the last day of October 1925, further consolidating its local position with a Dormy Shed in Crowthorne from the following Spring.

Those events seem to have put paid to any local links from the hotel, with the original Ford sold locally before 1930, when it was a goods vehicle a few miles away with a College Town owner near Sandhurst, whilst the last record with Mrs. Lester for the second one is the final day of 1927. After that it passed by September 1928 to *Archie Arlott*, the carrier based at Beenham, where of course the James family had lived many years before, so perhaps not a mere coincidence? However, he did not run the vehicle, which was either scrapped for spares or its body was perhaps re-used, as he had several others of that make and size.

C.E. & V.M. Jeatt
White Bus Services
North Street Garage, Winkfield, Berkshire

The long and interesting story of this operator has already been dealt with in White Bus Services – Berkshire's Oldest Independent, published in 2015, so see the website at www.paullaceytransportbooks.co.uk

So, for the purposes of this volume, we will fast-forward to events in the Bagshot area in 1938. Now, a *White Bus Service* had for many years operated from Windsor to Bagshot via the Great Park and Sunninghill and terminated at The Square, where connections were afforded with *Aldershot & District* services onwards to Camberley or Egham, plus the *Direct Bus Service* to Guildford or Bracknell.

The latter had been started by *Harry Lintott*, and its full background will be found under his heading on page 83, as we now deal with the aftermath of its sale to *Sidney Ansell*. He had been an operator based in Peckham in South London, who came to Lightwater to take over from *Lintott*, but by early 1938 had concluded that he wished to dispose of the bus service and just continue with some coaching work in semi-retirement. To that end he advertised the service as a going concern, complete with 3 buses, a Chevrolet (UR 5780), a Bedford WLB (ACG 89) and Dodge RBF-type (BOR 501), all of which are detailed under *Lintott*. In his advert in Commercial Motor on 28th February 1938 he sought £1750 for the buses and £750 for the license.

At Winkfield the *Jeatt's* spotted the advert, so their father Will (who still dealt with all correspondence) got off a letter to *Sid Ansell*, which led to Will and him meeting at the garage in Lightwater to discuss the sale.

At the same time, Easthampstead RDC had heard of the possible sale of the only bus link to Bracknell from Bagshot, so they advised *White Bus* of their support for the proposed transfer of that section. In the meantime, the local territorial operators did not discuss the route, straddling the territorial divide of the A30. However, the *Aldershot & District* was interested in acquiring the southern portion from Guildford to Bagshot, which in fact fitted in nicely with the *White Bus* proposal to replace the northern section as Bagshot to Bracknell.

The *White Bus* proposal was not in fact to extend the existing service, but to run an additional route from the common section which would upgrade the route from Windsor through the Great Park as far as The Crispin. That would increase the service from the original Tuesday/Saturday/Sunday operation to a full Monday to Saturday service. From The Crispin it would run down Lovel Road to the junction at Shepherd White's Corner, then alongside the Race Course western flank and across the London Road into Kings Ride, then onto Bagshot (The Square). The initial journey would start from The Crispin at 8.33am towards Bagshot, which took 23 minutes, though the full route from Windsor was 51 minutes. It then left Bagshot at 9.10am for Bracknell running via Cricketers Bridge – Swinley Turn – Golf Links – Nine Mile Ride Turn – Bagshot Road (Horse & Groom) – Bracknell (Hinds Head, top of High Street), where it arrived at 9.27am, to turn and form the 9.30 return, after which the bus did the same on a 4-hourly headway until when the bus reached The Crispin at 10.28pm from Bagshot, sliding off service at that point near to the North Street Garage.

In is also interesting to note that Will Jeatt noted at the time that *White Bus* was considering a service from Windsor to Virginia Water, though nothing more came of that proposal. In the meantime, as the detailed map was being drawn up and added to the application placed with the Traffic Commissioner, *Sid Ansell* decided he would instead sell out to *Aldershot & District*, although that would not actually affect the proposal as such.

However, when the application was heard on 5th October 1938, the Commissioner decided to agree with the *A&D* assertion that the northern section 'had too few chimney pots' to warrant a bus service! It was of course true that almost all the route did lack housing as it was Crown Land, but as a link between two small towns it would have been useful. As a result of that decision, no such service existed until April 1954, when *Thames Valley* and *Aldershot & District* finally started a joint service 75 as Reading – Bracknell – Bagshot – Guildford, by which time the New Town developed Bracknell in that direction. And so, what might have been an interesting addition to the local transport scene was thwarted, though recently *White Bus* has started to run a bus service from Bracknell to Frimley Park Hospital via Camberley, so maybe one day it will also provide a link to Bagshot?

Brookhouse Keene
Cody Bus Service
Cody Coaches
Binfield, Berkshire

Including the transport activities of
Charles Scott Barker, William Sharpe and
George Lamb (Reindeer Bus)

When *Brookhouse Keene* came into the story as a carrier from Binfield in 1924, he did so as successor to service which can be traced back to at least 1883, so firstly we shall examine its back-history.

Charles Scott Barker had been born at Greenford in Middlesex in 1850, the son of blacksmith William Barker of Finchampstead, Berkshire and his wife Sarah, who hailed from Odiham in Hampshire. By 1861 the family were living in Finchampstead, with William having a blacksmith's shop in Eversley Road.

It is not clear what Charles initially did for employment, though he chose not to follow his father, and in 1871 he is found as an attendant at the newly opened Broadmoor Criminal Lunatic Asylum, just a few miles eastwards at Crowthorne, Berkshire. The next we hear of him is in London, or rather still Surrey at that time, when he married Exeter-born Helen Chamberlain at Camberwell St. Giles in April 1879. Their marriage certificate notes him as a servant living in Hawkhurst Road, whilst her address is nearby in Peckham at Marlborough Road. Their son Charles William Barker is born in Peckham early in 1880, but although also christened there, it is noted that his parents are now residing in Finchampstead, with his father now a licensed victualler.

By the Spring of 1881 the above trio, together with the mother-in-law Jane Chamberlain, are all residing at the Jack of Newbury pub, situated in Terrace Road, on the northern fringe of the spread-out village of Binfield, Berkshire. Whether merely coincidental or not, it is worth noting that there were other Barkers also on that same road as blacksmiths.

Apart from running the pub, aided by his wife and her mother, Charles soon established a horse-drawn carrier's service from those premises through to the market town of Reading, though by way of an indirect route taking in Allanby Park Corner – Shurlock Row – Whistley Green – Hurst – Sandford Mill – Woodley, operating one return journey each Wednesday and Saturdays. In Reading he used the Lower Ship Hotel in Duke Street as his lay-over point, leaving from there at 3pm. As was usual at that time the main trade was in goods and parcels, though some passengers were carried at times, the latter being restricted in respect of the horse-power available. In the carriers list of 1892 he is noted as providing a link to Easthampstead, the

southerly neighbour to Bracknell, though not necessarily the same day, and indeed he may well have run to both on other days from Binfield.

By 1895 a definite link to Bracknell was indeed in place, in the form of an 'omnibus service' between Binfield and the London & South Western Railway station at Bracknell, some 3.5 miles away. This ran at 8.40am and 7.25pm from the Jack of Newbury pub, and appears to have been primarily intended for the better off local residents, who would use it to go about business or shopping in London or Reading by train. By 1899 he was using the telegraphic address of 'Bus, Binfield', and by that date the afternoon carrier's journey had been put back to 3.30pm.

Contemporary adverts also note a cab for hire, and on the 1901 census he was employing 40-year old locally born Harry Wetts as a 'fly driver', and he probably also handled the Bracknell journeys. Charles and Helen's family were steadily added to with Edward (1882), Sidney (1884) and Bertie (1887), though none would feature in the business. Another relative, 15-year old Lily Chamberlain had also arrived by 1901, probably Helen's niece, who assisted with the pub.

Both the carrier's van and other wheeled vehicles were housed in a large brick-and-clapperboarded barn which fronted the pub site and opened straight onto the road, the licensed premises actually occupying an elevated position further back from the road with a terraced garden to its front.

The 17th Grade II former bus garage is still standing.

The carrier's service had been altered by 1912 to operate on Tuesdays, Wednesdays, Thursdays and Saturdays, still departing from Reading at 3.30pm from an undeclared point, whilst by 1914 that is given as the Royal Oak at No. 14 Broad Street, with a time of 4pm and the Wednesday journey now omitted. By 1916 the departure had reverted to 3.30pm, though still from the Royal Oak. In respect of the Bracknell station link, it was still listed until 1915, so it was probably curtailed through the loss of horses to the army requisitioning officers?

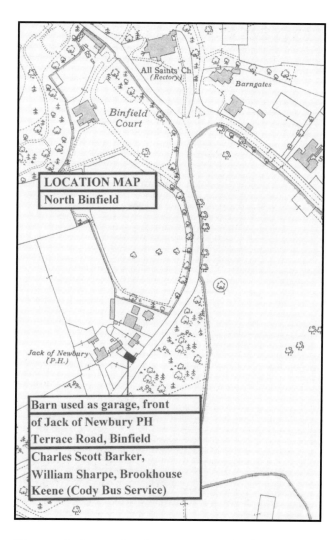

LOCATION MAP
North Binfield

Barn used as garage, front
of Jack of Newbury PH
Terrace Road, Binfield
Charles Scott Barker,
William Sharpe, Brookhouse
Keene (Cody Bus Service)

The carrier's service became motorised from May 1920, when the 70-year old *Charles Barker* put a 20hp Buick 1-tonner (BL 7278) on the road. It carried an open brake body with seating for 13, and bore a dark green livery. Although not specifically noted in the motor taxation records as not being a new vehicle, most Buicks of that type in Britain at that time had origins in War Department service, often as ambulances. It is not known whether Charles actually drove this vehicle, or indeed was covering the service personally at the time, but in July 1922 he ceases to be the landlord of the Jack of Newbury, passing away in 1928 locally aged 79.

His place was taken by *William Sharpe*, who also took over the Buick from 15th July 1922 along with the carrier's service. The 1924 local directory confirms that *Sharpe* was running the service only on Thursday and Friday, and was still leaving the Royal Oak at 3.30pm. However, he did not wish to continue with that business, so in that Summer *Brookhouse Keene* comes into the frame to take over the carrier's route, at a time when the population of Binfield was about 1920.

Firstly, it should be noted that the new owner's name has at times been mistaken for a double-barrelled one, though Brookhouse was indeed his Christian name, and amongst his 13 siblings there were also brothers Hanley Garnet and Oakley Rufus, though others had the standard names of that age! Brookhouse had been born in 1881 in the Hambleden valley, just a few miles

north-west of Marlow in Buckinghamshire, the son of a farmer of Chisbridge Farm in the hamlet of that name. He duly married local girl Mildred Alice Gibbs in 1908, and by 1911 they were at Upper Nook End Farm in Hambleden, whilst they duly had daughters Doris (1912) and Gladys (1916).

There are no military records for *Brookhouse Keene*, so his transformation from a farmer to involvement with transport is without further known evidence. However, as his location was only a few miles from Lane End, it is understood that he already knew *Bernard Richard ('Cody') Smith*, a local garage owner who was also already established as a bus operator.

In respect of his transfer to Binfield it should be noted that in the post-Great War years the holdings of the Hambleden Estate were being built up through the acquisition of local small farms. And So Mr. Keene came to Binfield to take over the carrier's service, though evidently with a view to expanding its role for passengers, being free of responsibilities for the pub.

With such changes in mind he licensed a new 1-ton Chevrolet (MO 3220) on 12th July 1924, which carried a dark green front-entrance saloon bus body seating 14. This was kept in the barn at the Jack of Newbury, and he also took over the Buick (BL 7278) from *Bill Sharpe* with effect from 3rd September 1924, now listed as a 14-seater. Although the vehicles were based there, the Keenes had also bought a plot of land in London Road, just to the western side of Popeswood, where The Bungalow was constructed, see location map page 62.

Brookhouse Keene is shown with his new Chevrolet in front of the pub barn at the Jack of Newbury.

The level of service noted in local directories remained the same for 1924/5, but the 1926 edition shows he had relocated to The Sun in Castle Street, which had a large yard much favoured by carriers. It seems that the Chevrolet was in daily use, with the Buick probably retained as a back-up vehicle, and nothing is known of its departure. Not only did the fully-enclosed body of the Chevrolet attract further passenger use on the service, but it also opened up the regular hiring for taking sports teams and other private parties at other times, providing valuable additional revenue.

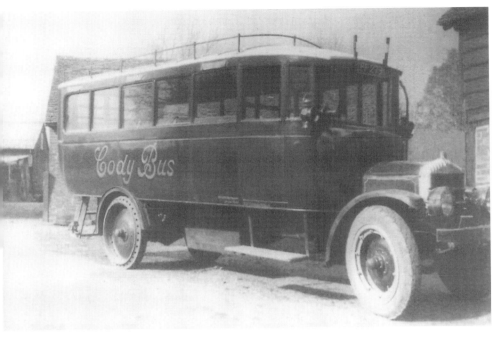

The Garford which brought with it the long-lasting name of Cody to Binfield, fitted with pneumatic tyres on the front wheels only at that point, parked beside the barn at its pub base. Note that the lighting was also a mix of electric headlamps and side oil lamps, whilst the large roof-mounted rack was accessed by a rear ladder just visible behind the rear wheels. The make of body is not recorded, but the brackets on the front dome indicated the use of a route board or number?

Such was the increase in passengers that later in 1925 *Brookhouse Keene* found it necessary to obtain a 20-seater to cope. Up until this point the long-established link had not been given a name, but the bus acquired was to change all that! The new arrival came from the aforementioned *Bernard 'Cody' Smith* of Lane End, his nick-name being derived from a childhood fascination with the wild-west showman William Cody ('Buffalo Bill'), who the youngster had seen in High Wycombe on 11th June 1904. The body had in fact originally been built for Smith to use on an ex-WD Caledon 40hp (LR 9683) chassis in 1921, being transferred to an ex-WD Garford (PP 2791) in October 1924. This blue liveried body had *Cody Bus* emblazoned along its sides, which was retained by Keene to identify his bus service. This Garford was shedded at the Jack of Newbury, and when acquired it had solid rear tyres but with pneumatics fitted at the front. Its body had a front entrance, but also featured a large ladder in the centre rear end for access to the almost full-length roof cage.

Mention of the roof-cage reminds us of the very diverse goods then carried by the carrier's bus or van – old residents talk of crates of hens or ducks, trussed pigs or goats, plus large laundry baskets delivered in exchange for last week's consignment were just a few of those.

Once their bungalow had been completed, the next phase during 1925/6 was to construct a garage for the passenger vehicles, and the association with the Jack of Newbury finally came to an end. *Mr. Keene* also took on a hired driver around the same time, *George Lamb*, who lived nearby by his base at Amen Corner. However, by 1928 he had relocated to Waltham St. Lawrence, where he had been born in 1903, and decided to try his hand with a bus service through Shurlock Row. His *Reindeer Bus* ran twice daily on Tuesdays, Thursdays, Fridays and Saturdays, using the Lower Ship in Duke Street as his Reading terminus. That venture had ceased by 1930, after which he just

concentrated on his garage business at Waltham St. Lawrence, and by 1939 he had moved to Cookham.

After gaining the experience of various operations *Keene* decided in June 1927 to dispose of both the Garford (PP 2791) and the Chevrolet (MO 3220), their replacement being a new Chevrolet LM-type (RX 283), which carried a blue-liveried 14-seater all-weather coach body. This move saw him with a vehicle which was suited to the bus service, whilst also providing a more attractive type for private hire, a quite common solution for the small country operator at that time. Although the bodybuilder for this is not recorded, it is worth bearing in mind that Vincents of Reading were the Chevrolet main agents at that time, so it may well have been their handiwork.

No details of how the bus service developed in terms of frequency has surfaced for the 1920's, though at 1931 it was still quite similar to the original timetable, but now with twice-daily journeys on Mondays, Tuesdays, Thursdays and Fridays, and six journeys on Saturdays, there being no service on Wednesdays and Sundays.

The original route from Hurst turned just before the Jolly Farmer pub into Sandford Lane, a lane of variable widths interrupted by several narrow arched bridges, where the River Loddon and mill-race streams passed under, along with some blind bends. In that respect the passage of a bus service came to the attention of the County Surveyor during early 1926, as the *Thames Valley Traction Co. Ltd.* put on a rival service between Reading and Hurst using its somewhat larger forward-control Thornycroft J-type 32-seater saloons. Indeed, in places the roadway was only 11 feet wide, of which over 7ft would be taken up by such a bus, and the Surveyor noted that the other operator (*Brookhouse Keene*) used a smaller bus and also did not concern him in respect of weight-damage to the brick-arched bridges which had never been designed for such heavy traffic. In respect of that stretch of road, it was also very prone to flooding, which also no doubt contributed to the *Cody Bus* being re-routed straight along from Hurst to Sindlesham (at what we now call Winnersh Cross Roads), where it turned right and passed over the River Loddon at the more reliable Loddon Bridge by The George pub.

Despite the comments of the County Surveyor and Wokingham Rural District Council, *Thames Valley* did carry on using the route via Sandford Mill, and from 11th April 1926 this 'experimental' service was placed on a firmer footing with a basic 3-journey through service from Reading (St. Mary's Butts) – Hurst (Townsend's Pond) on Mondays to Fridays, plus an extra run on Saturdays and Sundays, though the latter services ran later in the day as was typical of that time. 5 or 6 other short-workings also ran from Reading out as far as Woodley (Post Office), but it would not be until the next timetable booklet of the Summer of 1927 that the route number 1a was used.

Also in that general area, the Road Motors of the *Great Western Railway* had made an appearance on the road between Reading and Hurst, when its existing Reading (Stations) – Bath Road – Twyford (Station) route was extended onto Hurst from 24th August 1925. However, it was once again cut back to Twyford from 2nd February 1926.

The next stage in *Thames Valley* developments saw the 1a extended onto Maidenhead in April 1929, and that ran via Shurlock Row – Waltham St. Lawrence (The Bell) – White Waltham – Heywood Park – Cox Green. Indeed, *Marlow & District Motor Services Ltd.* had operated between Maidenhead and Waltham St. Lawrence, though control of that company had passed to *Thames Valley* in 1929, leading to that route being incorporated into the extended 1a.

The development of these *Thames Valley* and *Great Western Railway* services had little competitive effect on the *Cody Bus*, though they would contribute to the shape of future events. It should also be noted that another relevant factor to the future was the established *Beta Bus Service* which ran to Binfield to Maidenhead. This was operated by *Charles Fuller*, who had been a *Thames Valley* driver at Maidenhead between 1921-3, after which he drove for *William Carter (Alpha Coaches)* of Maidenhead, before partnering *Alfred William Pomroy* in April 1925, a fairly typical example of an experienced driver teaming up with a motor engineer. In fact the choice of their fleetname *Beta* stemmed from the fact that *Alpha* was already in use, and was a play on the word 'better'!

The first that was heard of the bus service is in December 1930, when the inspecting officer for hackney carriages for Wokingham BC, Sergeant Goddard, refused to approve the vehicles offered for licensing by *Beta,* which also indicates that the original plan was to link that town with Maidenhead. Certainly a more suitable vehicle was noted as acquired in March 1931, whilst their original license application under the new Road Traffic Act of 1930, which took effect from 1st January 1931, saw them applying to continue running between Maidenhead and Binfield, 'as operated during the past year', so it is possible that Binfield was actually being served when the approach was made to enter Wokingham's area?

The *Beta Bus Service* also operated from Maidenhead and Burchetts Green, though out of the scope of this study. The service to Binfield started from the Clock Tower, just outside Maidenhead Station, and opposite their base at the Fancourt Garage, before continuing as Boyne Hill (The Crown) – Tittle Row (Post Office) – Heywood Park – White Waltham (PO) – Waltham St. Lawrence (The Bell) – Shurlock Row (Royal Oak and Church) – Allanby Park Corner – Binfield (Church) – Binfield (The Standard) – Binfield (The Shoulder of Mutton), the latter terminus being just 100 yards from the *Cody Bus* garage on the A329. However, the full account of that operator will be found in the *Early Independents of the Maidenhead Area.*

Returning to the direct events concerning the *Cody Bus Service,* the 1930 Act saw *Brookhouse Keene* applying to continue the bus service, as was outlined above, and also to continue his established practice of running excursions and tours from both Binfield and Woodley areas. Indeed, under the new legislation all advertised excursions and tours required prior approval. So, *Mr. Keene* applied for the following destinations in respect of E&T's from Binfield – day excursions to Bournemouth and Southend, and half-day circular tours to the Chiltern Hills and Savernake Forest, all of the above (other than Southend) being routed through his familiar territory of Hurst, Shurlock Row and The Walthams, were picking up points were included. Also, he gained a license for other special occasions, which he could use for the many popular annual events of the Summer calendar.

If the above list seems rather limited, that was made up by the extensive E&T's emanating from Woodley, which were also routed through Hurst, The Walthams and Binfield, with pick-ups throughout, and these comprised full-day excursions to Bognor Regis, Brighton, Epsom Downs, Goodwood Downs, Littlehampton, Southsea and Worthing, whilst half-day tours catered for Hindhead, Ascot Racecourse and Aldershot Military Tattoo, the latter two specifically for the dates of those events.

Despite this fair-sized list, it must be appreciated that there was still only the one Chevrolet coach available for both the bus service and the excursions, which in time would make him consider whether the bus service was his priority now. Indeed, whilst the 1930 Act had provided smaller concerns protection from the often un-scrupulous competition of former times, it also gave such operators a saleable commodity in the form of the Road Service Licenses.

Another relevant factor was the change in strategy by those railway companies that had been involved in bus operation, largely in connection with the new Act and other legislation, whereby they stood down from direct participation in favour of taking shareholdings in the established territorial bus companies. In that way, the *Great Western Railway,* along with a much smaller stake from the *Southern Railway,* came to have a controlling interest in *Thames Valley,* which would greatly influence the latter's rate of expansion through the purchasing of other operators during the 1930's.

By early 1933 *Thames Valley* was considering how to recast the services in The Walthams and the links to Maidenhead and Reading from that area. Approaches made to the Maidenhead-based *Fuller & Pomroy (Beta Bus Service)* and *Brookhouse Keene (Cody Bus),* would give them the opportunity needed to remove the competition over those roads. Both were agreeable to the offers made, so on 1st April those operators ceased their bus operations to or from Binfield, allowing *Thames Valley* to alter its services from that same date so that the 1a ran only as Reading (Stations) – Woodley (PO), and a new Route 2a ran from Reading (Stations) to Shurlock Row via Loddon Bridge – Winnersh (Cross Roads) – Hurst – Waltham St. Lawrence. From the Maidenhead end a Route 21 left Bridge Avenue for Wokingham, running via Cox Green – White Waltham – Waltham St. Lawrence – Shurlock Row – Binfield – then along the Forest Road (Warren House) and into Wokingham via Wiltshire Road. Although the latter route would see a number of detailed changes over the following years, that would be the basic pattern for some time.

Both *Beta* and *Cody* only sold their bus services as noted above to *Thames Valley,* each continuing to trade, which in the case of *Brookhouse Keene* meant the coaching work, along with maintaining the goods element of the carrier's service, the latter travelling into Reading on Tuesdays, Thursdays and Saturdays only and using The Sun Inn yard in Castle Street, and running through until some time in 1939.

Although TV had only paid £175 for the goodwill of the service, without the distraction of that, coaching work was naturally increased, in particular private hire, and there can have be few local residents who did not at some time go on a trip in the little blue 14-seater Chevrolet (RX 283). Despite being some 12 years old when war broke out in September 1939, it was soon providing a daily aircraft worker's service from the Binfield area to Woodley Airfield. By then the all-weather hood was somewhat past its best, with bits flapping in the wind, but this remarkable little coach continued through to the last day of 1947 before finally being replaced!

In fact, the replacement was only some two years its junior, though a much larger forward-control AEC 'Reliance' of the original 660-type (UU 161) new in 1929 to *Keith & Boyle (Orange Coaches)* of London SE11, though it came to Binfield via other owners, arriving in January 1947. It carried a Hoyal 32-seater coach body, originally of dual-door layout, though altered to just a front doorway by then.

Post-war developments featured assistance by *Bill Jones,* who became *Brookhouse Keene's* son-in-law in early 1948 when he married Gladys, a move which saw the garage extended to also cater for the anticipated growth in private car ownership, and also to further develop the coach business. Back in 1937 his other daughter Doris had married Joseph Cove, though neither was involved in the business.

In January 1948 the fleet started to expand, with the arrival of a 1937 Bedford WTB-type 24-seater (HB 5421), which originated with *D.T. Breese* of Methyr. The main thrust of pot-war operations was to gain additional contract work, alongside the excursions and private hire.

However, the family suffered a series of losses during this period, starting with the death of Joe Cove at only 37 in early 1947. To compound that, his wife Doris went for an injection recommended to ease her chronic asthma, only to die from a violent reaction later that same year, aged 35 and leaving three daughters Sally (9), Wendy (7) and Cherry (5). If that was not trauma enough, Brookhouse's wife Mildred died in September 1948, with him also following her on 17th October!

It is certainly to the credit of the family, now in a new partnership of *Gladys D. Jones, E.W. Jones, V. Jones and A.E. Wright (t/a Cody Coaches),* that the business survived this series of tragic events, particularly as Bill and Gladys also took in the 3 orphaned girls.

As already noted, contract work was targeted, with Berkshire County Council providing opportunities for schoolday services to the Piggott School, which had been built on 'neutral ground' between Twyford and Wargrave in order to serve an area extending throughout the parishes of both those villages, along with The Walthams, Shurlock Row, Hurst and Binfield. Such a contract also fitted in nicely with advertised excursions and private hire work. The wartime aircraft contract did not end immediately, but was soon replaced with daily worker's contracts to the AWRE at Aldermaston and the AERE at Harwell, both during the construction and later phase of operation, each of these calling for the use of older types which would often be driven by part-time drivers who spent the day employed at the site, also saving the fuel of an empty return journey.

Bedford OB FBL 677 is seen after sale in later years.

Another secondhand Bedford followed in February 1949, being a 1944 Duple 30-seater front-entrance bus body on a wartime OWB-type chassis (GZ 2161), formerly employed by the *Northern Ireland Road Transport Board*. A new Bedford OB-type (FBL 677), with 31-seater Mulliner front-entrance bus body followed in July 1949, the first new vehicle bought since 1927! During 1949 the AEC 'Reliance' 660-type (UU 161) departed, leaving the fleet at 3.

A further new coach was ordered for 1950, this time a forward-control Guy 'Vixen' with a full-fronted 30-seater front-entrance coach body by Thurgood's of Ware, and it entered service as GBL 152 in August. Its arrival led to the end for Bedford WTB-type HB 5421, which departed in December of that year.

The local newspaper advert for April 1949 excursions.

With more vehicles now available out of school times it was decided to extend the range of E&T's starting from Woodley, with an application made in time for the 1950 season to add a further 9 destinations, though one of the existing local tours would be surrendered at the same time. The new additions were are follows-

Destination	Notes
Bournemouth	May to September
Cheddar	May to September
Chiswick Empire	Saturdays/Boxing Day
Elm Park, Reading	Reading FC matches
Hayling Island	May to September
London Zoo	May to September
Oxford Theatre	Throughout the year
Southend-on-Sea	May to September
Wembley Stadium	Up to 24 days p.a.

The tour taking in Frensham Ponds was surrendered.

Similarly, the E&T's starting from Binfield were increased by 12, with 3 of the local tours surrendered-

Destination	Notes
Bognor Regis	Throughout the year
Brighton	Throughout the year
Cheddar	Throughout the year
Chiswick Empire	Saturdays/Boxing Day
Elm Park, Reading	Reading FC matches
Littlehampton	Throughout the year
London Zoo	May to September
Oxford Theatre	Throughout the year
Portsmouth	Throughout the year
Southend-on-Sea	Throughout the year
Wembley Stadium	Up to 24 days p.a.
Worthing	Throughout the year

Kimble, Highmoor and Skirmett were surrendered.

A number of local pick-ups were already established at Binfield (Royal Standard), Woodley (Post Office), Hurst (PO), Waltham St. Lawrence (PO), Shurlock Row (Royal Oak) and at Bracknell (PO), with booking agents at Binfield (F. Auger, PO and Mr. Gooday, Corner Shop), Woodley (A&E Skevington) and Bracknell (R. Stevens in the High Street) and Charlie Fry (Priestwood Garage), and at the Cody Garage.

The Thurgood-bodied Guy 'Vixen' coach GBL 152.

Another Bedford OB with Duple 29-seater 'Vista' front-entrance coach body (NUM 13) came third-hand, having been new to *Neill* of Leeds in October 1950, then passing within that same city to *Heap's Tours* in January 1953. It is shown below in *Smith's* livery.

In January 1955 the final addition to the fleet arrived in the form of a new Bedford SBG (KMO 681), which had a Thurgood 36-seater front-entrance coach body, seen below after sale and repainting by *Smith's Coaches*.

However, Bill Jones was suffering with his health as the 1950's wore on, so it was decided to dispose of the coach business, and a ready purchaser was found in *Smith's Luxury Coaches* of Reading, and the takeover was finalised for October 1956. The latter also took Bedford OB NUM 13 and the SBG-type KMO 681 into stock, but the Mulliner-bodied Bedford OB FBL 677 was sold to *Geddes (Burton Cars)* of Brixham, and the Thurgood-bodied Guy 'Vixen' (GBL 152) went to *Kemp* of Tillingham for further public use, those two seeing no use by *Smith's*.

Mr. Jones then concentrated on developing the garage business, taking Barry Handley as a partner under the continuing title of Cody Garage. The Jones's sold out their interest to Barry in 1977, who continued to run the garage until it was would up in 1990. And so, *Cody*, a name which had come to the area by means of the purchase of the Garford bus way back in 1924, finally ended its long-standing local connection.

Frederick George Lansley
The Mount, Hurst, Berkshire

Fred Lansley was born in 1878 south of Newbury in the Hampshire village of East Woodhay. At 1901 he still lived with his parents at 'Baker's Buildings', but was employed at a local large house as a groom. By 1911 he embraced motor transport and become a domestic chauffeur, now living at 'Coombe Cottage' north of Newbury at Chieveley. In fact, he had married Harriett Thorngate from nearby Hampstead Norreys in 1902, probably when he moved to that position. Also to note was that a 14 year-old niece from Binfield was living with them in 1911, so that may have had a bearing on his next relocation to East Berkshire.

Indeed, by May 1915 he was living in Church Street, Crowthorne, now described as a chauffeur-mechanic, and at that point he enlisted for the Army Service Corps (Motor Transport), being initially sent to Grove Park at Lee in South London for assessment. He was posted to the island of Malta, driving staff cars mainly, though he had progressed to lorries and had been promoted to Corporal in March 1917. He stayed there until 1918 when he was shipped to Alexandria in Egypt, where he remained until selected for demob in January 1919. It is interesting to note that he was a skilled driver, also able to deal with others with confidence, qualities that undoubtably contributed to his desire to be his own master once he was discharged, though it is not known what he initially did, or when he relocated to the village of Hurst, some 6.5 miles east of Reading.

In the 1927 local directory the carrier for Hurst into that market town was still Charlie Grant of Church Farm, who can be traced back to about 1907. *Fred Lansley,* based at 'The Mount' in Lines Road, now assumed that role, along with the small-holding he developed. Whether he acquired his vehicle, is not recorded. The only known vehicle used by him was a Chevrolet which carried a green and cream-painted 14-seater 'sun-saloon' body and was initially supplied as a private vehicle to H. Walters of 'Highgrove', Wallingford in March 1930, and it is not known when it reached Hurst.

Certainly by 1928 the carrier's service operated on the same basis as the predecessor, on Mondays, Tuesdays, Thursdays and Saturdays, and used The Royal Oak at No.14 Broad Street as his base in Reading. It was possibly from then that regular runs on Friday or Saturday evenings into that town for the cinema, the proprietor enjoying a fish'n'chip supper in the vehicle with his paying passengers. It is difficult to fully appreciate now what a treat it was to leave their dark and cold cottages for the escape to the latest films with all their glamour and drama. It is known that he also undertook other local journeys for dance parties, whist, darts and other sporting teams, plus a few day trips to the coast on Summer Sundays.

When the 1930 Act came into force he applied for a license for excursions to Bournemouth and Southsea, the Aldershot Military Tattoo and other annual local events. Those to the coast ran on Sundays and Bank Holidays, whilst the tattoo was an evening event held during June.

The carrier's service did not require a license, as it did not ply for hire and by then used the private yard at the Lower Ship at No.22 Duke Street, but with the improvements to the service offered by *Thames Valley* from soon after then, the carriage of passengers had probably come to an end. In fact, the operation was then increased to daily excluding Wednesday (the early-closing day for shops in Reading) and Sundays, the route continuing to be via Sandford Lane and the then sparsely-populated area of Woodley. The return run was at 4pm, and it would seem that it continued through to the outbreak of WW2. The Chevrolet survived with another operator to 1945, and even after that as a lorry through to 1951. Fred passed away at Gosport in 1968, but nothing is known of his post-war activities.

Ledbury Transport Co. Ltd.
Thackray's Way
Reading & London

The full and interesting 90-year saga of *Thackray's Way – A Family In Road Transport* has already been told in the 2001 volume of that name, still available at the time of writing -so see the website for full details- www.paullaceytransportbooks.co.uk

For the purposes of this volume we shall concern ourselves only with the operations that reached our catchment area, of which there were two. The major route was one of the two operated between Reading and London, taking the A329 out of Reading and running via Earley – Winnersh – Wokingham – Binfield – Bracknell – Ascot – Egham and Staines, after which it joined the A4 on the Great West Road and entered London on the same road as taken by the alternative route along the Bath Road, which also included the westwards extension onto Newbury. This service had commenced on 31st July 1930, taking the established other operator *Thames Valley* by total surprise, that firm having pioneered the link in May 1927. However, the *'Valley's* operation had continued at a low level, with only a couple of daily return journeys, aimed at the better-off shoppers and theatre-goers. From the outset, the *Thackray's Way* coaches brought improved comfort and frequency, thereby increasing the social range of passengers, and inevitably a 'war' followed between the parties over fares and resulting in the

'Valley' having to field some new coaches. However, with the passage of the Road Traffic Act from 1st January 1930, the Traffic Commissioner gave the license to *Thames Valley* over that road, and even after an appeal and support from Wokingham BC, the *Thackray's* service had to cease from late August 1931.

Gilford coach GC 1867 enters at The Colonnade on the route via Ascot and Wokingham from London.

With the loss of that route, allied to the evident level of support from Wokingham people, *Robert Thackray* came to the decision to run a feeder service in the form of a local bus route between Wokingham and Wargrave, a link not then served by *Thames Valley*. It started from 1st October 1932, though the optimistic original timetable (*see page 25 of the Henley & Marlow volume*) was reduced from 13th January 1933. In order to make a neater connection with the express coaches on the Bath Road, the route was extended on through Upper Wargrave to Kiln Green from August 1933, but its usefulness as a local service linking Wokingham seems limited. Certainly, when *Ledbury* was acquired by *Thames Valley* from 1st January 1936 that operation was not continued.

JANUARY 1933

THACKRAY'S WAY

THE LEDBURY TRANSPORT COMPANY, LTD.
5 and 6, Crown Colonnade, Reading. Phone 2673.

WOKINGHAM—WARGRAVE
TIME TABLE

Wokingham Town Hall ..	2 50	4 50	6 50	8 50
Dog & Duck, Embrook ..	2 55	4 55	6 55	8 55
Green Lane Turning ..	2 58	4 58	6 58	8 58
"Castle Inn"	3 2	5 2	7 2	9 2
"Cricketers"	3 5	5 5	7 5	9 5
Twyford Station	3 10	5 10	7 10	9 10
A.A. Box	3 13	5 13	7 13	9 13
Wargrave, George & Dragon	3 17	5 17	7 17	9 17

				s.o.
Wargrave, Grge & Drag.	2 5	4 5	6 5	8 5	10 5
A.A. Box	2 9	4 9	6 9	8 9	10 9
Twyford Station ..	2 12	4 12	6 12	8 12	1012
"Cricketers".. ..	2 17	4 17	6 17	8 17	1017
"Castle Inn" ..	2 20	4 20	6 20	8 20	1020
Green Lane Turning..	2 24	4 24	6 24	8 24	1024
Dog & Duck, Embrook	2 27	4 27	6 27	8 27	1027
Wokingham Town Hall	2 32	4 32	6 32	8 32	1032

s.o.—Sundays only.

Henry Thomas Lintott
Direct Bus Service
Lightwater, Surrey

'Harry' was the senior of the two bus men of that same name, and indeed around 1930 he, along with sons Alfred, Harry and Frederic were all operating bus services in various places in the Counties of Berkshire, Hampshire, Hertfordshire and Surrey!

Harry had been born at Liss in Hampshire in 1874 and lived with his parents on Forest Road in East Liss in 1881, but by 1891 he had taken employment as a page in 'Larchwood' at Burstow in Surrey, some 23 miles to the east. He married Ada Dalton in 1895 back in his home area at Petersfield, and by 1901 he was working as a domestic gardener and living at No.2 Rock Pit Cottages in Liss, the couple having 7 children in total. By 1911 he was earning a living variously sweeping chimneys and labouring, by then living in East Liss at Princes Bridge, whilst in 1920 they were at The Manor House in East Liss, and Harry senior is shown below.

Frederic duly emigrated to Canada, but later returned, whilst after Harry junior had war service he turned to a chauffeur before starting the family off in the direction of bus operation. He ran in the St. Albans area of Hertfordshire, and in due course Frederic ran from Odiham in Hampshire to Reading in Berkshire, whilst Albert tried his hand with buses in the Liss area, where of course they had family connections and the area was not well served by others. Young Harry, on the other hand, came to work for his father as a motor fitter by the time he married in July 1929.

So, to return to the senior Harry, he had purchased The Garage in Guildford Road, Lightwater, Surrey at some point before his late 1927 application to Windlesham UDC for permission to run a daily bus service from Guildford to Bracknell via Bagshot, Lightwater, West End, Bisley, Brookwood Crossroads, Worplesdon and Stoughton, and approval was given in February 1928. Prior to that, to travel from Bracknell to Guildford was not possible direct by bus, despite only being 17 miles apart, so the choice of *Direct Bus Service* was indeed very apt, with the service commencing in April 1928.

The initial vehicle was actually transferred from the St. Albans operation under the _District Bus Service_ name operated by young Harry, being a 14-seater Thurgood of Ware-bodied Chevrolet LQ-type (RO 9447), painted green as were, it is believed, subsequent vehicles. It was joined in October 1928 by a similar bus but most likely bodied in Farnham by Arnold & Comben, also a 14-seater registered as PK 3709. The second bus allowed the original 6 daily operations to be increased to 9 from November 1928, though not all went over the Bagshot to Bracknell section, which was only sparsely populated between the built-up areas. A third similar bus arrived in May 1929 as PG 254.

The other operations were, by the early 1930's, largely winding down due to competition and the effects of the 1930 Road Traffic Act, so after Alfred gave up, his 5 buses came to Lightwater as a Dodge 14-seater by Strachan & Brown (RO 8804) new January 1928, 14-seater Chevrolet LQ's UR 4043/4 of July 1929, a Guy OND 20-seater of August 1929 (UR 4466), and a 14-seater by Thurgood on Chevrolet LQ chassis new in March 1930 (UR 5780), all arriving in February 1932, along with sons Harry and Alfred, leaving only the Odiham to Reading service under Frederic, soon to be sold to *Thames Valley* in May 1932.

Under the 1930 Act the license to continue the service from Guildford to Bracknell was issued in November 1931, with the weekday pattern still of 9 journeys, 4 of which extended northwards over the Bagshot to Bracknell section, whilst on Sundays only 6 journeys ran, though 4 still ran the full route.

With the obvious over-supply of buses and manpower, an application was made in May 1932 for a circular route from Lightwater via Sunningdale, Suunninghill, Ascot and Bagshot, but despite this pre-dating the later *White Bus Service* through from Windsor, it was not approved.

Private hire had featured once the surplus buses were to hand, which included the very popular Royal Ascot Races and the Aldershot Military Tattoo, both of which took place during the third week of June in the daytime and evening respectively

TIME TABLE.

WEEKDAYS. | SUNDAYS.

	a.m.			p.m.						a.m.		p.m.				
Bagshot Square......... dep.	7 10	9 43	11 45	1 15	3 15	5 45	6 40	7 20	9 45	9 15	11 15	2 15		5 45	7 15	9 40
Lightwater War Memorial...	7 13	9 49	11 49	1 19	3 19	5 49	6 43	7 25	9 49	9 19	11 19	2 19		5 49	7 19	9 44
West End, Wheatsheaf	7 16	9 52	11 52	1 22	3 22	5 52	6 46	7 30	9 52	9 22	11 22	2 22		5 52	7 22	9 47
Bisley, Hen and Chickens...	7 19	9 56	11 56	1 26	3 26	5 56	6 49	7 35	9 56	9 25	11 25	2 25		5 55	7 25	9 50
Bisley Post Office	7 20	9 57	11 57	1 27	3 27	5 57	6 50	7 36	9 57	9 26	11 26	2 26		5 56	7 26	9 51
Knaphill, Garibaldi	7 22	10 0	12 0	1 30	3 30	6 0	6 54	7 45	9 59	9 28	11 28	2 28	3 25	5 58	7 30	9 53
Brookwood Cross Roads ...	7 24	10 2	12 2	1 32	3 32	6 2	6 56	7 47	10 1	9 30	11 30	2 30	3 27	6 0	7 33	9 55
Brookwood Cemetery Gates	7 26	10 4	12 4	1 34	3 34	6 4	6 58	7 49	10 3	9 32	11 32	2 32	3 29	6 2	7 35	10 0
Pirbright, Fox Inn	7 28	10 5	12 6	1 36	3 36	6 5	7 0	7 52	10 5	9 35	11 35	2 35	3 32	6 5	7 38	10 3
Worplesdon, New Inn	7 30	10 8	12 8	1 40	3 40	6 8	7 2	7 54	10 8	9 39	11 39	2 39	3 36	6 8	7 40	10 6
Pitch Place	7 34	10 12	12 12	1 48	3 42	6 12	7 5	7 57	10 12	9 41	11 41	2 41	3 38	6 14	7 43	10 10
Stoughton	7 38	10 16	12 16	1 50	3 50	6 16	7 7	8 0	10 14	9 45	11 45	2 45	3 41	6 16	7 46	10 15
Guildford P.O. .... arr.	7 48	10 26	12 26	2 0	4 0	6 26	7 16	8 10	10 28	9 56	11 56	2 56	3 50	6 26	7 56	10 25

	a.m.		p.m.							a.m.	p.m.					
Guildford P.O.......... dep.	8 10	10 30	12 30	2 15	4 20	6 30	7 20	8 20	10 30	10 0	12 0	3 0	4 0	6 30	8 15	10 30
Stoughton, Royal Arms ...	8 20	10 40	12 40	2 25	4 30	6 40	7 30	8 30	10 40	10 10	12 10	3 10	4 10	6 40	8 25	10 40
Pitch Place, Ship Inn	8 24	10 44	12 44	2 29	4 34	6 44	7 34	8 32	10 44	10 14	12 14	3 14	4 14	6 44	8 29	10 42
Worplesdon, New Inn	8 28	10 48	12 48	2 33	4 38	6 48	7 38	8 34	10 48	10 18	12 18	3 17	4 18	6 48	8 33	10 48
Pirbright, Fox Inn	8 30	10 50	12 50	2 35	4 40	6 50	7 40	8 36	10 50	10 20	12 20	3 19	4 20	6 50	8 35	10 50
Brookwood Cemetery Gates	8 32	10 52	12 52	2 37	4 42	6 52	7 42	8 38	10 52	10 22	12 22	3 21	4 22	6 52	8 37	10 52
Brookwood Cross Roads ...	8 34	10 54	12 54	2 39	4 44	6 54	7 44	8 40	10 55	10 24	12 24	3 23	4 24	6 54	8 39	10 55
Knaphill, Garibaldi	8 36	10 56	12 56	2 41	4 46	6 56	7 46	8 42	10 58	10 26	12 26	3 25	4 26	6 56	8 41	10 58
Bisley Post Office	8 38	10 58	12 58	2 43	4 48	6 58	7 48	8 44	10 59	10 28	12 28		4 28	6 58	8 43	10 59
Bisley, Hen and Chickens	8 39	11 0	1 0	2 45	4 49	6 59	7 49	8 45	11 1	10 29	12 29		4 30	6 59	8 44	11 1
West End, Wheatsheaf	8 42	11 5	1 5	2 50	4 52	7 2	7 52	8 48	11 5	10 32	12 32		4 35	7 2	8 50	11 4
Lightwater War Memorial...	8 45	11 10	1 10	2 55	5 0	7 9	7 55	8 51	11 9	10 35	12 35		4 40	7 6	8 55	11 7
Bagshot Square .... arr.	8 48	11 14	1 14	3 0	5 8	7 15	7 58	8 54	11 12	10 40	12 40		4 45	7 12	9 0	11 10

	a.m.				p.m.					a.m.	p.m.				
Bagshot Square .... dep.	8 50	11 14	...	...	5 10	...	...	8 55	...	10 42	12 42	...	4 46	...	9 2
Cricketers Bridge	8 52	11 16	...	...	5 12	...	...	8 57	...	10 43	12 43	...	4 48	...	9 4
Swinley Road turning	8 54	11 18	...	...	5 14	...	...	8 59	...	10 45	12 45	...	4 50	...	9 6
Golf Links	8 56	11 20	...	...	5 16	...	...	9 1	...	10 47	12 47	...	4 52	...	9 9
Nine Mile Ride	8 58	11 22	...	...	5 18	...	...	9 4	...	10 49	12 49	...	4 54	...	9 12
Horse and Groom	9 2	11 24	...	...	5 20	...	...	9 8	...	10 51	12 51	...	4 56	...	9 16
Hind's Head, Bracknell arr.	9 10	11 26	...	...	5 22	...	...	9 20	...	10 55	12 55	...	5 10	...	9 20

	a.m.				p.m.					a.m.	p.m.				
Bracknell Station Road dep.	9 20	11 28	...	...	5 26	...	...	9 20	...	11 0	1 0	...	5 20	...	9 24
Horse and Groom	9 22	11 30	...	...	5 29	...	...	9 25	...	11 2	1 2	...	5 22	...	9 26
Nine Mile Ride	9 24	11 32	...	...	5 32	...	...	9 28	...	11 5	1 5	...	5 26	...	9 29
Golf Links	9 28	11 34	...	...	5 35	...	...	9 31	...	11 8	1 8	...	5 30	...	9 35
Swinley Road turning	9 30	11 36	...	...	5 37	...	...	9 34	...	11 12	1 12	...	5 35	...	9 37
Cricketers Bridge	9 35	11 40	...	...	5 40	...	...	9 40	...	11 14	1 14	...	5 40	...	9 38
Bagshot Square .... arr.	9 40	11 45	...	...	5 43	...	...	9 43	...	11 15	1 15	...	5 42	...	9 40

The timetable after approval under the 1930 Act, though the times are believed to be similar since it commenced.

There was also a special service operated on the occasion of a large popular golf tournament at the Royal Berkshire Golf Club off Swinley Road and north of Bagshot. Buses were run 'on demand' at either end of the competition from both the Ascot and Bagshot railway stations to form a through route between those points on 11th September 1934.

Despite no actual expansion of the bus service, 2 more vehicles were duly purchased in March 1935 as Bedford WLB-type 20-seater with Thurgood body as ACG 89, followed by a Dodge RBF-type 26-seater by REALL coachworks in September 1936 as BOR 501. The original Chevie (RO 9447) had gone back in 1932 after the other buses arrived, probably along with PK 3709, whilst UR 4043 went in 1935 and Dodge RO 8804 after the new Dodge entered service.

It seems that the sons soon drifted off to other forms of employment, with young Harry returning to St. Albans, so once Harry senior became unwell around 1937, his wife Ada found it difficult to keep things running, and that led to some warnings from the Traffic Commissioner, leading to a suspension of license from January 1937. In order to give some lee-way for the service to be properly maintained, arrangements were made for *Aldershot & District* to supervise the service, but by November the decision had been made to sell out, not to *A&D* but to Peckham-based *Sidney Ansell!* What came after that was an interesting time and will be found under the heading for *C.E.&V.M. Jeatt*, on page 74, whilst *Harry Lintott* moved about 7 miles to Horsell near Woking at passed away in June 1955.

The 1935 Thurgood-bodied Bedford ACG 89 awaits departure from Guildford for Bagshot.

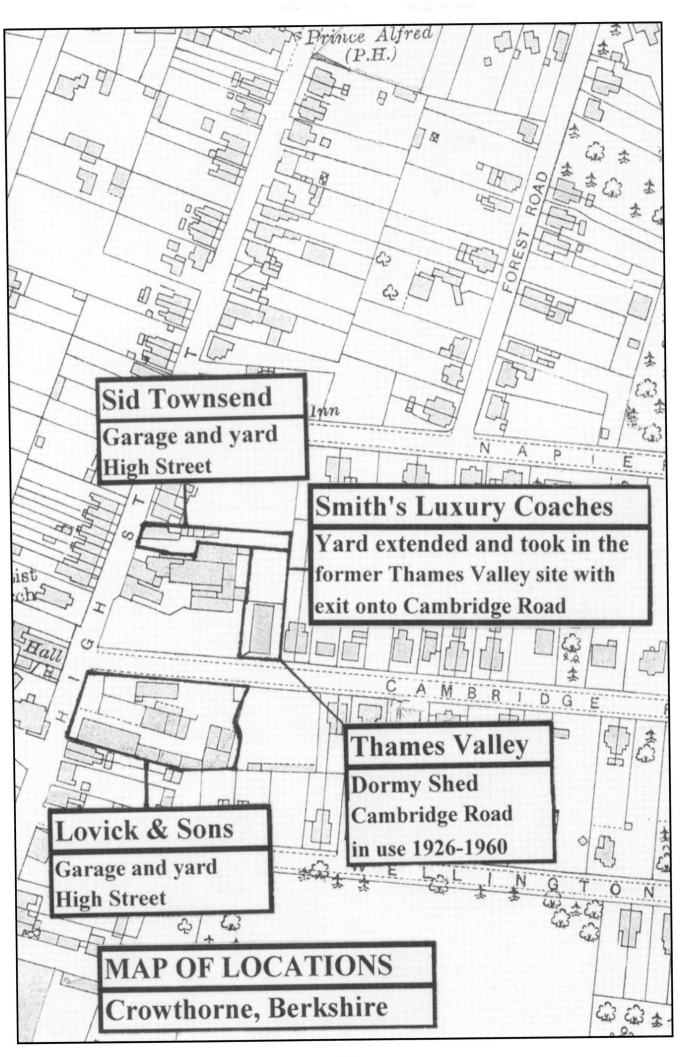

Sid Townsend
Garage and yard
High Street

Smith's Luxury Coaches
Yard extended and took in the
former Thames Valley site with
exit onto Cambridge Road

Thames Valley
Dormy Shed
Cambridge Road
in use 1926-1960

Lovick & Sons
Garage and yard
High Street

MAP OF LOCATIONS
Crowthorne, Berkshire

Charles Lovick & Sons
Lovick's Coaches
Crowthorne, Berkshire

The origins of the Lovick family at Crowthorne have been attributed to the construction of the Broadmoor Criminal Lunatic Asylum just to the south-east of that village and some 2 miles short of the Berkshire/Surrey border. Family sources also accredit *Charles Lovick* as the pioneer associated with the family move from Norfolk, whilst also noting that he had originally left school aged 9, after which he did gardening work and duly held posts with the Duchess of Montrose, Lord Cadagon and Lord Ulmsdale.

Whilst not necessarily disputing some of the above, research shows a different sequence of documented events, none of which distracts in any way from his achievements over the years.

Indeed, it was not Charlie who first brought the Lovicks to the area, but his brother John, who was 16 years his senior, and in 1861 both can be found at Riddlesworth, some 6 miles east of Thetford, Norfolk and just above the Little Ouse River that forms the border with Suffolk. On the 1871 census their father James was at The Stud, part of the Riddlesworth Hall estate, and famed for the breeding of racehorses that won at the Newmarket track some 25 miles to the south-west in Cambridgeshire. Within that household was Charles, then aged 8, which fixes his birth year as 1863, though subsequent records do vary, and 10 years later he was still there, most likely employed on the same estate.

However, by 1871 John had made his way down to Berkshire, being employed as a groom at Wick Hill House, just off the Maidenhead Road between Bracknell and Warfield. Also employed there as the cook was 23-year old Emily Taylor from Dorking in Surrey, and the couple married in nearby Wokingham in early 1876. John's early careers varied according to opportunity, and in 1881 he was a night watchman living at Crowthorne, along with a 1-year old son James born in that village. By 1901 he was a domestic gardener and residing in Crowthorne High Street, by which time additional sons Harry (1883) and William (1888) had been added. However, John died in 1908 and his widow and children remained in the area, so we shall hear more of some of them in due course.

The first reference we have of Charles independent of the family home is when he married Kezia Drake on 21st January 1887 at Wandsworth in Surrey, when both gave their address as No.50 Corrunna Road, in Battersea, with Charles as a gardener. As it was Kezia had been born in 1858 at Barrow in Suffolk, near to Bury St. Edmunds and only some 15 miles from the Riddlesworth Estate. She is also found on the 1881 census in service as a cook, along with her sister Ziliah in a small household at Bury St. Edmunds. As Culford Hall, the residence of Lord Cadogan was only a few miles away from Barrow, it would seem that Chalres was likely to have been in his employ at the time he met Kezia, confirming family tradition.

The original phase of building for the Broadmoor Criminal Lunatic Asylum had taken place prior to 1868, so clearly neither John or Charlie were involved, but another phase took place in 1902, so that is probably when the cartage work attributed by family sources to Charlie actually took place. However, Charlie and Kezia had arrived at Crowthorne by the birth of their first child Harriett ('Hattie') in 1888, and he recognised that the relative remoteness of the railway station, then known as Wellington College Station some 1.5 miles to the west, provided an opportunity for the operation of passenger transport in the form of horse-drawn flys.

Based in the High Street, he would transport staff and visitors for the asylum, and also Wellington College, which had been set up by Queen Victoria in honour of the Duke of Wellington, who often passed through the area when he rode from his estate at Stratfieldsaye along the Nine Mile Ride to Windsor Castle. The college was primarily intended for the education of the sons of army officers, often as a prelude to their acceptance at the Royal Military Academy just a few miles further east at Sandhurst. At term ends and half-holidays the boys would arrive complete with trunks, and ferrying them from the station was a busy time. The area also had numerous large to medium houses, which saw a steady trade in the need for taxi work, and Charles added other types of vehicle as trade developed. Haulage also featured from an early date, and in order to accommodate the expansion a large plot of land in the High Street, and on the southern side of Cambridge Road was developed into a yard and stabling. The horses kept there included those available for hire, both as hackney horses and smaller ponies for householders to hire to power their own carriages and pony-traps.

All off to Royal Ascot Races! Lovick's horse-drawn days, with Charles senior stood outside the Crowthorne Inn to see 3 of his two-horse carriages off for the day, a journey of about 8.5 miles.

On 5th December 1893 he further expanded his business interests by taking over the license of The Crowthorne Inn, on the northern corner of Napier Road at its junction with the High Street, just about 100 yards or so from his yard, and a greengrocer's shop was also opened on the opposite side of the High Street and next to The Prince Alfred pub by 1895. A lot of the subsequent expansion of the businesses would come with the maturity of Charles and Kezia's children, who were Hattie (1888), Charles Edward (1889), Bertie Cecil (1892), Archibald (1896) and the twins Cecil Victor and Lily (1898).

As already noted, the railway station provided regular trade for the carriages, but other seasonal events were also catered for, in particular Ascot Races, whilst in the pre-Great War era there were a number of regular point-to-point meetings locally, some associated with the various local military establishments. There was also a steady trade for wedding and funeral parties, and carriages could also be hired for family picnics to local beauty spots.

The 1911 census shows Hattie as working at home as part of the business, but in that year she married William Alfred ('Bill') Jaycock. He had originated at Dadham, near Stowe in Buckinghamshire in 1884, though his family had drifted a short distance into the neighbouring County of Oxfordshire in due course. He was still in the Stoke Lyne area, near Bicester in 1901, but by 1911 was one of a number of single young men attracted to working at Broadmoor as an attendant by the provision of board and lodgings built for that purpose. Although he was not involved in the transport business, we will hear of him again later on.

1911 is also that year in which we first hear of *Charles Lovick & Son,* marking the entry into the business of young Charles, soon followed by Bertie, and at that point some half-a-dozen horse-drawn vehicles ranging from light flys to the larger enclosed carriages were on offer. The cartage also continued, and as funds permitted a coal yard was added behind the stables and accessed via Cambridge Road, the raw materials being transferred from railway wagons at the station. Charlie also acquired a sizeable plot of land to the east of Napier Road, which was rich in gravel deposits, another facet to the business. Indeed, for some years that area was known as Lovick's Hill, and for many years he would arrange a huge bonfire there each November for the extended family, though being on an elevated position the entire village could enjoy the fireworks too! Much later on that land was sold by him for post-WW2 housing, completed in April 1949 when both Charlie and his son-in-law Bill were elected members of the Easthampstead Rural District Council, and the two got on well together, though one of Bill and Hattie's daughters recalled him as (quote) 'a miserable and mean old sod'!

However, not all the sons followed into the business, and in 1911 we find Archie as a 15-year old engineer's apprentice and lodging at No.8 Woodstock Road in Fulham, West London. It would seem that he had intended to contribute these skills to the business in due course, as he did return to Crowthorne and was also later described as a motor driver.

Also, of the sons of John Lovick, the nephews of Charles, only one came to work for him, with William in the role of carter by 1911. The other sons of James were James, who became as an assistant at Broadmoor and Harry, a domestic gardener.

The family business had therefore reached a quarter of a century in development before the younger generation embraced the still developing motor car. Another family tradition notes that the Lovicks 'owned the first motor car in Crowthorne', though it is probably more likely it was the first for public hire. Certainly, the first car recorded with them was a Napier 15hp first licensed on 9th January 1912 as BL 2334, and fitted with a landaulette type body seating 4 and painted dark blue with a yellow stripe, supplied by Vincents.

With young Bertie at the wheel, the first Napier (BL 2334) is seen by the Wellington Station Hotel.

The Napier proved a reliable purchase, and it was joined by another of that type on 17th February 1914 as BL 3467, which also carried a 4-seater landaulette body but in black with yellow lining. At that point in time few of the local larger households had gone over to motors, so there was a steady trade in taxi work, with *Charles junior* and *Bertie Lovick* as the drivers. The trade directory entry now showed *Lovick & Sons,* jobmasters, carmen and cartage contractors, motors for hire and garage, High Street, Crowthorne. The last mentioned was in fact a natural progression from the stabling facilities, as the early motorist had frequent need of servicing and repairs, unless they could afford a dedicated chauffeur-mechanic, something in short supply before the Great War. Similarly, not everyone wished to run a car just for occasional transfers.

Another shot of Bertie with Napier BL 2334 outside the Wellington Station Hotel, complete with the Manager boot-boys and buttoned-holed passenger. The hotel also features elsewhere for its own transport enterprises.

However, when indeed that event did come in August 1914, the fortunes for the Lovick boys would be rather mixed. *Archie* gave his trade as a motor driver, and he served with the British Expeditionary Force in France from September 1917 as part of the 30th Labour Corps, receiving a gunshot wound to his arm in December of that year. Returning to England as unfit for further service, his record is then amended to note that he died in February 1919, one of many of those who managed to survive the initial slaughter only to subsequently die of their related injuries.

The detailed records for *Bertie* have not survived beyond the fact that he joined the Army Service Corps in December 1914 and he served in France. *Cecil* gave his trade as motor engineer, and although qualifying as a motor driver-fitter for the army, he was sent to Longmoor Camp, near Liss in Hampshire, shortly after joining up in November 1916, where he became a train-driver! Initially he went to France as part of the Light Railway 4th Army under the Royal Engineers (Railway Operations) in February 1917, then later as 18th Train Crew Section before safely returning home.

The records for *Charlie junior* consist only of the medal record card, which show that 4 men of the same name served in the Army Service Corps, though he did also return safely, though his cousin Harry was not so fortunate, perishing in the large-scale fighting of September 1917 when serving with the 2/4th Battalion Oxfordshire & Buckinghamshire Light Infantry on the Western Front. His brother William is believed to have gone into the Army Veterinary Corps, a suitable role for someone so familiar with horses, but there are no records for his brother James, though both returned home safely from wherever the war had taken them, all experiences they would build on within the business as it developed.

Whilst her brothers were away, Lily worked in the office throughout the war years, until her marriage to Charles Hyatt in 1919.

In the meantime, *Charles Lovick* senior had a house built opposite The Crowthorne Inn on the High Street and known as 'Sherwood House', but despite that he continued with the license for the pub until late 1935, making it a total of 42 years! Of course, apart from the absence of his sons during the war years, he would have also lost most of his horses, especially being so close to the military establishments at Arborfield, Aldershot and Sandhurst, which left the transport side unable to expand.

However, once the war was over, the *Lovicks* were well placed to resume their activities and also make the changeover fully to motor power. As it was, *Bertie* had married in late 1917 to Jessie Weaver, whose father was another local publican at the Fox & Hounds in Sandhurst, while *Charles* married widow Beatrice Fells in 1923. The latter is also noted in November 1919 as the first owner of a 6hp Harley-Davidson motorcycle (BL 6665), the first of that make noted in the area, though he sold it again after only 4 months. In respect of the disposal of the horse-drawn vehicles, Charlie's son-in-law Bill Jaycock was offering on his behalf in July 1919 a one-horse brougham with rubber tyres and a wagonette, both in splendid condition for inspection at The Crowthorne Inn.

By 1922 a total of 5 hire cars were available, though exact details are lacking, other than that the pre-war Napiers were still with them at 1921. The old stables were adapted for housing the motor cars, but by 1923 the yard was becoming inadequate, so plans were drawn up for a new garage to include petrol pumps for public use, these being approved by Easthampstead RDC in January 1924.

In the meantime, charabanc outings were added from April 1921, with the purchase of an ex-WD Daimler Y-type. This did not come direct from the Slough Sales, but was one of a number reconditioned by the Shepherds Bush dealer (and London 'pirate' bus operator) Josiah Roberts for passenger use, and registered as MD 6090 it carried a 26-seater charabanc body painted dark blue. As the first such vehicle in the village it proved very popular for both the advertised excursions and private hire, with such a machine at last putting the South Coast in reach, albeit on solid rubber tyres and with only a canvas hood for protection if it rained! *Bertie* was usually found behind the wheel of the chara, as anyone venturing afar need to be a competent mechanic, and he was of course already familiar with the sleeve-valve engine. The general lack of other local providers in highlighted in 1926, when the congregation of Warfield Church choosing the firm for its annual outing to Southsea, even over *Thames Valley* or others based at Reading or Maidenhead.

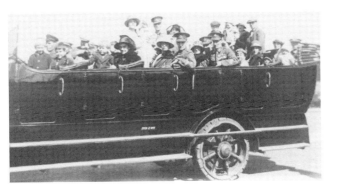

The Daimler off to Southsea with Bert Woods driving.

On the lighter side, the Ford Model T had already made a name for itself with its simple controls, and *Lovicks* purchased a number for various roles. The oldest had been built in 1920, but was new to a Birmingham operator as OP 3470, and exactly when it arrived in Crowthorne is not recorded. Initially it carried a 14-seater bus body, though there may have also been an alternative lorry body when not required for smaller passenger parties, and in its final phase it became a laundry van.

The first of the Fords 1-tonners purchased new arrived in January 1924 (MO 2543), again with a 14-seater saloon body and finished in stained brown and black trim, and again this was no doubt also used on goods work at times, ending its days as that class only with the firm in June 1937. The other Ford 1-tonner came in July 1925 as MO 5820 and is recorded with a lorry body and an alternative 14-seater open wagonette body, ending its days on goods duties in November 1935. All of the bodies fitted to these Fords were of course inter-changeable without much effort, being held on by just a few coach-bolts.

By 1924 the family residences had become that *Charles senior* and Kezia were at 'Sherwood House' in the High Street, accompanied by the still single *Cecil*, while son *Charles* and his wife Beatrice were nearby at 'Clevedon'. *Bertie* and Jessie were at 'Whitfield' in Broadmoor Road, whilst the nephews were *William* and his wife in the High Street and James and Edith at No.42 Broadmoor Road.

The Daimler Y-type (MD 6090) lasted with *Lovicks* until September 1931, though latterly on haulage work as the pace of coach design passed through rapid phases throughout the 1920's. Indeed, it was replaced on the coaching side from May 1927 by a Graham Bros. 24hp chassis, which was supplied and bodied by Vincents of Reading with a 20-seater all-weather chara body. Registered RX 127 it also had a brown and black livery when new, and it embodied a much lower design of chassis frame and a 6-cylinder engine of American origins, being the precursor of later Dodge developments in the UK.

The Graham Bros. RX 127 is shown at Southsea also with Bert Woods at the wheel. The development of the motor coach in those few years is evident.

Around the time of the purchase of the Daimler chara Bert Woods was taken on as a driver, but with such a vehicle as the Graham Bros. the range and frequency of excursions could be much expanded. Once again, this vehicle would end its days on haulage duties, lasting until March 1945, by which time it was in a blue and black livery and assigned to coal deliveries. Bert had actually been born Harry Ernest in 1891 a few miles away in Wokingham, moving to Crowthorne with his marriage to Fannie Lizzie Fox in 1911, residing at 'Chez Nores' in the High Street for many years.

Indeed, by 1938 the all-weather style of body with its removable celluloid side windows and canvas hood, was becoming rather outdated, so on the passenger duties it was replaced in August of that year by a third hand Gilford 166SD-type coach (UW 2615), which had a 26-seater front-entrance saloon coach body by Duple of Hendon. By that date the once widespread Gilfords were becoming a rarity, but this had always been fairly local, being new to the *Ledbury Transport Co. Ltd.*, which traded as *Thackray's Way* and used on its Newbury – Reading – London express services in

October 1929. It became No.38 in that fleet in due course, a number it retained after *Thames Valley* acquired those operations in January 1936. As such it would become *Lovicks* sole coach throughout World War Two, when it was used on contract work, and did not finally go until early 1952.

In May 1931 Morris 'Minor' 8hp van (RX 8585), of the same type much favoured by the Post Office, had been purchased from the main dealers Hewen's Garages of Maidenhead, and it was mainly used for the long-established parcels service based on railway arrivals at Crowthorne Station, for which *Lovicks* were paid on a contract basis.

On the car front, disposals of the earlier types are lacking, but in February 1932 a new Ford saloon (RX 9816) was received, whilst a 1934 Armstrong-Siddeley 15hp (RD 5794) came to them when about a year old.

On the excursions side, they had continued with much the same range of trips, and when Road Service Licenses were granted in 1931 they had authorised excursions to-

Aldershot (evening excursion)	For tattoo only
Ascot	On race days
Bognor Regis	Day excursion
Brighton	Day excursion
Goodwood	On race days
Portsmouth & Southsea	Day excursion
Windsor	Afternoon trip
Worthing	Day excursion

A lot of trade also resulted from various special shows at venues such as Wembley in North London, as well as the pantomime season at the theatres and the many other one-off annual shows within striking distance.

As already noted, *Charles senior* held the license of the Crowthorne Inn until January 1935, when he persuaded a not entirely enthusiastic Bill & Hattie Jaycock to take it over, presumably because he was so used to a free beer! However, despite their reluctance, they did continue through to September 1950, making the family connection of 57 years in total. Charles was of course well into his 70's by the outbreak of war in 1939, and in that year we find the first reference to *Lovick Bros.* However, their father continued to take an active interest in the business until he 'retired' in 1948. Their mother had died in 1942, but *Charles* lived until 1953, reckoned at the time to be his 94th year. After Bill and Hattie gave up the pub they lived nearby at 'Redvers' in Church Road, though Bill only outlasted his father-in-law by one year, passing away aged 70.

With another world war now out of the way, thoughts turned to meeting the pent-up demand for excursions as an antidote to the continuing years of austerity. New coaches were very scarce, with shortages of good

timber, aluminium and steel, so it would be some years before any such vehicles were likely. As it was, the *Lovick* boys were on good terms with *Reg Try* of *Windsorian Coaches*, who made some coaches available to them in April 1949. These consisted of a pair of the rare forward-control version of the Dennis 'Ace' of January 1936 (JB 7736/7), and these carried Duple 24-seater front-entrance coach bodies. Both were re-painted as two-tone blue, as indeed the earlier Gilford is believed to have been so treated.

The following month *Windsorian* also released 1931 Dennis 'Arrow' coach RX 8569, with a Duple front-entrance 31-seater 'sunsaloon' body. Evidently, with this came another identical coach (RX 8570), though not required by *Lovicks,* and it was re-sold to *Harry Luff* of Leatherhead. The other side of this good relationship was that if *Reg Try* was short of coaches, he would often turn to them for hire-ins.

Alan Lambert caught the Dennis 'Arrow' RX 8569 at Southsea in the Lovick twin-blue livery.

Following *Charlie Lovick's* retirement a number of changes came about, the most notable being the ending of taxi work from April 1949. The car fleet included the 1932 Ford (RX 9816), the Armstrong-Siddeley (RD 5794) and a Hillman saloon car (CPA 126) which had been reputedly purchased following the death of the Duke of Connaught at nearby Bagshot Park in 1942. These, along with the Morris 'Minor' van (RX 8585) all went to a Reading car dealer for disposal during April, the van's primary role now being redundant with the nationalisation of the railway's road parcels traffic. This is no record of exactly when haulage work ceased, though it is believed it ceased when the war ended.

A new partnership was then formed with another long-established local family with business interests, with the Lovick brothers joining with *Charles Bell.* The latter had originally worked at the Royal Aircraft Factory a few miles away over the Hampshire border at Farnborough, after which he had developed his shop selling electrical goods in Crowthorne High Street. The new partnership came into effect on 1st September 1949 and was known as *Lovick Motors Ltd.,* one of the other shareholders being local sheetmetal-worker *C.F. Taylor,* who would go on to head a considerably larger concern in due course in Molly Millars Lane, Wokingham. However, at that time he was merely renting space from the Lovicks, though his presence there did lead to them being listed locally as bodybuilders in the 1950/1 local directory.

Under the new partnership all the garage facilities continued to be offered, along with the coaches, and there was even a revival of some taxi work again, along with self-drive hire cars and a 24-hour breakdown service, with *Charlie Bell* as Managing Director. The coal business also continued for a little longer, before being sold to the other local merchants, the Masons, who had their office just around the corner of the High Street in Dukes Ride. Other Lovick and Bell lines also had other local business interests in the village, including a wool shop, something no place would be without in those days of popular knitting.

The Austin GMO 14 at Wembley hired to Windsorian.

There was also some investment in the coach fleet during 1951, a year of increased optimism fuelled by the staging of the Festival of Britain. Delivered in May was an Austin K4/CXD-type with a fully-fronted 32-seater front-entrance coach body (GMO 14), followed in July by a half-cab Guy 'Arab' MkIII with a Meadows 6DC630 engine of 10.35 litres (GMO 418) and carrying a 35-seater front-entrance coach body. Both bodies were by Thurgoods of Ware and finished in light blue with dark blue trim, whilst on their sides was a circular area with an 'L' monogram, surrounded by *Lovick Motors Ltd.* and Crowthorne and incorporating a winged device.

The arrival of the above coaches saw the disposal of the Gilford coach (UW 2615) in February 1952, leaving the pair of Dennis 'Aces' and the 'Arrow' to make up the 5-strong fleet. However, the 'Arrow' (RX 8569) went at the end of June 1953, whilst one of the 'Aces' (JB 7737) was withdrawn at the end of September 1954, followed by the other example (JB 7736) during the following March, leaving only the 1951 deliveries still active. Although the second 'Ace' was sold, the other had been retained and still lingered in the yard.

Charlie Bell had not married, and as a keen follower of horse-racing he kept a couple of retired horses in the nearby stables of the Prince Alfred pub. Sadly, however, he collapsed and died whilst attending the Cheltenham Gold Cup meeting in March 1954 at the age of 51. Following that tragedy, his business interests passed to his elder brother *George Francis Bell* (born 1899), so the Bell-Lovick partnership did continue through to 1956, the year in which *Bertie Lovick* reached the age of 65.

The decision was taken to sell the garage business as a going concern, after which it would become Crowthorne Motors, but it was also decided not to continue coaching into the 1956 season. Again, this aspect of the business found a ready buyer in *Brimblecombe Bros.* just a few miles away in Wokingham, who took over in January 1956, inheriting the road service licenses and the private hire diary. They also acquired the 1951 Austin (GMO 14) and Guy (GMO 418) of that same year, both of which were repainted into their red, maroon and cream livery for further service until 1962 and 1961 respectively. Also passed to them was the 'Ace' still in the yard, but that was sold to a dealer direct from the Crowthorne site. Other photos of former *Lovick* vehicles will of course be found under the *Brimblecombe* heading.

Bertie Lovick lived to reach 74 in 1965, whilst *Charles* passed away in 1972 aged 83, having moved to Weston-super-Mare. The other brother active in the business was *Cecil* (known as 'Ticker'), who died in 1962 aged 65. The family and its various businesses have long been remembered in Crowthorne, and it was through its pioneering charabanc that many from the village got their first glance of the seaside.

This advert appeared in the local press during 1952.

Marlow & District Motor Services
Marlow, Buckinghamshire

The full account of the development and operations of this concern were covered in the Early Independents of the Henley & Marlow Area, so here we shall only look at the service that reached Wokingham, after the established Marlow – Henley – Twyford route was projected onwards from the Autumn of 1929.

Way back in 1919 the *British Automobile Traction Co. Ltd.* had listed a Henley to Wokingham service as one of its proposed routes, but it had not come to fruition. So perhaps that the *Thames Valley*-associated *Marlow & District* did put that in place was at last an attempt to plug that gap.

The latter applied to Wokingham BC for licenses on 5th September, which were granted, though the exact date the service commenced is not known. 4 journeys were extended on from Twyford to the town, using a route past Twyford Station and via Hurst village and on to Winnersh Crossroads.

Quite how the service fared is not recorded in the GM's reports of the parent Thames Valley concern, though when newer buses came in December 1929 all were licensed with Wokingham BC. It seems that the curtailment of that section had much to do with the decision to extend the Marlow – Henley – Twyford route through to Reading from May 1931, which also linked the Marlow – High Wycombe section to form a 23-mile long route. No doubt it was necessary to better use the new buses to cover those operations, so as part of that re-organisation the Wokingham part of the route map was discontinued from 4th February.

Marlow & District Karrier CL4-type KX 3901 was one of the batch licensed by Wokingham BC, seen here in a photo by John Parke outside The Crown Hotel at Marlow on a departure to Twyford.

Povey & Smith, Povey Bros. and Bernard A.W. Smith
Sonning & Woodley Bus Service
Sonning-on-Thames, Berkshire

The riverside village of Sonning-on-Thames lies some 3.5 miles east of Reading and had actually been on the original route of the *British Automobile Traction Co. Ltd.* service between Maidenhead and Reading which started in July 1915. The *BAT,* and from July 1920 those of the succeeding *Thames Valley Traction Co. Ltd.* continued to serve the village in some form.

Although the mainline railway passed very close to the village, the nearest stations were Reading and, for those heading east, at Twyford some 2.5 miles away by road. Indeed, the Road Motors of the *Great Western Railway* would provide a link from 21st October 1924 using a small Chevrolet bus at suitable times for trains at either Twyford or Reading, whilst there had been a horse-drawn service between the French Horn Hotel and Reading to meet trains in pre-Great War days, which was operated by a local coachbuilder but presumably killed off when horses were requisitioned.

However, in the meantime *John Caleb Povey* had been born at Mortimer in Berkshire on 8th July 1892, though by 1901 the family had relocated to Swyncombe, some halfway between Nettlebed and Watlington in Oxfordshire, where his father John was a carter on a farm. By 1911 they had again moved to 'Millers Cottages' at Sonning Eye, over on the Oxfordshire bank of the River Thames but within hailing distance of Sonning-on-Thames, young John now having joined his father as the under-carter on the farm, whilst his 9-year old brother Arthur was noted as born in Reading.

There is no surviving military service record for John for the Great War, though he may have been the driver recorded with the Royal Garrison Artillery. However, John started undertaking haulage work in his own right in due course, though the precise date has not been discovered, and the first motor vehicle known to be licensed to him was BL 9702 of March 1922, the make of which is not recorded, though perhaps an ex-WD vehicle from the nearby Slough Dump? By the time of its arrival the partnership of *Povey & Smith* was evident. Again, it is unclear if any passenger-carrying featured at that point, as vehicles often had inter-changeable bodies at that time.

The service records for *Bernard Albert William Smith* have, however, survived, so we shall review them now. At the time he enlisted he was living with his mother at 'Hemingford Cottage' over at Farnham Common in Buckinghamshire, and gave his calling at driver/motor engineer and his birth year as 1898 and his place of birth as Painswick in Gloucerstershire.

He joined the Army Service Corps (Mechanical Transport) on 1st March 1916 and some 6 months later was mobilised at Grove Park ASC Deport in Lee, south London as part of 373rd MT Coy, subsequently transferring to the 478th in 1917 and the 615th in 1918, all around the Bulford Camp area of Salisbury Plain or other southern army locations. He was sent to France from Southampton in October 1918 as part of the ASC 1129nd MT Coy under the 47th Ambulance Convoy as part of a mass clearance of injured soldiers from the continent as the war came to a close, before being demobbed himself in February 1919. Why he came to Sonning is not known, but his first recorded vehicles was BL 9007 in August 1921, likely an ex-WD type.

However, for their entry into bus operation *John Povey* and *Bernard A.W. Smith* placed a 1-ton Model T Ford on the road from 18th July 1922 as MO 203. It carried a 14-seater bus body, whilst later details note that it had a blue-liveried bus body as well as a black-painted truck body.

The Ford was followed by a similar bus on 12th September 1922 as MO 508, and this time the 14-seater bus body was finished in white and brown, the variance in colour schemes suggesting they purchased it as ready-made stock from a dealer.

The service ran from Sonning (French Horn Hotel) to Reading (Blagrave Street) and operated via Pound Lane Turn – Sonning Golf Course – Woodley Avenue. It should be appreciated that Woodley was at that time just a small settlement surrounded by several large private estates such as Bulmershe Court.

This had probably started with the arrival of the first bus, but in order to comply with the hackney carriage bye-laws of Reading Borough Council, *Povey & Smith* had both buses licensed with that authority from 19th September 1922. On that same date a driver's license was approved for *John Povey* of 'The Pit', Sonning, as well as a conductor's license for his brother *Arthur Povey* of the same address, whilst John married local girl Daisy Cullum on 2nd April 1923.

Tickets confirm that the title *Sonning & Woodley Bus Service* was used, whilst advertising on the reverse promoted the haulage work under *Povey & Smith*. No timetables have survived regarding the service, but it must surely have operated at least several times per day, probably with a reduced service on Wednesday for the early-closing day.

To judge by later events it would seem that *Bernard Smith* was primarily occupied with the haulage activities, as well as some charabanc work, making use of the vehicles noted above. However, when RBC renewed licenses on 22nd May 1923 they did so as him and *John Povey* both as drivers and no further listing of any conductors. By that date *Bernard Smith* was at 'Vine Cottage', Pound Lane in Sonning, whilst *John* was now at Thames Terrace nearer to the riverside. As both buses were still licensed with RBC this also would seem to mark an increase in the frequency of operation, though no actual timetables have survived.

John Povey also undertook coal deliveries from the 1920's, though again no firm dates have been found. By May 1925 the *Poveys* and *Mr. Smith* had gone their own ways, with the latter then advertising as a haulage contractor and owner of an 18-seater owner-driven pneumatic-tyred charabanc. He was still at 'Vine Cottages' and could be found advertising until at least 1929.

Despite the ending of the partnership with *Smith*, the bus service continued, along with some haulage work, and on 30th May 1925 *Povey Bros.* put a third Ford 1-tonner on the road as MO 5436, equipped with a 14-seater bus body.

Although *Thames Valley* had fielded its own Ford T-type 'chasers' on the A4 between Maidenhead and Reading to harass the buses of *Ranger & Simmonds (Reliance)* during 1922-3 it does not seem to have particularly targeted the Sonning-based concern. However, the Board of the '*Valley*' heard on 20th May 1926 that a letter had been sent a week before from *Povey Bros.* to indicate that they were mindful of disposing of their bus service in order to develop the haulage business.

The offer of £100 for the goodwill of the service was accepted by *Povey Bros.* and soon afterwards *Thames Valley* started a new un-numbered service to run as Reading (St. Marys Butts) – Woodley – Sandford Mill – Hurst in order to serve the Woodley area, with Sonning passengers catered for by the main Route 1 (Maidenhead – Reading) with the competition gone.

Povey Bros. continued with the coal deliveries and general haulage work, though MO 293 was elsewhere by September 1927, and even the 1925 model MO 5436 had been sold by May 1927. There is little information on MO 508, which was still with them, but had gone elsewhere to be last licensed by a Dorset owner on 30th September 1929.

Certainly *Povey Bros.* were still listed as haulage contractors in the 1928 directory, but by 1929 only *John C. Povey* is included as a coal merchant, that trade having probably continued throughout the period under review. Indeed, he is still found as such in 1932, listed as of 'The Elms', Sonning Eye in 1933, but had gone from local directories by 1934, but he died in 1972 in Sutton Coldfield in Warwickshire.

Bernard Smith continues to be shown as a charabanc proprietor in the 1928-9 directories, but is absent by 1932, from which it can be concluded that he did not continue under the new more stringent requirements of the 1930 Road Traffic Act.

Some examples of the tickets used on the bus service will be found in colour on the back cover.

Perkins Bros.
Wokingham, Berkshire

The Perkins Brothers only had a fairly brief involvement with charabanc work, though their effect on the wider history of motoring in Wokingham was considerably more.

Their father had been born at Hobart in Tasmania, duly reaching Wokingham with his London-born wife, and they ran a stationer's and fancy goods shop. Son *Eric Heard Perkins* had been born at Hobart in 1879, but his brother *Frank Stanley* was born in Wokingham in 1889. The family were at No.8 Denmark Street in 1891, but had relocated to No.78 Rose Street by 1901.

By 1901 we find *Eric Perkins* as a boarder at No.18 Aldershot Road in Willesden, Middlesex, where is working as a cycle-maker. However, by 1905 he was back in Wokingham, living at 'St. Kilda' on the East Heath, just south of the town centre. Although his business was that of cycle and motor-cycle repairer, he was an early advocate of the motor car, placing a chocolate-and-yellow-painted 5.5hp Astor with Speedwell 2-seater body (plus rear 'spider' seat) on the road on 3rd May 1905 as BL 572. He retained the car for 9 years, a remarkable feat at the time, whilst he is also generally acknowledged as being the first person in the town to offer a motor taxi, though fuller details are not known.

By 1911 the cycle repair shop was established at No.39 Market Place, though developments on the new motor garage post-Great War would be centred on Nos.40/42 Broad Street, at the junction with Shute End and Rectory Road, ideally placed to attract the attention of most motorists passing through the town.

However, at 1911 *Frank Perkins* was not yet involved in the business, as he was a confectioner at that time, though the war years would see both brothers driving motor vehicles, leading to their post-war ventures. Also in 1913 *Ernest* had married in Wokingham.

Eric Perkins was the elder by a decade, though being older than the initial recruitment group, entered war service in February 1917, by which time he was living at No.19 Milton Road in Wokingham. He had wanted to join the Royal Flying Corps., but he was assigned to the Army Service Corps and sent to Grove Park in south London for assessment, where he was passed as a light car driver and motor mechanic. From October 1917 to December 1918 he was in East Africa, whilst he records show he contracted malaria in Daresalaam.

Frank also entered the war in November 1917, and served as a driver for the French Red Cross, both brothers returning home safely after the conflict.

Post-war the focus was understandably on motor vehicles, though the cyclist was not forgotten, and for some years the CTC (Cyclist's Touring Club) emblem was displayed to show that repairs were available. A short way east of Wokingham was Easthampstead Park, the seat of the Marquis of Downshire, himself a very keen early motorist, who regularly placed orders with *Perkins Bros.* for his stable of motors, though at times he also favoured Vincent's of Reading.

Apart from taxi work from an early date, other passenger transport waited until 7th July 1920, when the brothers placed a charabanc based on a French Delauney-Belleville chassis on the road. That was, however, not a new vehicle, originating as a large car in 1907, but now carrying a 13-seater chara body painted blue and re-registered in the Heavy Motor Car Series as BL 0343. Under the 1920 Road Traffic Act from January 1921 such a category was discontinued, so it was re-registered yet again as BL 8446.

The brothers ran some excursions to various local and seaside destinations, making them Wokingham's original charabanc operators, whilst the vehicle was also popular for private hire. Despite that apparent success, it seems that after the 1921 season they took the decision to cease such work, in order to expand the garage facilities, the vehicle being sold to an owner at Whitby on the North Yorkshire coast.

And with that sale *Perkins Bros.* left the scene as regards large-scale passenger activities, though their garage went from strength to strength, whilst as late as 1922 the cycle repair premises at Market Place were still in use. The garage by then had space for 6 cars under repair, along with RAC and AA accreditation, with a 7-day 24-hour breakdown service on offer. At that point they were agents for Singer and Overland, but would in time become the local Morris agency.

The Perkins Bros. Garage at the eastern end of Broad Street, this 1928 photo showing Morris demonstrators of various models for a local motor show hosted there.

Thomas Spragg & Johnny Wooff
The Progressive Bus Company
Bracknell, Berkshire

Tom Spragg had been born at Glastonbury in Somerset in 1874, and his parents then lived in Old Road. By 1891 he was working as a baker, still living at home but now relocated to Wells Road. However, by 1900 he was evidently in Faringdon, in north-west Berkshire, where he married Georgina Emma Pinniger from nearby Buckland. A year later the couple were to be found at No.36 Bennett Road in the seaside Hampshire town of Bournemouth, where he was a bread baker on his own account.

Further business moves saw them at Bromley-by-Bow in East London by 1907, where their only son Bertram Henry was born, then by 1911 they were at No.6 Kincraig Street in Cardiff, where Tom was a foreman bread baker. However, the family moved once again by 1915, with Tom having his own baker's shop yet again, now at 'Tregea', towards the western end of the High Street in the market town of Bracknell in Berkshire. In that location he duly becomes a general grocer, provision merchant and purveyor of patent medicines, and by 1918 he had opened another branch in the village of Binfield, a few miles west of the town, known as The Up-To-Date-Stores. He also owned a parcel of land at that location and would also take on other houses which he continued to rent out.

In what appears to be his first brush with the provision of public transport, in May 1919 he purchased a secondhand Ford Model T 20hp car (BL 5460), new in 1917, which he had the classification changed to a public conveyance. It had a blue and black body and is reckoned to be the first motor taxi on offer in the town, but for how long he continued that type of work is not known, and possibly driven by Johnny Wooff?

Sometime shortly before 1923 he sold the Binfield store to another, along with the plot of land, in order to make money available for his next venture.

In the meantime, the younger *Johnny Wooff* had been born at Bracknell in May 1894, the son of George Wooff, who had a blacksmithy in Stanley Road, just a short way off the High Street, and where the he lived with his wife Jane in 'Church Villas'. However, Johnny did not follow his father's trade, and by 1911 he was a motor mechanic. In due course he opened The Central Garage, some three-quarters of the way up the eastern (top) end of the High Street. As such, there seems little doubt that *Spragg and Wooff's* paths will have crossed, and as the garage is also attributed as being the original taxi provider in the town, it seems likely that both were involved with the Ford as already noted above.

The two men brought their respective resources together from Easter Sunday 1st April 1923, when they started a bus service between Ascot (Horse & Groom) and Reading, in direct competition with the buses of the *Thames Valley Traction Co. Ltd.* However, that operator was using its mostly ex-War Department J-type Thornycrofts, which carried former *London General* B-type double-deck bodies of an ancient design and were running on solid tyres.

In comparison, *Spragg & Wooff* bought a pair of Ford T-type 1-tonners from Rice & Harper, the Ford agents at Guildford, who also built for them the 14-seater bus bodies. These were registered as MO 1196/7 on 24th March 1923, and they bore a grey and green livery. At that point the venture was shared equally between the two partners, and both were also licensed with Reading Borough Council as drivers, aided by George Probert of No.6 Temperance Cottages in Binfield Road.

Reading BC had by then brought in various measures in order to control town centre traffic, mainly with the idea of keeping certain roads free for the passage of the Corporation tramcars, so this new service was given the Butter Market as its terminal point, reached from London Road by way of London Street and Duke Street, whereas the *Thames Valley* service entered from London Road, then Southampton Street and Bridge Street to terminate in St. Mary's Butts and took 70 minutes between Ascot and Reading.

From the outset the rationale of the competition was to provide a much faster service between the towns, with the bus running as Ascot (Horse & Groom) – Bracknell (High Street) – Binfield (Popeswood) – Wokingham (Town Hall) – Winnersh (Crossroads) – Earley (Three Tuns) – Reading. In order to out-run the opposition, these small buses carried conductors, with 18-year old Terrance ('Ted') Brennan of 'Oak Hill Cottages', Old Bracknell and 16-year old James Thomas ('Jimmy') Matthews of Bay Road, Bullbrook being the first pair licensed, neither wishing to follow their fathers into the local brickworks. They were joined from 17th April by 16-year old Cecil Charles ('Charlie') Tate of 'Kingsley Terrace', Wokingham Road, Bracknell, having been born at nearby Chavey Down as a policeman's son.

The service certainly proved a popular one, and a third Ford Ford 1-tonner was obtained from Rice & Harper's showroom stock and licensed as MO 1647 on 8th June 1923. This had a rather larger bus body seating 14 and it was painted as smoke grey, and its purchase allowed the as yet untapped potential traffic from Binfield village, which at the time only had the limited facilities offered by local carriers. Indeed, *Tom Spragg* had written to Easthampstead Rural District Council in May 1923 stating the intention to run some buses through the village, and although that authority did not exercise any powers over hackney carriages, it was responsible for the upkeep of the highways. It did agree to the principle of such a service, but stipulated that only the small buses currently proposed were to be used, and also that it would review the situation after 14 days. As it was also concerned that *Thames Valley* would follow suit in running via Binfield, the Clerk was instructed to inform that company of such restrictions, adding that if the operators flouted the requirements the Council would refer the matter to the Minister of Transport. However, both Reading BC and Wokingham BC were happy to license the buses.

Whereas the first pair of Fords had only perimeter seating, and are believed to have been entered through the centre of the rear, the third example featured all forward-facing seats with a front entrance, whilst for the first few months of operation the service was only known as the *The Grey Bus.* Also, earlier tickets are annotated 'TS', for Thomas Spragg, though later ones carried no title, but are identified by the stages shown.

The journeys through Binfield village proceeded down the Binfield Road – Stag & Hounds Y-roads – Binfield Crossroads (Royal Standard) – Terrace Road (The Roebuck) – St. Marks Road, to emerge again onto the A329 at Popeswood (Shoulder of Mutton). By June 1923 an evening journey left Ascot (Royal Foresters) and ran along the High Street (Horse & Groom) before extending onto the Sunninghill & Ascot Picture House, and that month patrons could see Pauline Frederick in 'The Sting of the Lash', Mandie Dunham in 'Sheer Bluff', as well as looking forward to the 'Four Horsemen of the Apocalypse'' and the Prisoner of Zenda', with a suitably timed bus home for patrons.

Tom Spragg had originally lived over the shop in the High Street, but around the time the bus service started he had a new house called 'Edenfield' built a short way over the summit of the High Street eastwards on the London Road. Accommodation for the buses had not been practical at either his shop yard or the Central Garage, and the trio of Fords were kept in the yard of George Wooff's blacksmith yard and accessed via Sawmill Lane, just to the south of the High Street.

As envisaged by the ERDC, *Thames Valley* soon began to divert some buses via Binfield village to counter the competition, leading to a motion to prevent that being placed before the Council on 23rd August 1923, such objection centring on the Company not having previously applied for the same. However, at the meeting the Clerk noted that *Thames Valley* had phoned its request, and that it had also undertaken not

to use buses larger than 14-seaters, so the objection was removed.

The buses transferred to cover these duties were a pair of 1922 Ford T-type 1-tonner 'chasers' as Cars 54/5 (MO 773/4), which carried Vincent B14F bodies and were in an all over red livery without fleetnames, earning them the local nickname 'the scarlet runners'. These had previously been used against competition between Maidenhead and Reading to good effect, and extra crews were drafted into Ascot Dormy Shed to man these, with working hours approaching 100 a week being clocked up.

Whereas the little grey Fords of the Bracknell-based concern could easily out-run the lumbering J-type Thornycroft double-deckers, *Thames Valley* now used its similar little buses to overtake those Fords, effectively sandwiching the grey machines, or just raced ahead to cream off the traffic!

However, the advent of the grey buses had attracted much local support, so the venture was not that easily defeated, especially as Binfield now had a new service thanks to *Spragg & Wooff.* Of course, Tom still owned properties in the village, and on one occasion he was driving the bus when he was approached by a tenant, who told him that grass was growing up through the floorboards, and demanding he did something about it. To that he said he would come around with his shears and cut it personally!

Having pioneered these faster links, the next phase was to build on the popular aspects of the routes, and that was achieved in several ways. Firstly, there was a call for a permanent extension to serve Sunninghill, and in that connection a larger bus would be needed. In order to resolve both issues, the route was extended about a mile further east-wards from Ascot High Street onto the Cordes Hall in Kings Road, Sunninghill, and that started with the delivery of a 20-seater.

The new bus was a sleek and speedy Italian-built Lancia 'Tertaiota' on pneumatic tyres. It was registered as MO 2213 on 16th October 1923, and its front-entrance body was by Bartle of Notting Hill, who bodied a number of such chassis. It bore a livery of 'aluminium and maroon', the latter colour applied to the mudguards only, and for the first recorded time *Progressive,* made its appearance as a fleetname, painted in large gold script lettering along the body sides, confirming that the title *The Progressive Bus Company* had now been adopted. The riding qualities of this bus were such that many locals chose to use it for the pleasure of the journey, and there is little doubt that its arrival stole the march over the *Thames Valley* buses in use, which would not receive pneumatic tyres for another 4 years. With the new bus added another crew was found, as 39-year old former gardener Harry

The first Lancia MO 2213 at the Reading terminus by St. Laurence's Church and near the Butter Market. Queen Victoria turns her back on the rivalry between Thames Valley and Progressive, whilst the building to the left of the church was lost in the WW2 bombing raid. The window stickers read 'REDUCED FARES'.

Headington as a driver and 15-year old Bertram Spragg now joining the family business as a conductor.

The tickets used on the buses from the outset were mainly standard issue Bell Punch stock for the values of 2d, 4d, 6d, 8d and 1 shilling, but once the 'fares war' phase started by *Thames Valley* was entered, after the chasers had failed to defeat *Progressive*, some other values were printed up by the High Street printing department of Lawrences Stores to give intermediate values of one penny and a ha'penny and 3 pence (as shown in monochrome and actual size below). All known tickets of either variety offered redemption of their face value against purchases at Lawrence Stores, of which there were branches at Ascot and elsewhere.

In keeping with the earlier undertaking not to use buses of over 14 seats on the journeys via Binfield, the new Lancia was to be found on the main-line along the A329. Unfortunately, no actual timetables for the Ascot/Sunninghill – Reading service have come to light, but suffice it to say that the journey time by little Ford or speedy Lancia was about two-thirds of that taken by the Thornycrofts, despite the legal speed limit then being 12mph for larger buses.

Although the original partnership between *Tom Spragg* and *Johnny Wooff* had been on an equal basis, funding for the Lancia had come from Spragg, and as Johnny could not match that investment, he duly sold his interest to his partner. Indeed, once established the buses were in the daily care of the other licensed drivers and conductors. Harry Headington is seen below from his service during the Great War as a motor driver.

The Fords remained garaged in the blacksmiths yard, but the Lancia could not be kept there, so it was stabled in a large shed at the coachbuilder and garage owner

Frank Gough, about 100 yards further eastwards on the London Road from *Mr. Spragg's* home and on the opposite side. However, in order to better address the garaging needs, perhaps also in connection with *Wooff* no longer being responsible for maintenance, plans were drawn up for the construction of a proper brick-built garage on a plot of land between *Tom's* house and Larges Lane at its junction with London Road. In fact adjacent to that was another sizeable shed in use by James Dow Manners, a coachbuilder. He had been born in Dundee, Scotland in 1867 and had been established in Bracknell since at least 1903, in Stanley Road and then Wokingham Road, before relocating there as a tenant of *Tom Spragg,* and his fuller significance to this story will reveal itself in due course.

The building plans were laid before ERDC and given approval on 7th February 1924, after which work started immediately to produce a garage large enough for 6 full-size single-deck buses. There is little doubt that the intense competition with *Progressive* caused the *Thames Valley* management to consider its own accommodation issues, as the double barn at Englemere Farm, just west of Ascot High Street was becoming insufficient and lacked facilities for maintenance. It therefore resolved that it would build a new garage off the High Street in Course Road and re-arrange its services to form a through Windsor – Ascot – Bracknell – Wokingham – Reading route, with four journeys taking in Binfield village. It should of course be noted that its forebear *The British Automobile Traction Co. Ltd.* had continually served the Sunningdale – Ascot – Bracknell – Wokingham – Reading route since December 1915, though the advent of the 'silver Lancia' had been the biggest upset to date!

The Progressive garage is seen in later years when it was used by Jackie Strachan of Wokingham Road as a satellite site. See Location Map on page 61.

As already noted, the *Thames Valley* Ford 'chasers' were taken off with the opening of the Ascot Garage in May 1924, though Car 54 (MO 773) found a more peaceful role as the Depot Lorry based there. However, the *'Valley'* now used its size to start a fares war, with the Ascot to Reading fare slashed from 2s 9d to just 2s, so *Progressive* responded and put 'Reduced Fares' posters in its bus windows.

Tom Spragg also had another vehicle, registered in 1920 as a van (BW 2402), of unknown make but new to E.J. Butler of Henley, though it is understood to have been used in connection with the shop – home deliveries also being undertaken, quite likely a Ford.

In order to maintain the seating capacity throughout the day a further 20-seater was needed, and the chance arose to purchase another Lancia quite cheaply. It was one of a number of the earlier Z-type chassis which had become available as reconditioned but previously un-registered items, and was mechanically similar to the 'Tetraiota'. The body for this was contracted to a Reading firm, believed to be Vincents, but *Spragg* came to note its rather slow progress. The suspicion was that the coachbuilder had been 'got at' by *Thames Valley,* perhaps through the possibility of a larger order from that Company, and that go-slow tactics were in use. So, as soon as the framing was complete, he had it driven away and brought back to Bracknell!

The task of completing the 20-seater front-entrance bus body then fell to James Manners, though the work took place inside the bus garage, where he used the Bartle example as a pattern to complete what was certainly the largest project he would ever handle! The completed bus was registered as MO 3530 on 3rd July 1924, some 8 months after the chassis was purchased. A further driver was taken on that month, being 33-year old Fred Willoughby, a former postman who lived in Camberley. With a pair of Lancias now in use, more passengers could enjoy the faster ride, though the antics of the bus drivers saw Wokingham BC threatening to withhold licenses if matters did not improve.

Sometime after the arrival of the second Lancia, another route was pioneered, but the exact date is not known, though a timetable appeared in the local press on Saturday 13th October 1924. As a new link entirely, this was a major coup by *Progressive,* in that it had spotted a weakness in the territorial agreement that had for many years existed between *Thames Valley* and *Aldershot & District*, which had identified the A30 as the boundary between operating areas. For much of that time the two concerns had shared the same Chairman in Sidney Garcke, and the understanding was that each would not cross that road without consultation with the other, which had left Crowthorne without bus links to other towns.

The new route ran from Reading and far as Wokingham, before turning south to serve Nine Mile Ride – Crowthorne (Station) – Crowthorne – Sandhurst – Camberley (Duke of York), which also gave end-to-end competition with the *'Valley's* route from Reading to Camberley via Shinfield – Eversley – Yateley. *Progressive's* 19-mile route was timetabled at 1 hour 10 minutes, whereas the TV Route 9 of only 16 miles took 1 hour and 25 minutes. The full timetable for the *Progressive* service included the bus working out or back between Bracknell and Wokingham before taking up the duty-

PROGRESSIVE BUS TIME TABLE UNTIL FURTHER NOTICE.

WEEKDAYS ONLY.

READING (Market Place) TO CAMBERLEY (Duke of York).

	a.m.	a.m.	p.m.	p.m.
READING .... dep.	—	11 30	2 55	5 55
King Street	—	11 52	3 17	6 17
Embrook	—	11 56	3 21	6 21
Wokingham	9 15	12 0	3 25	6 25
Hand Post Corner	9 20	12 5	3 30	6 30
The Bridge	9 24	12 9	3 34	6 34
Wellington College	9 29	12 14	3 39	6 39
Crowthorne (Prince Alfred)	9 34	12 19	3 44	6 44
Little Sandhurst	9 40	12 25	3 50	6 50
Sandhurst Halt	9 43	12 28	3 53	6 53
Wellington Arms	9 47	12 32	3 57	6 57
Jolly Farmer	9 50	12 35	4 0	7 0
CAMBERLEY (Duke of York Hotel) ...... arr.	9 55	12 40	4 5	7 5

CAMBERLEY (Duke of York) TO READING (Market Place)

	a.m.	p.m.	p.m.	p.m.
CAMBERLEY (Duke of York Hotel) ... dep.	10 0	1 45	4 25	7s 10
Jolly Farmer	10 5	1 50	4 30	7s 15
Wellington Arms	10 8	1 53	4 33	7s 18
Sandhurst Halt	10 12	1 57	4 37	7s 22
Little Sandhurst	10 15	2 0	4 40	7s 25
Crowthorne (Prince Alfred)	10 21	2 6	4 46	7s 31
Wellington College Station	10 26	2 10	4 51	7s 36
The Bridge	10 31	2 15	4 56	7s 41
Hand Post Corner	10 35	2 19	5 0	7s 45
Wokingham	10 40	2 23	5 5	7s 50
Embrook	10 44	2 27	5 9	—
King Street	10 48	2 31	5 13	—
READING .... arr.	11 10	2 52	5 35	—

s To Wokingham only.

A further pair of Lancias was ordered as complete vehicles this time, both being of the more powerful and larger 'Pentaiota' type and fitted with 25-seater front-entrance bodies by Strachan & Brown of Acton, a regular combination at that date. These arrived in February 1925 as MO 4648 and in May as MO 5443, and both carried the full *Progressive Bus Service* on the body sides and were in the silver-grey and maroon scheme.

The arrival of the further Lancias saw the demise of the original pair of Fords (MO 1196/7), both of which found owners elsewhere, with the later Ford (MO 1647) carrying on its duties via Binfield village until about July 1925, when it was replaced by one of the 20-seater Lancias.

As already noted, the local police were not amused by the tactics used by the drivers of the competing bus operators, and in May 1925 driver Harry Headington of *Progressive* found himself before the Wokingham Police Court summonsed for dangerous driving. Giving evidence PC Fletcher said that at 11.20am on 6th May the defendant's bus arrived at Wokingham slightly before that of *Thames Valley*, and both buses stopped outside the Town Hall. The *TV* double-decker set off first, followed by the *Progressive* bus which, along by the Post Office, then shot out to the wrong side of Broad Street in order to overtake the double-deck bus, a dangerous practice the witness considered.

George Edmunds, the driver of the *Thames Valley* bus, gave evidence that the defendant's bus cut in front of him dangerously. However, the defendant stated that the *TV* driver was well out towards the wrong side of the road, but as soon as he had passed it he returned to his correct side. The Mayor and local JP Admiral J.B. Eustace noted there had been many complaints about the way buses came through Wokingham, particularly along the narrow Shute End exit from Broad Street (where he lived!), adding that he saw no reason for

immense hurry to get to Reading! Indeed, the TV General Manager's Report of June 1925 pointed out abstraction of passengers by over-taking smaller buses.

The Police had spoken well of the defendant, who had served in the Army Service Corps from 1915-9, so he was on this occasion fined £1 (about one-third his weekly pay), but he was warned that if he re-offended then fine would be considerably more. In 1939 he can be found working on his own right as a coal merchant based in Skimped Hill Lane, so still in Bracknell.

That the service to Camberley proved popular is borne out by the need to buy a larger bus at short notice, so this time *Tom Spragg* turned to the nearest supplier of Dennis Bros. about 16 miles away at Guildford. They supplied him with a 2.5-tonner fitted with Strachan & Brown 30-seater rear-entrance bus body, probably from showroom stock. It was licensed as MO 6184 on 14th September 1925, gaining a hackney carriage license from Reading BC on 1st October, though used from as soon as it arrived.

Remarkably, the Dennis was posed for official photos by the chassis-maker, though its reign was to be short. The livery remained 'silver-grey' and maroon for all the larger buses.

However, the latest bus was to see only very short service with *Progressive*, as in the meantime *Thames Valley* had made *Tom Spragg* an offer to buy him out! Indeed, it was a measure of his competition that *TV's* offer was £5500 for the services, the 5 buses and also the garage at Bracknell. Apparently, he did of course realise that it was only a matter of time before the greater resources of *Thames Valley* and its financial backers would prevail. He also appreciated that such a sum would set him up quite nicely for a further business venture, and the takeover took place on 31st October 1925.

As soon as services finished for the day, the quartet of Lancias were taken into Reading Works, and literally overnight they given a quick repaint into the *'Valley's* livery of red and white, so the first the public knew of the event was when they re-appeared on some of their old duties the following morning!

One of the later pair of 25-seater Lancia 'Pentaiotas' was MO 4648, seen here outside the Horse & Groom in Ascot High Street, then a Noakes of Windsor pub. Ted Brennan was the conductor, whilst the driver was Fred Willoughby (correction to TV 1920-1930), plus Fred Keeley, a local man home on leave from the Army.

On the other hand, the Dennis was very much standard fare for the *Aldershot & District* fleet, so they agreed to buy it off *Thames Valley,* as well as providing £100 in recognition of competition removed along the A30 between Sandhurst and Yorktown. That bus then saw the usual life-span for its type before going on to become a lorry with the well-known dairy producers Cow & Gate of Wincanton, whilst the *A&D* also advised *Thames Valley* that it might in future wish to discuss operations from Camberley into the Sandhurst and Crowthorne area. The *'Valley* operations started from 1st November, initially using 3 Reading-based buses, whilst the Camberley terminus was moved across town to near the Station.

The Lancias were of course far from standard for the *'Valley* fleet, but they did see some use on the services through Binfield village and the long Camberley route until other solutions could be found. In that respect it was decided to erect a Dormy Shed for 3 buses in Cambridge Road, just off Crowthorne High Street, and to allocate some new buses as soon as they were available. As it happened, the batch of Tilling-Stevens B9A saloons then ordered with that in mind would be subjected to a slight delay after Tillings advised that some of the bodies would need to be subbed out due to pressure of work at its Peckham coachworks. These

arrived from May 1926, carrying 32-seater rear-entrance bus bodies, some taking up duties at the newly-completed Dormy Shed. Also reported in the last quarter of 1925 was that an income of some £500 had so far been derived from buses over the Wokingham to Camberley section already.

In respect of the operations between Ascot and Reading, these were soon absorbed into Route 3 by *Thames Valley,* whilst any passengers requiring Sunninghill were obliged to change bus at Ascot.

The quartet of Lancias had become *Thames Valley* Cars 94-7 (MO 3530, MO 2213, MO 4648 and MO 5443), and all were sold in April 1926 to *George Askew* of Loughton in Essex for further passenger service.

In the meantime, *Thames Valley* set about recovering much of the cost of purchasing *Progressive,* as *Tom Spragg* obligingly bought his former bus garage back in January 1926 for £1000, whilst the Lancias brought in £1750, along with the £1100 for the virtually new Dennis taken by *Aldershot & District.*

Tom Spragg then bought a small fleet of Peerless lorries, from the Slough Sales it is believed, with which he undertook mainly sand and gravel haulage for a few years before selling that on as well. Although *Progressive* had gone, it would be well remembered for many years, especially the 'silver Lancias', which had made a great impression locally. Indeed, it would not be until the covered-top Leyland 'Titan' TD1's came into use at Ascot from the Summer of 1928 that such comfort would once again be experienced on that route.

The former *Progressive* bus garage remained evident for many years in use as a satellite site for Strachan's of Bracknell (Austin dealership), then a removals contractor, and later as a tyre-fitting shop, until it was finally demolished in the '80s as the New Town expanded still further. *Johnny Woof* continued with his garage activities in his own right for many years and continued to live at No.2 Church Villas in Stanley Road until that too was buried under town centre re-development. He passed away in 1971, preceded by *Tom Spragg* six years earlier. The latter had, by 1939, returned to baking, with a bread and cake shop in the High Street at Lymington in the New Forest, with wife Georgina running the counter and tea-room.

Sid Townsend
Crowthorne, Berkshire

Sid Townsend had been born with that abbreviated Christian name at Wokingham in 1888, moving to Crowthorne by 1911 to work as a laundry assistant to Susanna Webb, marrying her daughter Helen in 1912. Unfortunately, she died at an early age, so in 1924 he was re-married to Laura Watts. By then he did cycle repairs in premises on the eastern side of the High Street, duly progressing to motor cars. Passenger work began when a Ford Model T (MO 6318) arrived in October 1925, which was a lorry sometimes fitted with up to 14 seats. The addition of a charabanc was no doubt not found worthwhile earlier on, given the coverage by the local jobmaster-turned-operator *Charles Lovick & Sons*, so it was not until 1928 that Sid added such work in a small way. He purchased a 20-seater Bean 11W-type, which went on the road as MP 7028 in June, the chassis also have an alternative lorry body for haulage work, in fact surviving in the latter form through to March 1942.

With the 1930 Road Traffic Act he applied for an excursions and tours license, but a similar one from the longer established *Lovicks* left Sid only obtaining a quite restricted range, half-day tours to Virginia Water, Windsor and Stratfieldsaye (the Duke of Wellington connection with Crowthorne being well known), along with the important annual events in June as Royal Ascot Races and the Aldershot Military Tattoo. Those to coastal destinations were for restricted to maximum numbers each season, with Southsea (12), Bognor Regis (7) and Brighton, Worthing and Littlehampton at 5 each, that being due to objections by the *Lovicks*.

The Bean continued on passenger duties through to 1934, so was presumably updated with its bodywork, but then was replaced by a secondhand Gilford AS6-type with Duple 20-seater coach body (GO 9697), new in 1931 to *Harris Coaches* of London E5. That side of the work did not expand in pre-war years, though the garage did to offer taxi, haulage and a 24-hour breakdown service, the latter duly facility contributing to his poor health as the years wore on.

Some contract work was undertaken during WW2, there being no shortage of military establishments and shadow factories in the area, so after the war there was in fact an expansion in coaching work. The haulage side was not neglected, with a Bedford MLD-type 2-ton lorry (DBL 860) purchased in October 1946.

On the coaching front, July 1949 saw the delivery of a new Bedford OB-type with Duple 'Vista' 29-seater coach body and registered FJB 267. Remarkably, that coach still survives to be used as a classic vehicle for wedding hires etc., though when caught by the camera it was going through a less glamorous phase of its life.

A similar OB new in May 1949 as KKH 127 to *Green's Auto Services* of Hull was added in August 1951, the contracts now consisting of a Local Authority school run and a worker's daily journey to the AWRE over at Aldermaston, with excursions still operating during school holidays, Sundays and Bank Holidays.

However, the toll of the varied work, involving long hours in the workshop or out in all weathers was by the mid-1950's affecting Sid's health, and in July 1956 he died. The Road Service Licenses were taken over by his wife Laura, who endeavoured to keep the business going, but issues with a deficit of maintenance led to Stop Notices being issued on the coaches, leading to her decision to offer the business to *Smith's Luxury Coaches* of Reading.

The latter already had a number of express licenses in or near the Crowthorne area, plus had acquired *Cody Coaches* in October 1956. The family there had given permission for a Binfield outstation, but were now hoping to expand the garage business and wanted that terminated, so the opportunity to take over *Townsend* at Crowthorne also solved the conundrum of how best to continue serving the area, which included the New Town being developed at Bracknell. *Smith's* did not run the Bedford OB's, though some former *Cody* coaches and their drivers were transferred to the Crowthorne base, which was duly expanded, whilst Laura Townsend continued to handle bookings, duly marrying the new Area Superintendent in due course.

J.H.A. Weaver
Slough & District Bus Service
Slough, Buckinghamshire

The main operations of *James Henry Absalom Weaver* were indeed centred on his base at Ledgers Road in Slough, but he ventured far from there with various attempts to set up services elsewhere, much of which is out of the scope of this study.

However, on 6th November 1923 he applied to Frimley & Camberley UDC for a hackney carriage license to provide a bus route to run as Camberley – Blackwater – Yateley – Crowthorne. As he was not a local man, and therefore an unknown risk, the Council discussed the matter on several occasions before they were satisfied to grant the license. According to the much-respected late researcher Peter Holmes, the service did in fact start, though no further evidence has come to light over the years. However, if that was indeed the case, then *Weaver* would have been the first to link Crowthorne by regular bus to any other town, preceding as he did the *Progressive* service that started about a year later.

But all was in fact not well with *Slough & District* at the time, leading to him not taking up licenses granted at Woking the same year, whilst his Guildford outpost ceased in late 1924. Whether he had abandoned the Camberley service before *Progressive* started is not known, so he could have been ousted by that, or his departure possible was the catalyst for that venture? A fatal accident at Slough in 1926 saw him give bus operations up completely on 23rd April of that year.

Amongst the mixed fleet of Slough & District was this former London General B-type with modified body and re-registered as PP 491 after its war service.

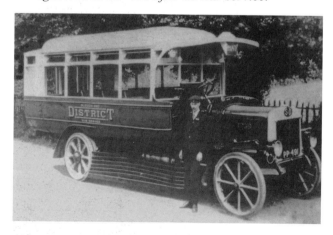

White's of Camberley
White's Garage, London Road
Camberley, Surrey

This firm started by *Peter White* offered passenger transport from its Camberley base, as well as from Baughurst in Hampshire, during some 7 decades from the 1920's to the '80's. However, here we shall only concern ourselves with its activities north of the A30 and in respect of its services and proposed operations to the Crowthorne and Reading areas.

Indeed, *Peter White* had tried as early as March 1926 to obtain permission to operate buses from Camberley to Reading, presumably on the direct route through Blackwater – Eversley – Arborfield – Shinfield. Even if he had envisaged using the less direct routing via Wokingham and Crowthorne, the proposal met with a refusal from Reading BC on the grounds that there was already an adequate service being provided by *Thames Valley*, the latter recently acquiring *Progressive* over that latter road, as well as being long established on the other route. Further attempts followed for buses from Reading in 1929, with 4 licenses requested for Aldershot in May, then following that refusal, another in September for 6 buses on a Farnborough service, also duly turned down.

Despite those specific set-backs, the firm prospered on passenger transport with excursions and private hire, building up a small but well-maintained fleet of white and black-painted coaches, along with a thriving motor garage and service station based on the London Road A30 in Camberley. It was therefore not surprising that the 1930 Act led to further consideration on operating routes, so in May 1931 an application was made for a rather over-long bus service as Aldershot – Frimley – Camberley – Crowthorne – Wokingham – Reading. The service had 10 return journeys daily, though the early and late departures were short-workings based on Camberley, but the Traffic Commissioner refused the license as both roads were already covered by *Aldershot & District* and *Thames Valley*.

In the meantime, an express coach service was started from October 1928 between Crowthorne and London, with another feeder from Finchampstead to meet that at White's Service Station, and under the Road Traffic Act 1930 was amended as below-

Service 1 was the weekdays version and started at Crowthorne (Iron Duke) at 8.45am, then ran via the Crowthorne (Station) – Sandhurst Halt (New Inn) – College Town (Jolly Farmer) – Yorktown (Duke of York) – Camberley (Recreation Ground and White's Service Station on London Road) – Bagshot (The Square) – Sunningdale (Post Office) – Kew – Chiswick – Hammersmith – Olympia – Kensington – Hyde Park Corner – Marble Arch to terminate at the Red & White Coach Station at Paddington (*Rickard's Coaches*). The return journey was at 6.20pm, so it was intended for shoppers and sightseeing rather than commuters. As indeed were most such services of that era, which often included a weekly late-night theatre-goers journey.

Service 2 left from Crowthorne (Station Crossroads) at 9.03am, then via Finchampstead (Post Office) – Eversley Street (New Inn) – Eversley Cross (The Chequers) – Yateley (White Lion) – Blackwater (AA call box) – Yorktown (Duke of York) and then as per Service 1, with a 5.50pm return journey.

In fact on Saturdays, Service 1 left 30 minutes later to pick up the Service 2 routing, but took the latter's earlier return time. On Sundays a further complication saw one coach as Service 1A from the Iron Duke at 9am, with another as Service 2A from Finchampstead at 8.55am.

These services were only part of a number running into to London by the firm, and continued to at least 1933, though latterly they were ousted by competition from the *Aldershot & District* service.

White's operated a number of Albion coaches such as this example with staggered waistrail bodywork.

White's would of course to continue to serve the area with a fleet of coaches for many more years to come, but did not attempt bus services again, another example of such an operator that 'just might have been'.

****

Regular Visitors To The Area

Not only were the local operators to be seen on the roads in the area covered by this volume, but several quite different venues attracted regular excursions.

Above *we see one of Charles Banfield's Peckham-based fleet picking up passengers outside St. Mary Abbots Court on one of the regular journeys to take visitors from 'the smoke' to see their relatives down at the Pinewood Hospital for TB patients situated near to Crowthorne, the coach being UMY 450, a post-war Leyland 'Tiger' PS2-type.*

Below *is a scene only a couple of miles westwards of Pinewood, where the attraction was California-in-England, a pleasant area of the same 'health-giving' pine trees set around Longmoor Lake. Elsewhere we have already heard of how that developed, along with dedicated transport links, but here we see a Leyland 'Tiger' TS3 (JO 1599) from South Midland of Oxford on a day excursion. Although dating from 1931, the coach had been re-bodied by Harrington during 1936.*

Minor Operators of the Bracknell Area

As we have found elsewhere, there were a number of persons who at times provided passenger transport by way of using a vehicle primarily intended for another trade. Such activities are poorly recorded and often of limited duration, but locally significant prior to the arrival of more dedicated facilities.

Herbert Laban Graves was far from a local man, being born at Newcastle-upon-Tyne in December 1899 and subsequently served in the Royal Navy towards the close of the Great War as a Stoker on HMS Sovereign, being paid off in early 1920. Apparently, his brothers had started a haulage business in London, from whom he obtained a Dennis lorry, probably ex-WD, with which he came to Bracknell to start a coal merchant's business, something he presumably was familiar with having shovelled many tons into the voracious boilers of a battleship!

The exact date for relocation is not known, but in 1921 he had married Alice Taylor at Woolwich in Kent, in fact where he had been de-mobbed. They were duly recorded at 'Puddledock Cottage' on the Wokingham Road, and the business expanded to cover haulage and secondhand furniture dealing. The lorry is recalled as having a canvas tilt, fitted as required with bench seats for carrying the Bracknell Wanderers Football Club, plus it is said some occasional seaside trips and each year to Royal Ascot Races, as Bracknell had no coach operator of its own until after WW2, though the 1930 Road Traffic Act would outlaw the use of such utility vehicles on passenger duties.

Reginald Andrew Gibson was born in 1904 locally and based at Prospect Place in Warfield Street, about 1.25 miles north of Bracknell, when on the last day of April 1924 he licensed a blue-painted Ford 1-ton truck also for 14 passengers as MO 3052. No other details have emerged of his activities, but by January 1929 the vehicle was as goods only for the Bracknell sawmill owner George Slyfield. Reg continued driving, and in 1939 was a lorry driver living at 'The Beeches' on Rounds Hill in Bracknell.

The Knight family of Winkfield Row are known for several business ventures based at nearby Chavey Down, about 2 miles east of Bracknell. By 1931 **Alec Knight** (born 1900) was listed as a haulage contractor, whilst his mother **Sarah Knight** (born at Oxford in 1867) was running the local laundry. No doubt connected with the latter was a Morris-Commercial 1-ton van with box body, painted blue and also licensed for 14 seats, placed on the road as MO 4763 in March 1925. It remained with her until late 1941 as a goods

vehicle, but what passenger work she undertook is only little known, though she was entrusted to take the Sisters and the girls from the local convent to Ascot Station or other local destinations.

Further still to the east and based in South Ascot was **William Sole**, who established himself post-Great War as a corn and coal merchant, duly joined by his son, though born at Kelshall in Hertfordshire in 1877, arriving in the area by 1911 as a Railway Signals Labourer living at 'Bishopwick' in South Ascot. In May 1923 he licensed a 25cwt Guy J-type fitted with a green-painted lorry body with 14 seats as MO 1405. It is understood he provided transport for local outings, sports and social events until other firms came along, but by its last licensing in October 1930, though still with that owner, it was for goods cartage only. His son Stanley was born in 1908, and at 1939 William was living at 'Beech House' in South Ascot.

Also, within Ascot there was **George Wheeler**, a man from 3 generations of that same name. His father had been born in Reading in 1831 and was a coach-painter, which no doubt steered the second George (born 1862 in Reading) to become an apprentice as a coach-builder, so in 1881 he can be found under the household of Thomas Mackrill at No.8 East Street in Reading, a coachbuilder who was still evident in the 1920's, who was also his uncle-by-marriage.

By 1871 the first George had moved to Sunninghill at 'Walnut Cottage', still as a coach-painter. The younger George duly relocated to Sunninghill by 1891, perhaps with the passing of his father, as his widowed mother was next door to his residence at 'Jubilee Cottage' on the Ascot Road. His trade was by then coach-builder and farrier, followed by his marriage in 1896, and by 1911 the couple had moved back in the family home at 'Walnut Cottage', their son George now 15 and as an assistant in the business, now termed coach-builder and motor works. Separate business premises had been established in the High Street, Ascot by 1892, on the northern side between the Horse & Groom and Stag pubs, duly known as 'The Garage'.

The youngest George went off to the Great War in October 1915 with the Worcestershire Regiment, but survived to be de-mobbed in July 1920. A new project started after his return was to overhaul a large old Gladiator car chassis, a French-built type, which was then rigged out as a 14-seater brake and painted green, given the registration BL 5349. When declared under the 1920 Act on 1st January 1921 it was a 12-seater.

As is usually the case with such localised operations, no evidence has survived of the uses to which the vehicle put, but after the death of George senior in late 1924, it remained in use, being transferred to his wife from motor tax renewal on 1st January 1925. Then it was again re-licensed through to the end of 1926, after which nothing more was heard of it or similar activities by the family, the son continuing with the garage.

Eastwards a little further is Sunninghill, where **Salter Bros.** had established the Queens Road Garage by 1920. In March of that year they placed a proper charabanc on the road with 16 seats mounted on a 20hp Maxwell chassis and painted dark red. However, that venture evidently did not live up to expectations, so the following January BL 7022 found a new owner in Brighton instead.

In the opposite direction, west of Wokingham by several miles, and off the Winnersh to Hurst road, will be found Sandford Mill, set in a large area duly given over to gravel extraction. It was that trade that attracted **Wilfred James Chaffey** to that location by 1927. He had been born at Bishops Caundle in Dorset in 1904, but in June 1927 he put a 1-ton Chevrolet X-type lorry with a blue-painted body on the road (RX 281), also fitted with 14 seats. It was with another owner by March 1932, but in the mean-time he did provided some regular local trips for sports and social events when not engaged on gravel, sand and general haulage. Indeed, although his passenger carrying no doubt ended with the 1930 Act, his main business prospered, so he relocated to 'Santoi' at Wheelers Green in Woodley by 1930 until at least 1935, but he was a short way from there at 'Santay' No.56 Colemans Moor Lane by 1939. His aggregate lorries were still to be seen in the 1960's.

In another area of Winkfield Row **Samuel Nickless** had come to settle with his parents at their general grocery, though he had been born in 1900 at Hockley in Essex. In fact his father had been a brickfield labourer over at Binfield, so knew the area already, but as Samuel got to working age he did neither trade, and in June 1928 he placed a Willys Overland Crossley 25cwt truck on the road as RX 2475, painted blue with white lining out and at times fitted with 14 seats. He duly went to work on the Warfield Hall Estate, rising to Farm Baliff at the Home Farm by the mid-1930's, and indeed the vehicle was elsewhere locally on agricultural goods work. As far as is known he used the vehicle for local outings to darts matches, dances and other party hires just for a couple of years, certainly ceasing before the 1930 Act.

Minor Operators of the Crowthorne Area

As in most rural villages or towns, early transport for various purposes came not necessarily from dedicated transport operators but was often provided by those with motor vehicles for another primary purpose. In the case of Crowthorne, the rather distant Railway Station and the neds of the satellite communities at Wellington College and Little Sandhurst saw some short-lived provision until other local operators were established.

Thomas James Whittaker of The Maisonette in Ellis Road, just of the High Street in Crowthorne, was by 1920 a Coal Merchant, collecting his supplies from the Station which was then known as Wellington College. On the last day of March 1922 he placed a new Ford 1-tonner on the road as BL 9742, the body of which was painted dark blue and described as an open-type with 14 removeable seats. It is believed it mainly saw use to transport local sports teams, probably in which he also participated, but no evidence of other hire or excursion work is evident. His involvement no doubt faded once more suitable vehicles were available locally.

Percy Evan Thomas was a Land & Estate Agent based in Crowthorne who resided at 'Cenarth' in Wellington Road, but had been born in 1877 at Brandon in Suffolk. He was established by 1911 as Auctioneer & Surveyor at St. George's Hall., living at 'Holly Bank'

On 30th August 1920 he placed on the road a Rocket-Sneider 30-40hp 'van wagonette' with the new registration of BL 7815. However, the vehicle was actually new in 1908, probably having in the meantime seen wartime service as a staff car or ambulance, but now painted as chocolate with red stripes. It is further noted as a 14-seater charabanc with seats that were removeable and kept at Williams Garage by the Railway Station. There are no known references to any public excursions by him, but it is thought that he used the vehicle and his local connections to take shooting parties and other persons visiting the local estates that dominated the local area. That vehicle was last licensed at the close of September 1922, after which he seems not to have undertaken any passenger-carrying work.

Thomas Henry Cooper had been born at Portsmouth in 1875, but was based in 'Nutwood' in Longdown Road at Little Sandhurst, some three-quarters of a mile from the centre of Crowthorne by 1911 and established as a coal merchant. In June 1921 he licensed a Daimler as BL 8783, which mark was cancelled for some reason to be replaced by BL 9183 on the 27th of that month. Little detail was given of its type, but it seems likely to be a large car chassis, now carrying a slate-coloured lorry body with seating for 14. It is believed he was mainly concerned with local journeys for teams of sportsmen, inter-pub darts and events such as dances. Although he kept the vehicle until 1929, by then noted as goods only, such work probably ceased once the Crowthorne operators, along with *George Hodges* of Sandhurst provided better facilities.

The Mason family of Wokingham and its transport activities appear elsewhere under that town, but their

Finchampstead relatives also had some vehicles that also sometimes carried passengers. Once again, their main business was as coal merchants, but the mere ownership of a motor vehicle in that rather seasonal trade invited some diversification. Also, it seems that such work was largely for sporting teams and other local social events such as dances or whist-drives. In October 1924 **Edward James Mason** from Finchampstead put a Ford 1-ton truck on the road as MO 3971, painted grey and licensed for 14 passengers. In March 1925 his son **Jim Mason** of No.10 Council Cottages in Finchampstead had a similar green-painted vehicle with 14 removeable seats. Although both those vehicles had good working lives on the coal transport, it seems that passenger-carrying was only short lived.

Also based in Crowthorne was a local carrier, who regularly took passengers at a time when the village had no bus link to Wokingham and Reading. **Alfred Cooper** was, however, not of local origins, being born in 1865 at Englefield, a few miles west of Reading. By 1891 we find him at No.2 Wellington Terrace in Caversham and working as a sawyer, his son Alfred Frank born in 1890, and who would later assist him and was duly known as Frank. By 1901 he had again relocated to New Farm at Bradfield, a village a short way father west than his birthplace, possibly because his wife came from nearby, when he had established as a coal merchant and haulage contractor. In the 1902 directory he was at the Southend side of the village and had added a grocery, but entries ceased there in 1907.

Certainly, he had moved to Crowthorne by 1910, establishing himself as a greengrocer, florist and coal merchant with a shop in Church Street. It is assumed he used a horse-powered waggon for the 14-mile journey to Reading, with a motor van following at an unconfirmed point. The service started out by 1910 as Tuesdays and Fridays only, with Thursdays added from 1911 and also Saturdays from 1912, which may be a pointer to motorisation, when DP 267 (as seen on this page) arrived, somewhat earlier than an advert of January 1919, which offered 2 carrier's vans, one single horse and the other for a pair, with detachable tilts and 2 sets of harness, along with a chaff-cutter, so may represent something of a clear-out post-war.

With the motor van, it was more practical to carry passengers, who were charged a return fare of 6d, and the areas served by 1916 were Earley, Wokingham, Easthampstead Park, Crowthorne, Wellington College, Broadmoor, Owlsmoor, Sandhurst, Blackwater, Frogmore, York Town and Camberley. As the van was lettered A. Cooper & Son, Frank was then assisting his father, though the shop was manned by Alf's wife Eva and their daughter Elsie (born Reading 1890). The van Reading at 4pm from The White Hart Hotel.

The family, however, were residing a short walk away in Pinewood Avenue by 1924, and it was to that address in 1930 that a former *Thames Valley* Brush double-deck body was delivered for use as a garden shed, but Alf died in the Spring of 1928, when his listing for the shop ceased. However, his son was still operating the carrier's service for goods only after the 1930 Act to at least the start of the Second World War.

Alf Cooper's carrier's van based on a Darracq car chassis was almost certainly bodied and supplied by Vincents of Reading, fully sign-written with the route.

Minor Operators in Wokingham
Frederick Langman
William Palmer

Frederick Langman had been born at Crazies Hill, near Wargrave in Berkshire in 1862, coming to Wokingham via Fawley in Buckinghamshire and Emmbrook, just to the west of the town centre by 1903. His sons Ernest (born 1886) and David (born 1903) also joined him in the business as Carpenters and Builders, which was based at No.4 Station Road in Wokingham by 1911. Shortly after the Great War he had a motor lorry or van, which at times he fitted with seats and used on some outings. It is likely that one of the sons drove the vehicle, but such work ended once other purpose-built vehicles became available in the town.

William Palmer was born at nearby Binfield in 1873, by 1911 we find him living in Wokingham at No.72 Westcott Road and working as a plasterer's labourer. By 1922 he had relocated within the same road at No.28, when he placed a new Ford Model T truck (BL 9557) on the road. Painted in a blue livery it was described as a hackney-truck, used for light haulage or fitted with seats for passenger use. This would seem to mark the start of his occasional public trips, either for local sports teams or to horse-racing meetings. Noted as a man of a nervous disposition, he was at the wheel on a trip to Goodwood Races, when his Ford rolled back on the steep access road from the valley floor at Singleton, after which he discontinued taking passengers. The exact date of that accident is not known, but the truck was elsewhere before 1926.

BRIMBLECOMBE BROS., WOKINGHAM

Reg. No.	Chassis Make & Type	Bodybuilder	Layout	Date New	Date In	Date Out
YW 939	Lancia Pentaiota	London Lorries	C26F	May-28	by Jun-41	Dec-41
CNO 716	Fordson V8	Willett	C26	Jul-35	by Jun-41	Oct-51
WJ 1916	Leyland Tiger TS1	Duple (1937)	C31F	Jul-31	Nov-42	May-52
COD 71	Commer PLNF5	Heaver	FC26F	May-39	Aug-43	Feb-48
RS 8306	Albion Viking PM28	Cowieson (1934)	B32F	Dec-26	??-43	May-49
RX 6923	Star Flyer VB3	Star	C20D	Jun-30	Feb-46	Oct-49
DWL 918	Morris Commercial Leader	Duple	C26F	Nov-36	Feb-46	Jul-50
CBL 502	Bedford OB	Thurgood	C26F	Nov-39	Feb-46	Jul-53
CUL 8	Maudslay Magna SF40	Duple	C36C	Aug-35	by Apr-46	Oct-52
DRX 489	Maudslay Marathon III	Whitson	C33F	May-47	New	Dec-61
	Re-bodied in 1953 as	Strachan	FC35F			
ANW 443	Albion Valkyrie PW67	Whitson (1948)	C33F	May-34	Jan-48	Jul-53
DOV 973	Leyland Lion LT8	Duple	C37?	Feb-38	Nov-48	
AOV 272	Leyland Tiger TS7	Burlingham	C32C	Mar-35	May-49	Jul-54
FWJ 902	Bedford WTB	??	C26?	Mar-39	Aug-49	Nov-53
FJB 733	Austin K4/CXB	Whitson	C29F	Oct-49	New	Dec-59
FJB 734	Austin K4/CXB	Whitson	C29F	Oct-49	New	Jan-60
FJB 735	Austin K4/CXB	Whitson	C29F	Nov-49	New	Jan-60
FGC 869	Dennis Lancet II	Metcalfe	C33F	Aug-38	Jun-50	Nov-54
RN 8396	Leyland Tiger TS8	Burlingham	B31F	Jul-38	May-52	May-55
MMT 866	Bedford OB	Duple Vista	C27F	Apr-47	Oct-53	Dec-59
ECK 316	Bedford SB	Duple Vega	C33F	Jun-51	Nov-53	Mar-55
WH 7578	Leyland Tiger TS7	Duple	C33F	May-36	Jan-54	Oct-55
FCJ 844	AEC Regal III 0962	Burlingham (1959)*	FC35F	Aug-48	Jul-54	Sep-66
FCJ 843	AEC Regal III 0962	Burlingham (1957)*	FC35F	Aug-48	Sep-54	Feb-67
KMO 939	AEC Reliance MU3RV	Burlingham Seagull III	C41C	Feb-55	New	Jul-66
LJB 264	Bedford SBG	Duple Vega	C38F	Jul-55	New	Oct-72
GMO 14	Austin K4/CXD	Thurgood	FC32F	May-51	Jan-56	Jun-62
GMO 418	Guy Arab III	Thurgood	C35F	Jul-51	Jan-56	Aug-61
KOC 662	Foden PVFE6	Lincs Trailer	HD43F	Jun-50	Jun-56	Dec-57
JGD 116	AEC Regal IV	Plaxton Venturer III**	C41C	Jun-51	Nov-57	Sep-58
DRD 382	Bedford OB	Duple Vista	C29F	Mar-49	Oct-58	Jan-60
RJB 292	Bedford SB3	Duple Super Vega	C41F	Nov-58	New	Nov-75
RBL 655	Austin J2BA	BMC	M11	Sep-58	New	Non-PSV
GCA 388	Bedford OB	Duple Vista	C29F	Jan-50	Mar-60	Jan-61
YMP 553	Bedford SBO	Burlingham Seagull	C35F	May-53	Mar-60	Feb-65
2040 FH	Ford 570E (ex-demo)	Plaxton Embassy	C41F	Dec-60	New	Oct-72
XBL 477	Trojan	Trojan	C13F	Feb-61	New	Aug-68
WOT 144	Bedford SB1	Duple Super Vega	C41F	Aug-59	May-61	Mar-76
188 ARX	Ford 570E	Duple Yeoman	C41F	Apr-62	New	Jan-76
933 FJB	Bedford VAL14	Plaxton Panorama	C52F	Nov-63	New	Jan-76
FDL 318	Bedford OB	Duple Vista	C29F	Mar-48	Jul-64	Nov-65
NDF 751	Bedford SBG	Duple Vega	C36F	Mar-54	Jul-64	Mar-68
VPD 488	Bedford SBO	Duple Vega	C38F	Jul-54	Jul-64	Mar-68
2652 VF	Austin J2VA	Kenex	M12	Nov-60	Jul-64	Oct-72
149 SPB	Trojan (ex-van)	Trojan (ex VBX 298)	C13F	Sep-60	??-65	
ADY 188B	Commer LBD	Harrington	M12	Aug-64	Aug-66	Dec-70
ADY 189B	Commer LBD	Harrington	M12	Aug-64	Aug-66	Dec-70
7197 HX	Ford 570E	Burlingham Seagull 60	C41F	Jun-60	Jan-67	Feb-72
7198 HX	Ford 570E	Burlingham Seagull 60	C41F	May-60	Jan-67	Oct-72
7199 HX	Ford 570E	Burlingham Seagull 60	C41F	Jun-60	Jan-67	May-72
PBL 362F	Commer 2500LB	Rootes	M12	Jun-68	New	Jan-76
NJH 814D	Bedford VAL14	Plaxton Panorama	C52F	Apr-66	May-70	Mar-76
HNJ 182D	Commer 1500LB	Rootes	M12	Sep-66	Dec-70	Jan-73
JNJ 670D	Commer 1500LB	Rootes	M12	Sep-66	Dec-70	Jul-75
KNM 412G	Ford Transit	LCM	M12	Dec-68	Jun-71	Feb-83

Reg. No.	Chassis Make & Type	Bodybuilder	Layout	Date New	Date In	Date Out
895 DBL	Bedford SB5	Plaxton Embassy MkII	C41F	Mar-63	Jun-71	Jan-76
GMF 180B	Ford 676E	Duple Maurader	C52F	Apr-64	Jul-72	Dec-73
JNK 682C	Bedford SB5	Plaxton Embassy	C41F	May-65	Jul-72	Feb-76
YVN 214	Bedford SB1	Duple Super Vega	C41F	Apr-61	Nov-72	Feb-76
POT 503G	Bedford VAL70	Duple Viceroy 37	C53F	Apr-69	Nov-72	Feb-76
TXD 696L	Ford R226	Duple Dominant	C53F	Apr-73	Jan-74	Feb-76
SDP 342M	Ford Transit	Dormobile	M12	May-74	New	Feb-83
JKK 300E	Bedford VAS1	Duple Vista 25	C29F	Mar-67	Oct-74	Feb-76
MRO 996P	Ford Transit	Dormobile	M12	Mar-76	New	Feb-83
MRO 997P	Ford Transit	Dormobile	M12	Mar-76	New	Feb-83
VLY 629M	Ford Transit	Tricentrol	M12	Feb-74	Jul-75	May-80
SBH 909R	Ford Transit	Dormobile	M12	Mar-77	New	Sep-87
SBH 910R	Ford Transit	Dormobile	M12	Mar-77	New	Aug-78
JTF 141W	Ford Transit	Smith	M12	Mar-81	May-84	Sep-87
JNE 837V	Ford Transit	Deansgate	M12	May-80	May-84	Sep-87

Notes

*FCJ 843/4 were new with half-cab Strachans C33F coach bodies and ran in that form until rebodied

**JGD 116 was rebodied with the Plaxton body in March 1956

DRD 382 and GCA 388 were exported to Cyprus, where they were re-registered as TBK 735 and TBN 825

Hire cars

A number of hire cars were in use by Brimblecombes, firstly in their own right, then those acquired with the businesses of Herring Bros. and Costessey Coaches, but at present only incomplete details are known.

Commercial vehicles

??	acquired from Herrings	30cwt closed van		??	Feb-46	??/53
JBL 813	Morris 30cwt	van plus 8 seats		Sep-53	New	

Additional vehicles acquired but not operated

DY 7337	AEC Regal	Harrington (1939)	C32F	Feb-33	54/55	??

This coach was noted by Jimmy LaCroix as Brimblecombe Bros., but motor tax makes no mention. It may have been acquired for spares and subsequently scrapped, last owner recorded was in 8/54, but not run.

JB 7737	Dennis Ace F/C					

This coach had been sold to Lovick Motors by Windsorian, and is noted as last licensed to 30/9/54, next recorded owner was Baker (dealer), Dorking 7/56, and it is believed that this vehicle was still at Lovick's at the takeover by Brimblecombe's in 1/56 and traded into Bakers.

??	Trojan 3-cylinder	Van				

This van was formerly Brooke Bond Tea and was acquired for its engine and parts for others of the type.

VBX 298	Trojan	Trojan	C13F	??/60	??/65	??/65

This minibus came from Laverick, Bracknell and the chassis had been badly damaged in a bad smash at Warren House crossroads, so Brimblecombes placed the body on 149 SPB, which had been acquired as a van to create the resulting minibus, the Laverick chassis being dismantled for spares.

??	Leyland Comet	Lorries				

The engines of several lorries of this model were removed for use in upgrading Bedford SB-type coaches, with LJB getting the engine from WOT, the latter and RJB receiving Leyland 0.400 engines instead.

BROOKHOUSE KEENE (CODY BUS/CODY COACHES)

Reg. No.	Chassis Make & Type	Bodybuilder	Layout	Date New	Date In	Date Out
MO 3220	Chevrolet 1-ton		B14F	Jul-24	New	Jun-27
BL 7278	Buick 20hp		W14	May-20	Sep-24	by Jun-27
PP 2791	Garford 20hp		B20F	Ex-WD	??/25	Jun-27
RX 283	Chevrolet LM	Vincent?	AW14F	Jun-27	New	Dec-47
UU 161	AEC Reliance 660	Hoyal	C32F	May-29	Jan-47	??/49
HB 5421	Bedford WTB		C24F	Oct-37	Jan-48	Dec-50
GZ 2161	Bedford OWB	Duple	UB30F	Feb-44	Feb-49	Dec-54
FBL 677	Bedford OB	Mulliner	B31F	Jul-49	New	SC
GBL 152	Guy Vixen	Thurgood	FC30F	Aug-50	New	SC
NUM 13	Bedford OB	Duple Vista	C29F	Oct-50	Jan-53	SC
KMO 681	Bedford SBG	Thurgood	C36F	Jan-55	New	SC
Notes	Coaches marked SC were acquired by Smith's Coaches of Reading in October 1956					

RICHARD HERRING & SONS/HERRING BROS., WOKINGHAM

Reg. No.	Chassis Make & Type	Bodybuilder	Layout	Date New	Date In	Date Out
BL 2932	Napier 15hp	Vincent	Taxi 4	Mar-13	New	by Jan/21
BL 4298	Napier 15hp	Vincent	Taxi 4	May-15	New	post 1921
BL 2830	Briton 10hp	Vincent ?	Car 2	??/13	by Jun/17	
DP 680	Napier 15hp	Vincent	Taxi 4	??/11	by Jan/21	
AA 992	??				by Jan/21	
BL 8098	Ford T 1-ton		W13	Nov-20	New	Sep-23
BL 8843	Fiat F2	Ford	Ch14	Jul-21	New	Sep-29
XK 7162	Crossley 20-25hp	Ford	Ch14	Ex-WD	Apr-22	
T 8864	Crossley 20-25hp	Ford	Ch14	Ex-WD	??/24	May-33
RX 2379	Star Flyer VB4	Weybridge	AW20D	May-28	New	
RX 6923	Star Flyer VB4	Star	AW20D	Jun-30	New	BB
BL 8812	Ford T 1-ton		Van	Jul-21	??/31	Mar-36
TK 7376	Ford AA		C14F	Feb-32	??/33	
DWL 918	Morris Commercial Leader	Duple	C26F	Nov-36	Feb-38	BB
CBL 502	Bedford OB	Thurgood	C26F	Nov-39	New	BB
Notes	The late disposal dates of some earlier vehicles is due to their dual use as goods/hackney					
	Coaches marked BB were acquired by Brimblecombe Bros. in February 1946					

C. LOVICK & SONS/LOVICK'S COACHES, CROWTHORNE

Reg. No.	Chassis Make & Type	Bodybuilder	Layout	Date New	Date In	Date Out
BL 2334	Napier 15hp	Vincent	Taxi 4	Dec-12	New	post 1921
BL 3467	Napier 15hp	Vincent	Taxi 4	Feb-14	New	post 1921
MD 6090	Daimler Y	Roberts?	Ch26	Ex-WD	Apr-21	Sep-31
OP 3470	Ford T 1-ton		B14	??/20	c1922	
MO 2543	Ford T 1-ton		B14	Jan-24	New	Jun-37
MO 5820	Ford T 1-ton		W14	Jul-25	New	Nov-35
RX 127	Graham Bros 24hp	Vincent	Ch20	May-27	New	Mar-45
UW 2615	Gilford 166SD	Duple	C26F	Oct-29	Aug-38	Feb-52
RX 8585	Morris Minor 8hp	Morris	Van	May-31	New	Apr-49
RX 9816	Ford		Car	Feb-37	New	Apr-49
RD 5794	Armstrong-Siddeley 15hp		Car	Jul-34	??/35	Apr-49
CPA 126	Hillman		Car	Oct-34	??/42	Apr-49
JB 7736	Dennis Ace F/C	Duple	FC24F	Jan-36	Apr-49	Mar-55
JB 7737	Dennis Ace F/C	Duple	FC24F	Jan-36	Apr-49	Sep-54
RX 8569	Dennis Arrow	Duple	C31F	Apr-31	May-49	Jun-53
RX 8570	Dennis Arrow	Duple	C31F	Apr-31	May-49	Not used
GMO 14	Austin K4/CXD	Thurgood	FC32F	May-51	New	BB
GMO 418	Guy Arab MkIII (Meadows)	Thurgood	C35F	Jul-51	New	BB
Notes	The 3 Ford T's all had alternative bodies for goods work, later solely on such duties, OP 3470					
	later as a laundry van, others going onto coal deliveries. RX 8585 was for parcels deliveries.					
	Coaches marked BB were acquired by Brimblecombe Bros. in January 1956					

SPRAGG & WOOFF (PROGRESSIVE BUS COMPANY), BRACKNELL

Reg. No.	Chassis Make & Type	Bodybuilder	Layout	Date New	Date In	Date Out
BL 5460	Ford T		Car 4	??/17	May-19	
MO 1196	Ford T 1-ton	Rice & Harper	B14R	Mar-23	New	??/25
MO 1197	Ford T 1-ton	Rice & Harper	B14R	Mar-23	New	??/25
MO 1647	Ford T 1-ton	Rice & Harper ?	B14F	Jun-23	New	Jul-25
MO 2213	Lancia Tetraiota	Bartle	B20F	Oct-23	New	TV
MO 3530	Lancia Z	Vincent/Manners	B20F	Ex-WD	Jul-24	TV
MO 4648	Lancia Pentaiota	Strachan & Brown	B25F	Feb-25	New	TV
MO 5443	Lancia Pentaiota	Strachan & Brown	B25F	May-25	New	TV
MO 6184	Dennis 2.5-ton	Strachan & Brown	B30R	Sep-25	New	TV
Notes	Buses marked TV were acquired by Thames Valley in October 1925					
	The body on MO 3530 was started by Vincents but completed by Manners at Bracknell					
	The Ford car was used for taxi work prior to the commencement of the bus service					

S.R GOUGH (GOUGH'S GARAGE BUS SERVICE)/EAST BERKS SERVICES, BRACKNELL

Reg. No.	Chassis Make & Type	Bodybuilder	Layout	Date New	Date In	Date Out
VD 3503	Leyland Lion LT5A	Leyland	B32RP	Aug-34	Apr-48	May-52
GW 724	Bedford WLB	Wilmott	C20F	Dec-31	Dec-48	May-49
NV 8218	Commer PN3	Grose ?	C20F	Nov-36	Jun-49	Nov-52
UD 9831	Bedford WTB	Thurgood	C26F	Feb-38	Jun-49	Jun-56
VV8771	Bedford OWB	Duple	UB29F	Aug-42	May-51	Jul-54
CFV 677	Bedford OB	Duple Vista	C29F	Feb-48	May-52	Aug-62
BNL 676	Bedford OB	Duple Vista	C29F	Jan-46	Jul-54	Jun-59
HDG 473	AEC Regal 9621E	Duple A-type	C33F	Oct-48	Jun-56	Apr-61
DVH 531	Bedford OB	Duple Vista	C29F	Mar-48	Apr-58	Mar-63
XKV 121	Ford Thames 510E	Duple Yeoman	C41F	Jul-59	New	Apr-70
TOV 268	Commer Avenger MkIII	Plaxton Venturer	C41F	Mar-57	Apr-61	Mar-67
KET 888	Commer 44A	Plaxton Venturer	C41F	Mar-54	Jul-61	Jun-66
SWK 971	Commer Avenger MkIII	Duple	C39F	Jun-56	Jul-62	Aug-67
EBV 283	Daimler Freeline D650H	Duple Ambassador	C41C	Apr-53	Jun-63	Feb-64
4019 AW	Bedford SB5	Duple	C41F	Mar-63	Feb-64	Oct-70
1212 MG	Bedford SB5	Duple	C41F	Apr-62	Jul-65	May-70
294 BLB	Bedford SB8	Plaxton Embassy	C41F	Apr-62	May-66	Apr-70
1316 WA	Ford 570E	Plaxton Consort MkIV	C40F	Jan-61	Mar-67	Jun-70
1317 WA	Ford 570E	Plaxton Consort MkIV	C40F	Jan-61	Mar-67	Apr-70
Notes	Gough's at Bracknell passed to East Berks Services in 1962 with those coaches still in stock					

LEWIS & NEAL (COSTESSEY COACHES), WOKINGHAM

Reg. No.	Chassis Make & Type	Bodybuilder	Layout	Date New	Date In	Date Out
RMO 667	Bedford CAV	Martin Walker	M11	Dec-58	New	Mar-60
UJB 498	Bedford CALV	Martin Walker	M11	Feb-60	New	May-61
GYA 911	Bedford OWB	Duple	UB29F	Dec-44	Aug-59	Jul-60
DDP 912	Bedford OB	Duple Vista	C29F	Aug-48	Jul-60	May-62
HAA 168	Austin VBK2/SL	Lee	C21F	Jan-49	Oct-60	May-61
DCB 259	Bedford SB	Duple Vega	C37F	Apr-52	May-61	Aug-63
VPD 488	Bedford SBO	Duple Vega MkII	C38F	Jul-54	Apr-62	BB
2652 VF	Austin J2VA	Kenex	M12	Nov-60	May-62	BB
NDF 751	Bedford SBG	Duple Vega MkII	C36F	Mar-54	Jan-63	BB
FDL 318	Bedford OB	Duple Vista	C29F	May-48	??/63	BB
Notes	Coaches marked BB were acquired by Brimblecombe Bros. in July 1964					
	A large number of cars were also owned and these are detailed in the main text					

STANDARD BODY CODES USED IN THESE FLEET LISTS

Letters before the seating capacity -			Letters after the seating capacity -	
AW	All-weather coach		C	Centre entrance
B	Single-deck service bus		D	Dual doorway
C	Saloon coach		F	Front entrance
Ch	Charabanc		R	Rear entrance
F	Fully-fronted body		P	Rear platform-style entrance
HD	Half-deck coach			
M	Minibus			
U	Utility standard bodywork			
W	Wagonette body			

Notes	Fleet lists are derived from researched information, photos and motor tax or hackney records.
	I am also most grateful for the assistance of my fellow Provincial Historical Research Group
	members, the Bus Archive and the PSV Circle for their help in resolving some queries.

A final look at some of the fleets covered in this book, with 3 more photos.

First up is the Ford 570E-type in the Thames Trader range, new in April 1962 as 188 ARX to Brimblecombe Bros. It carried the Duple body designed specifically for that chassis range and designated as the Yeoman, with 41 seats and a front entrance. This coach would remain in the fleet until January 1976 and was noted by employees as very reliable and good to drive.

Another long-serving coach with Brimblecombe Bros. was this AEC Reliance with vacuum-braking and the reliable AH470 engine of 7.685 litres, along with the synchromesh gearbox also made this coach a popular one with drivers. It often appeared on excursions to the south coast destinations including Bognor, where it was photographed by Eric Surfleet. KMO 939 had been delivered in February 1955 with a Burlingham Seagull-style body seating 41, and it served until 1966.

One of my favourites in the fleet of Gough's Coaches was this AEC Regal 9621E-type of 1948, and HDG 473 came to Bracknell in June 1956, carrying an A-type Duple body seating 33. The 9.6-litre engine made it a lively performer, though the half-cab layout was by then becoming rather outdated. It was mainly employed on a contract run, but in this photo it has gone with a party to Wembley, driven by Jack Macro, and it left the fleet in April 1961.

Other Titles Still Available from the Paul Lacey Transport History Series

All prices include postage - A4 unless otherwise stated

A History of Thames Valley Traction Co. Ltd., 1920-1930
144 pages with 144 monochrome photos, maps and fleet list -published at £15 *on offer for £13* – very limited stock

A History of Thames Valley Traction Co Ltd., 1931-1945
208 pages with 300 monochrome photos, maps and fleet list – published at £25 *on offer for £13*

History of Thames Valley Traction Co. Ltd., 1946-1960
224 pages with 544 monochrome photos, maps and fleet list – published at £25 *on offer for £13*

Thames Valley – The Final Decade, 1961-1971
224 pages with 548 monochrome and 100 colour photos, maps and fleet list - published at £25 *on offer at £13*

50 Years of South Midland, 1921-1970 - Author David Flitton
192 **A5 pages** with 142 monochrome photos, maps and fleet list – published at £11 *on offer for £6*

Thackray's Way – A Family in Road Transport 136 **A5 pages** with 62 monochrome photos, maps and fleet list – published at £10 *on offer for £5.50*

The Newbury & District Motor Services Story
224 pages with 300 monochrome photos, maps and fleet list – published at £25 *on offer for £13*

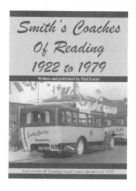

Smith's Coaches of Reading, 1922-1979
288 pages with 500 monochrome and 100 colour photos, maps and fleet list – published at £30 *on offer for £23*

Early Independents of the Henley & Marlow Area
96 pages with 81 monochrome photos, maps and fleet list – published at £15 *on offer £13*

Note - All offers are subject to stock being available and are correct at the time of publication, so please mention this book when ordering. Other promotions may occur via the website from time to time, so please check and use website form if using that method. Titles not listed are out-of-print or at very low stock, sorry!